MW01252888

Aristotle and Menander on the Ethics of Understanding

Philosophia Antiqua

A SERIES OF STUDIES ON ANCIENT PHILOSOPHY

VOLUME 138

The titles published in this series are listed at *brill.com/pha*

Aristotle and Menander on the Ethics of Understanding

By

Valeria Cinaglia

BRILL

LEIDEN | BOSTON

Library of Congress Cataloging-in-Publication Data

Cinaglia, Valeria.
Aristotle and Menander on the ethics of understanding / by Valeria Cinaglia.
pages cm. – (Philosophia antiqua: a series of studies on ancient philosophy, ISSN 0079-1687 ; VOLUME 138)
Includes bibliographical references and index.
ISBN 978-90-04-26975-0 (hardback : alk. paper) – ISBN 978-90-04-28282-7 (e-book)
1. Aristotle. 2. Menander, of Athens–Criticism and interpretation. 3. Ethics. I. Title.

B485.C56 2014
185–dc23

2014034593

This publication has been typeset in the multilingual "Brill" typeface. With over 5,100 characters covering Latin, IPA, Greek, and Cyrillic, this typeface is especially suitable for use in the humanities. For more information, please see www.brill.com/brill-typeface.

ISSN 0079-1687
ISBN 978-90-04-26975-0 (hardback)
ISBN 978-90-04-28282-7 (e-book)

This book is printed on acid-free paper.

Printed by Printforce, the Netherlands

To Pascal, Clelia and Ettore

∵

Contents

Preface

This book is a revised version of my PhD thesis. This project started in Exeter when, fresh from my Philosophy BA (Bologna), I approached the study of Menandrian comedy during my postgraduate studies: there, I started to appreciate the intellectual subtlety of Menander's technique of characterization and plot construction. In particular, like others before me, I was struck by what seemed to be similarities between the presentation of human character and action in Aristotle and Menander. Then, I gradually realised that the extent of the analogies between Aristotle and Menander was not limited to specific passages in which Menander seems to quote or reproduce ideas similar to those presented by Aristotle or Theophrastus: these analogies could indeed have had broader implications for the reading of most of Menander's extant comedies. This is why I have decided to undertake a more thoroughgoing investigation of the texts relevant to this comparision, so that I could locate the points of resemblance in the context of the philosophical work or drama in question. This inquiry brought out points of resemblance between Menander and Aristotle that go beyond parallels between isolated passages or ideas and which identifies key structural themes within their works. For instance, Knemon's misanthropy in *Dyscolos* is presented as based on a mistaken understanding of the value of social life and is criticised, within the play, on the basis of ideas comparable to those expressed by Aristotle in *Politics* 1. The presentation of the anger of Demeas and Polemon (in *Samia* and *Perikeiromene*) provides other clear examples of bad conduct which depend on a combination of intellectual mistakes and emotional lapses, and are comparable to cases of *akrasia* or lack of self-control in *Nicomachean Ethics* 7.

I was aware that the question of the relationship between Peripatetic philosophy and Menander had been debated since the early 1900s. However, I also recognised that a monograph bringing out fully the extent of shared or analogous ideas in Aristotle and Menander's comedies and exploring in equal depth both the dramatic and the philosophical texts, was still needed. That is why I decided to undertake this project.

A number of studies have been produced on the influence that Peripatetic philosophy allegedly had on Menander's comic production, especially in the 1950s and 1960s after the discovery of the Bodmer Codex (T.B.L. Webster, *Studies in Menander* (Manchester, 1950); A. Barigazzi, *La formazione spirituale di Menandro* (Torino, 1965); K. Gaiser, 'Menander und der Peripatos', *AA* 13 (1967), 8–40; A. Casanova, 'Menander and the Peripatos: New Insight into an Old Question', in A. Sommerstein (ed.), *Menander in Contexts* (New York, 2014), 137–151).

Also, since the 1980s, scholars have approached the question of the relationship of Menander to his intellectual and cultural context in a broader way. More specifically, in relation to the area I explore in this book, Menander's comedy has been studied with a particular attention to its social and ideological context (D. Konstan, *Greek Comedy and Ideology* (Oxford, 1995); A. Scafuro, *The Forensic Stage: Settling Disputes in Graeco-Roman New Comedy* (Cambridge, 1997); S. Lape, *Reproducing Athens: Menander's Comedy, Democratic Culture and the Hellenistic City* (Princeton, 2004); S. Basset, 'The Late Antique Image of Menander', *GRBS* 48 (2008), 201–225 and S. Nervegna, *Menander in Antiquity. The Contexts of Reception* (Cambridge, 2013)). There have also been studies of Menander's presentation of gender relationships (M.M. Henry, *Menander's Courtesans and the Greek Comic Tradition* (Frankfurt, 1985); V.J. Rosivach, *When A Young Man Falls in Love: The Sexual Exploitation of Women in New Comedy* (Routledge, 1998) and on the implications that gender relationships have for characterization and plot-construction (see in particular, A. Traill, *Women and the Comic Plot in Menander* (Cambridge, 2008). Some scholars have also attempted to analyse Menandrian plots and characters on the basis of Aristotle's ethical or aesthetic thought (L.A. Post 'Aristotle and Menander', *TAPA* 69 (1938), 1–42; W.W. Fortenbaugh, 'Menander's *Perikeiromene*. Misfortune, Vehemence, and Polemon', *Phoenix* 28 (1974), 430–443; D. Munteanu, 'Types of *Anagnorisis*: Aristotle and Menander. A Self-Defining Comedy', *WS* 115 (2002), 111–126; A. Scafuro 'When a gesture was misinterpreted: *didonai titthion* in Menander's Samia', in G.W. Bakewell and J.P. Sickinger (eds.), *Gestures: Essays in Ancient History, Literature and Philosophy presented to Alan L. Bolgehold* (Oxford, 2003), 113–135; A.M. Belardinelli, 'Filosofia e scienza nella commedia nuova', *Seminari romani di cultura greca* 11 (2008), 77–106; V. Cinaglia, 'Aristotle and Menander on How People Go Wrong', *CQ* 62 (2012), 553–566). More broadly, recent studies of the ancient theory of emotions and cultural studies have shed new light on the psychological complexity of Menandrian comedies (in particular, D. Konstan, *The Emotions of the Ancient Greeks* (Toronto, 2006); S. Halliwell, *Greek Laughter* (Cambridge, 2008); D. Munteanu (ed.), *Emotion, Genre and Gender in Classical Antiquity* (London 2011); E. Sander, *Envy and Jealousy in Classical Athens* (Oxford, 2014)).

However, a monograph that examines, in a comprehensive and systematic way, the extent and the implications of the analogies between Aristotle and Menander is still needed, and that is the project of this book. More precisely, my aim is to bring out the points of analogy or comparability between Aristotelian theory and Menandrian comedy in their respective presentations of human psychology and ethics. I believe that this comparison can help us to recognise the psychological depth and complexity both in Menandrian characterisation and Aristotelian analysis.

As the title of this book suggests, the idea is to stress that, for both Menander and Aristotle, ethics does not depend solely on goodness of character or having the right kind of motivations or emotions. Ethics is also a matter of reasoning correctly, having good judgment and understanding things in the right way. This idea is a distinctive feature of ancient ethical thought:[1] this book aims to show that this is also a key dimension of Menandrian comedy and that Menander elaborates this idea according to a pattern of tought that is analogous to Aristotelian philosophy.

As our understanding of Menander continues to evolve with the discovery of new fragments and the application of new interpretative approaches (C. Römer, 'A New Fragment of End of Act III, *Epitrepontes* 690–701 Sandbach (P. Mich. 4805)', *ZPE* 183 (2012), 33–36) and new approaches to New Comedy shed further light on the depth of Menander's work (A. Petrides and S. Papaioannou (eds.), *New Perspectives on Postclassical Comedy* (Newcastle upon Tyne, 2010), A. Sommerstein (ed.), *Menander in Contexts* (New York, 2014), and A. Pedrides, *Menander, New Comedy and the Visual* (Cambridge, 2014)), this book offers a fresh point of access to the question of the relationship between Menander and Aristotle and the implications of this relationship for the history of Greek ideas on ethics and human psychology.

1 See Chapter 1.1 for further discussion on this topic.

Acknowledgments

This book is the product of almost seven years of research, starting from the begging of my PhD at Exeter in 2007. Thus, the number of people that, in different ways, have kindly invested their time on this project, is quite conspicuous: to them I owe much gratitude and I hope I have made justice of the courtesy of their minds. All errors and shortcomings remain, of course, mine.

My two supervisors, Christopher Gill and John Wilkins, have been the ones that have encouraged, helped and assisted this project from beginning to end. When I arrived in Exeter for my Master in Classics, I would have never dreamed to be able to share with them my ideas at such length: it has been a privilege to be able to do so and I have benefited more than I can acknowledge here from the care of their exquisite, tireless supervision and precious comments and advices at every point of this project. To them goes my deepest gratitude as scholars and as inspirational models of human beings. In conjunction with them, I thank very warmly Dana Munteanu and David Konstan who have been constantly supportive and always available to read and comment on my PhD thesis first and, then, on my manuscript. The thoroughness of their comments and the warmth of their cheer has really meant a lot for this project. My two PhD examiners, Richard Seaford and Stephen Halliwell, have significantly influenced my thoughts on this latest version of my doctoral work. Working on my manuscript I could more clearly see the force of their comments in occasion of my *viva voce* examination: I am much grateful to them for the extended discussion they offered me on that occasion and their advice and support after that.

All the chapters of this book have been presented, at least in part, to various conferences, research seminars or colloquia. I would like, therefore to acknowledge my debt to the extremely helpful comments of my audiences. In particular, the comments received during the departmental research seminars and postgraduate research seminars in Exeter, during my PhD and after that, have incredibly helped my thinking on Menander and Aristotle. To each member of the department of Classics go my deepest thanks for creating the lively, intellectually stimulating and supportive environment that accompanied the first years of this project, and for allowing me, more recently, to rejoin their enthusiastic community as Honorary Research Fellow. The completion of this project would not have been possible without the support of the Philosophy department at King's College London, where I am completing my appointment as Teaching Assistant. In particular, I owe very much to the Ancient Philosophy group for sharing with me the privilege of their conversation and their feedbacks during research seminars, reading groups and informal conversations: my thinking on several aspects of this project has significantly benefited from this experience. Some of the chapters of this book have been drafted or presented while visiting Brown University in 2008/9 and 2010. I thank very warmly the Classics Department for having welcomed me and for having offered comments and feedbacks on my research. Discussions entertained at the time with David Konstan, Adele Scafuro and Marie Louise Gill were particularly relevant for writing Chapters 2, 3 and 4: I thank them very much for this. In the context of my visit to Brown, I owe a special thank to David Konstan and Pura Nieto, whose incredible enthusiasm, warmth and availability as hosts really made a difference during my stay in Providence.

In the latest stages of this project, I had the chance of receiving the brilliant support and advice of Antonis Pedrides and Sebastiana Nervegna, which I thank both for their time and kindness. I am also grateful to the thorough and much helpful comments of Brill's anonymous reader, to Tessel Jonquière and Laurie Meijers for the prompt and professional support they offered.

The research for this book and the preparation for the manuscript was made possible by the generosity of various funding bodies, including the Arts and Humanities Research Council, the Hellenic Society, the Classical Association and the University of Exeter grants scheme. Some of the texts discussed in this book have been the topics of various undergraduate seminars that I have been tutoring in Exeter and London. To their very much responsive students participant goes my gratitude for making me reflect once more, from jet another different angle, about certain ideas (in particular for Chapter 2, 4 and 5).

Finally, I want to record some more personal acknowledgements. Throughout this long, exciting adventure, and the upheavals of thoughts that this involved, everyone one in my family and circle of close friends had to deal with me, Aristotle and Menander. I thank them all for this. In particular, my parents have responded offering their characteristic vigorous love: their enormous help and their faith in me and this project has been unshakable and I thank them for this with much love. In conjunction with them, I thank my sister Claudia who has helped me throughout some of the most frightening (at least for me) computers' collapses with an unusual patience.

Finally, this book would have never been imaginable without the support, affection and care of my husband Pascal whose companionship and shared thoughts have meant more than he can ever imagine for this book. The preparation of the manuscript for this book has also coincided with the early childhood of our daughter Clelia and, more recently, the birth of our son Ettore. I do need to thank both my children for insisting vigorously and tirelessly to stand beside (or, more literally, to sit on) me for nearly every page of this book until the very end … I would have never made it without their special help! It is to them, to their dad and their unconditional love and smile that this book is dedicated.

Yens, August 2014

Notes on Conventions

1 Ancient Sources

In the footnotes I abbreviate names and works of ancient authors as in H.G. Liddell & R. Scott (eds.), *Greek-English Lexicon* 9th ed. (Oxford, 1996) and in P.G.W. Glare (ed.), *Oxford Latin Dictionary* (Oxford, 1982).

All Greek texts are based on the *Oxford Classical Texts*, unless otherwise stated. All Greek in the body of the text is translated, both in quotations and individual words: translations are generally my own unless otherwise specified. However, I have used published translations, usually modified by me, for the following works of Aristotle:

Apostle, H.G. 1969, *Aristotle's Physics*, trans. with introduction and notes, Bloomington: Indiana University Press.

——— 1975, *The Nicomachean Ethics*, trans. with introduction and notes, Dordrecht: Reidel.

Barnes, J. 1984, '*Eudemian Ethics*', in *The Complete Works of Aristotle*, trans. J. Solomon, vol. 2, Oxford: Oxford University Press.

———1994, *Aristotle: Posterior Analytics*, trans. with introduction and notes, Oxford: Oxford University Press.

Hicks, D.R. (ed.) 1907, *Aristotle: De Anima*, trans. with introduction and notes, Cambridge: Cambridge University Press.

Janko, R. (ed.) 1984, *Aristotle on Comedy: Towards a Reconstruction of Poetics II*, trans. with introduction and notes, Berkeley: University of California Press.

Kennedy, G.A. 2007, *On Rhetoric: A Theory of Civic Discourse*, trans. with introduction and notes, Oxford: Oxford University Press.

Reeve, C.D.C. 1988, *Aristotle: Politics*, trans. with introduction and notes, Indianapolis: Hackett.

2 Modern Works

The following modern works are abbreviated:

DNP H. von Cancik and H. Schneider (eds.), 1996/2003, *Der Neue Pauly*, 16 vols., Stuttgart; Weimar: J.B. Metzler Verlag.

LIMC Fondation pour le *LIMC* (ed.), 1981, *Lexicon Iconographicum Mythologiae Classicae*, 8 vols., Zurich and Munich: Artemis Verlag.

LSJ H.G. Liddell, R. Scott and Jones H.S. (eds.), 1996, *Greek-English Lexicon* (9th edition), Oxford: Clarendon Press.

All secondary literature is cited in footnotes with name of the author(s) and year of publication; it is given in full form in the Bibliography.

Introduction

1 Setting the Scene: Aristotle and Menander

The Preface has outlined the academic background and core project of this book. Here, I explain this project and its scholarly context more fully. Several studies have explored the influence that Peripatetic philosophy may have had on Menander's comic production,[1] and various scholars have attempted to analyse Menandrian plots and characters on the basis of Aristotle's ethical or aesthetic thought.[2] Here, I will not try to demonstrate the direct philosophical influence of Aristotle on Menander; my overall aim is to show that there are significant analogies between these two figures that reveal a shared thought-world and to explore the implications of these analogies on subjects ranging from theory of knowledge to ethics.

It has often been noticed that certain passages of Menander's comedies, fragments and *gnomai* reproduce ideas that are very similar to those presented by Aristotle and Theophrastus, or more generally, the Peripatetic school. In particular, it has been pointed out that Menander often makes statements about topics such as the role of accidental ignorance and fortune in human affairs that reflect Aristotle's thought.[3] It has also been claimed that Menander, in his construction of characters, virtually reproduces on stage the sketches given by Theophrastus in the *Characters*[4] and that he seems to hold the same view as Theophrastus about the education of character.[5] Nevertheless, there is still not enough evidence on Menander's life and work to confirm the hypothesis of a direct influence by Aristotle or Theophrastus on Menander. Menander was still very young when Aristotle died; and, even if it is possible that the mature Menander had some sort of interaction with the Lyceum and, particularly, with Theophrastus, the fragmentary nature of the work of both Theophrastus and Menander makes it difficult to assess the extent of their relationship. Hence, setting aside the question whether we can trace the direct influence of the

1 See Tierney 1935; Webster 1950; Steinmetz 1960; Barigazzi 1965; Gaiser 1967; Guzzo 1978, see also Casanova 2014 for recent discussion on this point.

2 See Post 1938; Fortenbaugh 1974; Gutzwiller 2000; Munteanu 2002; Scafuro 2003; Berardinelli 2008; Cinaglia 2012 and 2014; Cusset 2014.

3 See in particular Tierney 1935, Gutzwiller 2000 and Casanova 2014.

4 See in particular Steinmetz 1960, Barigazzi 1965.

5 Namely, that this is a process that requires both critical reflection and support from good friends. See on this topic: Steinmetz 1960, Barigazzi 1965; Gaiser 1967.

 | DOI: 10.1163/9789004282827_002

Peripatos on Menander, this book analyses the extent of the analogies between Aristotle's philosophy and Menander's comedy.

What I aim to do here is to study Menander's surviving plays as dramatic wholes (as far as our evidence allows us to do this) analysing their structure, the unfolding of their plots and the modes of presentation of the characters. Through this analysis I aim to bring out what Menander's plays convey about human life and psychology in order to reconstruct, as it were, a system of Menander's thought about specific topics. I think that this reconstruction offers us a better chance of understanding Menander's ethical and psychological viewpoint than we can gain simply by bringing together the scattered or fragmentary ethical reflections expressed in fragments or *gnomai* taken out of their dramatic context. I also aim to demonstrate that the set of ideas established in this way is highly comparable to the framework of thought in Aristotle's works on ethics and psychology. My claim is not that Menander provides his audience with a system of ideas that is as intellectually rigorous as the one that we find in Aristotle's treatises. Nevertheless, I believe that, in studying the structure, plots and characterisation of Menander's plays, it is possible to specify the way in which Menander understands the processes of rational and practical understanding, how he presents the psychology of his characters and how he deals with specific ethical issues. Thus, I aim to demonstrate that Menander and Aristotle—despite their different modes of writing and audiences—share an analogous system of ideas. Specifically, they seem to have a common understanding of human nature and its psychological and ethical aspects.

The Aristotelian ideas that I propose to correlate with the Menandrian themes are the following and they centre in Aristotle's ideas about ethical development. Aristotle believes that a combination of rational understanding and emotional training is needed if people are to form a stable character and framework of thought that will enable them to reason correctly in finding out factual truths and making practical choices. Achieving this sort of excellence in theoretical and practical understanding, and thus developing ethical and intellectual virtues, offers people the opportunity of living the best possible life that human beings can hope for. However, Aristotle also points out that the pathway towards this kind of life is not easy: one can fail in controlling one's emotions when responding to given circumstances, as happens in cases of *akrasia* (lack of self-contoll) or one can make mistakes in interpreting adequately one's own perceptions regarding certain particulars, or, finally, one can simply have bad luck and not be able to respond adequately to the sort of unfortunate circumstances one finds oneself involved in. These failings show that one's capacity to achieve successfully intellectual and practical understanding is not properly developed and needs to be further refined so that it may, eventually, become integral to one's character and psychological processes and, thus, provide the basis of living a truly happy life.

A few years later than Aristotle (who taught and wrote in the Lyceum between 335–323 B.C.), Menander's comedies (probably written between 325 and 290 B.C.), as reflected in the extant texts, present to a wider audience a type of drama which appears to reflect an analogously complex and sophisticated understanding of the interplay between intellectual or rational understanding and character or emotion. Menander presents us with characters who make factual and ethical mistakes because they are not able to handle adequately their emotional reactions under given circumstances; they are easily misled by their perceptions and they fail to respond appropriately to their bad luck. Their bad-tempered disposition leads them into troubles and prompts the other characters to blame them for their bad conduct. However, generally speaking, at the end of these comedies characters understand from their experiences what went wrong or finally recognise what the situation was that created their misunderstanding. Hence, at the end of the plays, we have the impression that they make progress in their ability to understand things and how to deal with them: generally speaking, the experiences they have gone through improve their characters and strengthen their resolution to become better persons.

My hypothesis here is that Aristotle and Menander offer analogous views of the way that people's perceptions and emotional responses to situations are linked with the presence or absence of ethical and intellectual understanding and their state of ethical character development. In order to show this, I will examine in detail analogies between the views given by Aristotle and Menander of the relationship between the formation of knowledge, character, choice and emotions, and of how these factors are affected by contingency and chance. By the end of this book, I hope to have shown that Menander and Aristotle share what is largely the same view of how people understand, reason and make factual and ethical mistakes (Chapter 2 and 3); how they face chance and accidental ignorance (Chapter 4); how they develop their character, and what the problems and factors are which are involved in this process (Chapter 5).

I am aware of the fact that this kind of study raises further questions: for instance, one may ask why we find these analogies in the works of Menander and Aristotle and whether this investigation can be extended beyond the works of these two authors and shown to reflect the thought-world of Athenian culture more generally at this time.[6] In addition to that, this book also invites

6 To respond to these questions it would be necessary to look at other kinds of literary sources produced around the same period. For instance, one way of addressing these topics would be

to reflect further on the relationship between Menander and previous forms of drama: that is, Greek Attic Tragedy, Old Comedy and also Middle Comedy.[7] My inquiry here does not attempt to cover this discussion: these topics go beyond the present enquiry and would require independent, sustained analysis. I hope, however, to provide here a solid discussion of the analogies between Aristotle and Menander that will trigger, in due course, dedicated reflections on these further lines of inquiry. In this book, therefore, I will limit myself to analysing the analogies that Aristotle and Menander share in matters of intellectual and ethical understanding, while recognising that the similarities thus brought out raise broader questions and have broader implications than can be pursued here.

2 Menander and Theophrastus on Character(s)?

Menandrian presentation of figures has often been associated with the analysis of types in Theophrastus' *Characters*.[8] Menandrian figures are often described as stock characters,[9] that is, as instances of predictable patterns that recur from

to undetertake a comprehensive examination of Athenian law-court oratory from the late fifth to the end of the fourth century, in the light of these questions. Law-court rhetoric, has, one might suggest, a special relevance for Menandrian comedy. The situations and key questions that are accentuated in Menandrian comedy are analogous to those discussed in Law-court speeches. For analogous comparison between oratory and drama see Dover 1974, pp. 23–36; essays of Bers and Harding in Worthington 1994; Hall 1995; Porter 1997; Goldhill 1999. See Scafuro 1997 for a discussion of the 'forensic' dimension of Greek and Roman comedy. For a broader discussion of Attic oratory in its social and intellectual context see Humphreys 1985 and 1988; Garner 1987; Cartledge, Millett and Todd 1990.

7 The study of Middle Comedy may help explaining the convergence of themes in Aristotle and Menander—although the extant evidence relevant to this kind of drama is rather fragmentary. Menandrian comedies, in fact, were probably strongly influenced by the works of poets such as Alexis, Amphis, Anaxandrides and Theophilus, belonging to this tradition and active during 404–323 B.C. For further discussion on these topics see Arnott 1996, pp. 18–24 and Papachrysostomou 2008, pp. 21–23. Further study on Middle Comedy in view of this topic would be interesting also because this kind of comedy may be also what Aristotel was familiar with (cf. Janko 1984, pp. 242–250) and, like Menandrian comedy, it could be comparable with Aristotle's mode of ethical analysis. See also Sidwell 2014 for further reflections on this topic.

8 See Diggle 2004 for a recent discussion of the authenticity of this title and, more generally, the aims of the treatise, which have been much debated.

9 See MacCary 1970 and, for a recent functionalist reading of Menander's characters, Macua Martinez 2008, especially p. 18.

play to play and represent well-acknowledged types of behaviour. However, as brought out shortly, there are problems in correlating Theophrastus' types and Menander's characters. In his treatise, Theophrastus gives examples of types of behaviour that recur constantly, and does so without explaining the underlying reason why this happens: he lists the various kinds of action that a certain kind of person is expected to perform. The assumption made by the treatise seems to be that it is everyone's natural inclination that shapes their ethical behaviour and not a series of reasoned choices as it is for Aristotle.[10] As noted in the previous section, Aristotle assumes that one's character formation, the shaping of one's ethical identity, depends on a complex interplay between natural inclinations, habituation and reasoned choices.[11] When reading Theophrastus' character-sketches, we do not find the same complex set of factors involved. The suspicious man (ἄπιστος), for instance, always behaves in the same way; every instance of his behaviour will reproduce the same pattern of choice and action: his natural inclinations alone seem to determine the way he behaves and they do not give scope for possible changes in his way of life and ethical understanding.

However, Menander's characters are not stock characters: they have their own opinions and a specific life-history that explains their deliberation and motivation for action. They might have specific natural inclinations that influence their choices and actions, but they also make reasoned choices, they recognise their mistakes and they try to change their way of life and their way of approaching people and situations. They formulate their reasoning on the basis of an identifiable framework of values and beliefs: they thus have social and biographical depth. In order to clarify this latter point, I will refer to a play that has often been treated as supporting the idea that Theophrastus may have influenced Menander: the *Dyscolos*. The purpose of this example is also to bring out more explicitly why it is worthwhile to explore possible analogies between Aristotle's philosophy and Menander's comedy rather than to concentrate on the alleged similarities between Theophrastus' character-sketches and Menander's characters.

The presentation of Knemon, in the *Dyscolos*, resembles the description that Theophrastus gives of two comparable character-types, that is, the suspicious man (ἄπιστος) and the self-centred man (αὐθάδης). What is particularly interesting in comparing these figures (that of Knemon and Theophrastus'

10 See Fortenbaugh 2005, pp. 87–92.

11 Although sometimes in *Rhetoric*, and in some passages of *Nicomachean Ethics* 4, Aristotle's description of types can be rather schematic.

suspicious and self-centred types) is to note their rigid standpoint in each case: both Menander and Theophrastus seem to describe extreme characters who are reluctant to change and who have grown old in habits that now constitute the way in which they naturally behave. Knemon and these two character-types appear particularly similar if we focus on the attitude that they maintain towards other people, especially towards the members of their family. Here is the description that Theophrastus gives of a suspicious character type:

> καὶ ὅταν ἥκῃ τις αἰτησόμενος ἐκπώματα, μάλιστα μὲν μὴ δοῦναι, ἂν δ' ἄρα τις οἰκεῖος ᾖ καὶ ἀναγκαῖος, μόνον οὐ πυρώσας καὶ στήσας καὶ σχεδὸν ἐγγυητὴν λαβὼν χρῆσαι.
>
> When somebody comes asking for the loan of cups, he would rather say no altogether, but if he has to oblige a member of his family or a close relative he will lend them only after he has all but checked the quality and weight of the metal and practically got someone to guarantee the cost of the replacement.[12]

As Diggle suggests, "loan for domestic objects would normally be made without interest, witnesses, or security".[13] But when a suspicious man such as Knemon is asked for something like that, the first thing he thinks about is whether the person who is asking has a sort of contract (συμβόλαιον) with him, on the basis of which that person could reasonably make the request. In the mind of the suspicious man, that would be the only reason why someone would think of asking him for something: he does not conceive any other way in which he could take part in relationships with other people. This is made clear in the exchange between Knemon and the slave Getas who knocks at Knemon's door to ask for the loan of a brazier. Knemon promptly refuses the loan as soon as he hears that he is not bound to Getas on the basis of a business contract and that Getas' request is that of a friendly, non-official, loan.[14]

We find some traits of Knemon also when we look at Theophrastus' description of the self-centred man. This kind of man is the sort of person who would not return a greeting[15] and who refuses to sing, recite or dance.[16] In this respect

---

12 Thphr. *Char.* XVIII, 15–18. Text and translation (slightly modified) by Diggle 2004.

13 Diggle 2004, ad loc. and Millett 1991, pp. 38–39.

14 Men. *Dysc.* 466–480. This point will be discussed in more detail in Chapter 5, pp. 154–155.

15 Thphr. *Char.* XV, 3.1.

16 Thphr. *Char.* XV, 10–11.

too, Knemon seems to fit Theophrastus' description: the self-centred man considers only his own perspective. Knemon refuses to speak with other people and to perform conventional acts, such as greeting, that would make him one of them. Like Knemon, the self-centred man also refuses to take part in parties where he needs to sing or dance; that is to say, he refuses to take part in those gatherings that facilitate the cultivation of interpersonal relationships and interaction with other people. On the other hand, we also know that, somehow, Knemon is induced to change his attitude as the play proceeds and, furthermore, we are told why the old man became the distrustful, self-centred person that we see on stage.[17] What we have left of Theophrastus' work does not offer scope for a possible change of mind of this kind: Theophrastus does not show characters who change and he does not explain why they become what they are.

It is possible to suppose that Menander had heard about, or even read, Theophrastus' *Characters* and that this had somehow influenced the construction of some of his plots; however, Menander's *Dyscolos* includes topics that go beyond the theme of the misanthropy of his main character. The *Dyscolos* as a whole includes a range of themes and its perspective embraces psychological insight and ethical or social reflection.[18] These topics, taken together, constitute a coherent design that has analogies with Aristotelian thinking about human nature and psychology in a way that goes beyond anything we find in the rather superficial sketches that Theophrastus offers in the *Characters*. As shown later in this book, in reading Menander and Aristotle we come to understand why doing certain things or responding to specific situations in a certain way is not good; we are also offered an analysis of the motivation that might lead someone to perform a specific act and the explanation of what is involved in the development of a certain kind of character. In Theophrastus' *Characters*, we are left without such explanations.

It is possible to argue that Theophrastus would have shared with Aristotle the same ideas about the development of intellectual and ethical virtue and the formation of character. We seem to have some evidence of this common ground from a testimony of Stobaeus that might help us in reconstructing the process that leads to the presentation of a self-centred and distrustful character such as Knemon.[19] In this passage, we learn that Theophrastus thought

17 Men. *Dysc.* 711–723.

18 See Chapter 5 for an extended discussion of this topic.

19 The testimony is quoted as evidence of possible influence of Theophrastus on Menander by Steinmetz 1960, Barigazzi 1965, p. 120 and Gaiser 1967, especially pp. 34–35. All of them

that the key to a good life does not lie only in having a liberal upbringing and good friends and relatives. Young people, in particular, should also know how to use their friends; they should engage with them in critical reflection; they should ask them for suggestions as they would ask suggestions from a guide when they travel.[20] In this way, as they become adult, they will be less likely to acquire the bad disposition of someone such as Knemon. It seems, therefore, that Theophrastus, like Aristotle, ascribed great importance to the role that human relationships and a shared life have in correct character development. It is, therefore, probable that Theophrastus' theories on the topic were actually very close to those ascribed to Aristotle earlier.[21] Consequently, it is also possible that there are analogies between Theophrastus' ethical thought and the way in which Menander constructs his characters (in this specific case, Knemon) and conceives their psychological processes. However, evidence and testimonies for Theophrastus' thought do not provide enough material to verify this hypothesis; this is why, in this book, I have chosen to focus solely on possible analogies between Menander and Aristotle, without getting involved in the discussion about links between Menander and Theophrastus or the later Peripatetic school.

3 The Structure of the Book and the Method of Enquiry

As already indicated, in this book, I will try to establish a comparison between two frameworks of thought (those of Menander and Aristotle) which brings out analogous features. In each chapter I have chosen to focus on one or two texts that enable me to specify Menander's treatment of specific topics. This approach is motivated by the thought that to reconstruct the framework of thinking that underlies a drama, whether tragic or comic, it is necessary to look at the whole structure of the play, to follow the progressive unfolding of the plot and the presentation of characters, as far as the extant text allows us to do this. To focus attention on specific lines without explaining the context in which they are spoken, or which kind of figure speaks them, would not help the present enquiry. This is the reason why I have deliberately chosen not to include

agree in saying that there are evident Peripatetic influences on the way in which Menander constructs and develops his characters; however, in fact, it is not possible to verify whether these influences include Theophrastus' thought specifically.

20 Stob. 2.31.124. On this point see Fortenbaugh 1992, pp. 292–293.

21 See pp. 2–3.

a discussion of some of Menander's more fragmentary plays, short fragments and *gnomai*.

Once I have outlined the main ideas that, I believe, underlie Menander's extant plays, in the second part of each chapter, I compare them with specific passages of Aristotle's works that identify an analogous set of topics. As with Menander, the discussion of specific passages is set in the broader context of Aristotle's thought so as to provide a comprehensive account of his ideas about certain topics, which can then be more effectively compared with what has been said about Menander. In some cases, I will integrate my analysis of Menandrian comedies with the discussion of texts belonging to the previous tragic and comic tradition. The aim of these brief discussions is not to examine in any depth the relationship between Menander and the previous dramatic tradition: their scope is to define and bring out fully the ethical dramatic mode which is characterist of Menander and that I show to be analogous, in themes and ideas, to Aristotle.

I now give an outline of the structure of the book and a more specific account of the topics to be treated.

In Chapter 1, I discuss the broader conceptual background of my enquiry about Aristotle and Menander. The aim of this section is to clarify the nature of the main themes of my account, such as the relationship between intellectual and ethical understanding, and the importance of this kind of understanding in living a full human life. I also discuss what is involved in applying this kind of account to drama as well as to philosophy.

In the following two chapters, I move on to interpretative discussion of dramatic and philosophical presentation of theoretical and practical understanding and to defective versions of this type of understanding. There, I suggest that Aristotle and Menander have similar views about how understanding develops, why it fails and what are the consequences of this failure. In order to illustrate this point, in Chapter 2, I will consider Menander's treatment of recognition and Aristotle's ideas about understanding (ἐπιστήμη). Generally speaking, the similarities between Aristotle and Menander will be shown to lie in i) the relevance that the individual's attitude has for the completion of a successful intellectual process and ii) the importance for the individual of forming a comprehensive framework of understanding that enables him or her to make sense of her experience in any given situation.

In Chapter 3, I will examine how, in both Aristotle and Menander, ethical issues are closely related to epistemological ones. In this respect, I will mainly stress two points. One is that, in both philosophical and dramatic contexts, an inappropriate factual understanding of something or someone is shown as often leading to practical error. Even though the reasoning that leads to the practical decision is virtuous in itself we might still misunderstand the circumstances of the action. Moreover, practical and factual understanding varies according to the state of mind of the person involved: failure to control one's emotions can influence the outcome of one's rational and intellectual activity so as to vitiate ethical reasoning and thus understanding. In this respect too, Aristotle and Menander will be shown to have an analogous framework of thought.

In the last two chapters, I will consider how Menander and Aristotle treat cases in which someone's intellectual and ethical insight, is challenged by situations that are not dependent on the agent but that happen by accident and influence in some way his life and his character. In these cases, Menander and Aristotle, in analogous ways, do not consider that a person, whose weaknesses are exposed by accidents or adverse situations, should be seen simply as the passive victim of events. Rather, they seem to believe that a person who has intellectual and ethical insight can respond effectively to what happens to him or her by accident. Hence, knowledge and ethics are not just dependent on the subject's theoretical and practical intelligence: they partly depend on variables that are external to the agent, but also on the response that the agent gives to these external factors. In Chapter 4, I will analyse the role of chance and accidental ignorance on human actions. Unforeseen events affect human life; these events are interpreted by rational beings who make choices and have different reactions to them. Depending on the character of people they affect, these events produce different responses and so the consquences of those events can be concurrent causes of other events that are the results of the decisions made by those involved. Thus, it seems to me that, from Menander's and Aristotle's point of view, chance events take on a different meaning according to the people concerned and their responses to these events, and, hence, according to people's ability to understand what is at stake and what should be done, that is to say, on their factual and practical understanding.

In Chapter 5, I offer broader reflections about certain shared emphases in the conception of human ethical life held by Aristotle and Menander. Accidental events and our interpretation of them are key factors that contribute in shaping our character, *ēthos*. Events, fortunate or unfortunate they might be, form an important part of ethical life and they offer a useful opportunity to build up one's character: they constitute the gymnasium in which we can exercise our skills and values. It seems that Menander and Aristotle share analogous ideas also in this respect. Self-formation, the building up of a consistent character and the progressive understanding of certain issues, develop as we respond to life's accidents and to our relationships with others. Ethical life is conceived by both Aristotle and Menander as functioning properly within a community of fiends and relatives: a correct understanding is achieved by communicating one's own thoughts to others in the context of a shared life. Understanding, therefore, also depends on the existence of a community and the public sharing of ideas.

CHAPTER 1

Setting the Broader Background

Having now specified the focus and the aims of this book, I dedicate this short chapter to discussing the broader theoretical context that underlies the ideas discussed so far. I have suggested that Aristotle gives special emphasis to the idea that rational or intellectual understanding is crucial for living an ethically good human life. In the following section (section 1), I will explain these ideas at greater length. In doing so, I will also specify the differences between ancient and modern treatment of understanding and its importance for ethical life. More broadly, I want to suggest that in ancient philosophy generally, and in Aristotle in particular, a close connection is seen between epistemology and ethics. Throught this discussion, section 1 also helps to explain at more length my choice of title for this book, as briefly discussed in the Preface.[1]

In section 2, I will explain how the framework of thought on this subject is also relevant for the interpretation of Menandrian drama. To speak about the theory of knowledge and ethics in connection with comic works risks transforming a piece of literature made for entertainment into an artificial expression of serious philosophical ideas—and this is not the view I want to convey. I believe that Menander, like any other playwright, wrote his plays with the intention of appealing to his audience and giving them an enjoyable dramatic experience. The aim of section 2 is precisely to explain the kind of pleasure that, I believe, Menander's comedy is meant to convey.

1 Understanding, Ethics and Ancient Philosophy

In contemporary philosophy, epistemology is the discipline that focuses on issues related to knowledge and, more generally, the process of understanding. As a discipline, contemporary epistemology attempts to answer such questions as: "What are the necessary and sufficient conditions of knowledge? What are its sources? What is its structure, and what are its limits?".[2] Typically, epistemology is seen as the study of justified belief. We know something because we first believe something. However, in order to be classified as true knowledge,

---

1 See p. XI.

2 Moser and Vander Nat 2003.

 | DOI: 10.1163/9789004282827_003

our belief needs to be i) true and ii) justified. Justification is an important element that enables true belief to become knowledge. We might just be lucky in believing something that finally turns out to be true;[3] therefore, if we want to claim knowledge, we should give a justification for our beliefs. Hence, generally speaking, in contemporary philosophy "knowledge is a belief of a special kind, belief satisfying certain conditions. These necessary conditions for knowledge, on the traditional approach, are the truth of what is believed and the justification or evidence of what is believed".[4]

In ancient Greek philosophy too, there is a concern with making sense of the interrelationship between knowledge, belief and truth.[5] For instance, the distinction between belief (δόξα) and truth (ἀλήθεια) is discussed in Xenophanes[6] and Parmenides[7] while Anaxagoras' fragments contain reflections on human intellectual power and the ability to infer from signs, and to understand what is invisible from what is visible.[8] Thus, the question of the nature of the difference between belief and knowledge was already a major issue in early Greek philosophy; and belief was, typically, regarded as an inadequate source of knowledge, because it was variable and qualitatively different from knowledge. However, it is not until the time of Plato and Aristotle, in the fourth century BC, that we find fully developed theories about human intellectual ability, the possibility and prerequisites of scientific knowledge, the problem of the distinction between knowledge and belief and the question of the possibility of error.[9]

It is, however, worth noticing that the characteristic approach of ancient philosophers to epistemology is different from the contemporary approach outlined earlier. Justified belief, in Plato and Aristotle, does not have the same status as knowledge as it has, typically, in the contemporary approach. In ancient philosophy, to know is not just to justify a belief: to know something means to raise one's own understanding to a level which is qualitatively different from that of mere belief. In this framework of ideas, to understand also means to realise that the higher status, that of understanding, *epistēmē*,[10] is

---

3 On the concept of 'epistemic luck' see Pritchard 2005.

4 Moser and Vander Nat 2003, p. 2.

5 See for extended discussion of this topic: Everson 1990; Brunschwig and Lloyd 2003 and Tuominen 2007.

6 DK 21, B 34.

7 DK 28, B 1 25–30.

8 DK 59, B 21b.

9 Brunschwig 2003, p. 19.

10 My translation of this word 'ἐπιστήμη' as 'understanding' follows Burnyeat 1981. See chapter 3.2 for extended discussion on this topic.

indispensable for explaining the lower one, that of belief. Consequently, the transition from belief to exact knowledge or understanding is treated differently in ancient thought. In the transition from belief to knowledge, ancient thought attaches great importance to the cognitive status of the subject who is in the process of gaining understanding and completing this process. To have knowledge implies understanding the explanatory power of knowledge in relation to belief.

To achieve understanding we need to have appropriate intellectual abilities but we also need to work on these in order to develop their full potential and to shape a consistent disposition as regards to finding the truth, that is (as they put it), to acquire intellectual virtue.[11] To possess intellectual virtue, in fact, involves the constant exercise and development of one's intellectual skills. An intellectually virtuous person would be one who has achieved a stable disposition that enables him or her[12] to be successful in finding the truth. This involves working on what reason, emotions, perceptions and particular situations suggest and following through a kind of reasoning that is rigorous and well-conducted and that, in this way, leads to knowledge of the truth.[13] Intellectual virtue depends on our knowing something properly because we do not just believe it on the basis of mere experience or hearsay but we also understand the cause of it and use the best possible reasoning to grasp its truth.

This approach suits an epistemology which is *person-based* instead of *belief-based*: to find out the truth we not only need a set of justifiable beliefs; we need to be the kind of person that is able to formulate them in the best possible way and to give an explanatory, comprehensive account of them. In contemporary thought this view (standard in ancient philosophy) is maintained by virtue epistemology.[14] Virtue epistemologists say that an agent *S* knows that *p* only in cases where *S*'s believing *p* results from a virtuous cognitive character. In virtue epistemology, the agent is "reliable": that is to say, starting from experiences, sensory appearance and beliefs, the agent is able to produce an

11 See Sherman and White 2003 for a broader dicussion on this topic and Montmarquet 1986 and Zagzebski 1996 for cognate modern theories.

12 In this book I will normally refer to indefinite subjects using the male personal pronoun. My reason for doing so is that ancient philosophers tend to speak exclusively from a male perspective and also that, in Menander's comedies, those who make the ethical and factual mistakes central to the dramas are mainly male characters.

13 Cf. Arist. *EN* VI 7, 1141a3–5.

14 See Sosa 1980; Montmarquet 1986; Code 1987; Zagzebski 1996; Greco 2000; DePaul and Zagzebski 2003.

additional state in a reliable, i.e. truth-conducting, way;[15] in this way, "knowledge is produced by a cognitive process that 'gets things right' or is 'accurate' a good deal of the time".[16]

These points should clarify what epistemology typically meant in ancient thought. According to Plato, for instance, the appearances offered by sense perception do not offer a precise or reliable account of what surrounds us: true knowledge must include the contemplation of objects of knowledge that can be achieved only through a sustained process of enquiry about the reliability of what we know, or what we think we know. Thus, sensory experience needs explanatory understanding which culminates in knowledge of the Forms in order for the individual to grasp fully what is perceived. To reach full understanding is a difficult process and knowledge of the truth is achieved only by exercising one's intellectual ability and expressing a sustained desire to achieve the ultimate, most complete understanding;[17] between knowledge and belief there is a gulf that few are able to bridge. For instance, according to Plato's *Republic*,[18] knowledge or understanding, thought (διάνοια), confidence (πίστις) and imagination (εἰκασία)[19] are the four kinds of cognitive states that human beings, like the prisoners in the cave, experience. The progress from one of those states to another depends on the subject's ability to discriminate between them, that is, to understand the difference between having a belief and possessing the explanatory power of understanding that makes sense of our belief.[20]

---

15 Greco 2000, pp. 167–168. See also Williamson 2002 who attemps to define knowledge as a truth-entailing mental state that is different from true belief (in particular: ch. 1, sections 4–5) and should be analysed and defined as fundamental and explanatory of belief and justification itself (ch. 9).

16 Greco 2000, p. 166.

17 These brief comments synthesise a complex set of ideas variously formulated in different platonic dialogues: Pl. *R.* V, 476b–e; 490a6–b7; 518b6–d1; *Symp.* 210a–d. On this point see among others Cornford 1935; Bluck 1961; Cooper 1970; Burnyeat 1976 and 1990; Fine 1990; Woodruff 1990. For recent discussions with a particular focus on late Platonic dialogues and Platonic dialectic method see M.L. Gill 2006 and El Murr 2006.

18 Pl. *R.* VII, 534a–b.

19 For a more detailed discussion of these four stages see Fine 1990, pp. 99–115.

20 At the level of imagination, the ordinary world of appearences, the prisoner in the cave sits bound in chains and sees shadows passing in front of him (Pl. *R.* VII, 514c–515c). What is crucial here is not what he sees: the point is that the prisoner cannot "discriminate between images and the objects they are of" (Fine 1990, p. 101). He understands the difference when he turns his head to the objects behind him (Pl. *R.* VII, 515c–d) and understands the explanatory cause of the shadows that he was seeing before. The prisoner should then be able to discuss what he sees by using his reason and discerning gradually

Aristotle, on the other hand, believes that we can gain a certain degree of knowledge, and not just belief, even at the lower level of sense perception; indeed, we cannot achieve any knowledge of truth without perceiving particulars. As explained later (Chapter 2), everyone, since he can perceive, should theoretically be able to achieve *epistēmē* by assimilating his experiences and sense perceptions according to proper reasoning.[21] Problems arise when perception of particulars is missing or we are simply not able to see them in a sufficiently comprehensive view.[22] It thus turns out that experience and insight are fundamental ingredients of theoretical understanding.

At the same time, the relevance of one's individual ability in getting to know something has its counterpart in the field of ethics.[23] In fact, in the Platonic-Aristotelian tradition, as well as in Greek philosophy more generally, knowledge has important implications for practical life. For Plato, to gain proper understanding is a prerequisite of an ethically good action. To understand the truth about what is good and bad should provide the basis on which we should measure the goodness or badness of our choices.[24] In Aristotle, by contrast, dianoetic virtues are not enough in the realm of ethics by themselves.[25] Someone who potentially has knowledge of what is good and what is not also requires the ability to deal with human emotions[26] or accidents[27] appropriately and to make sure that he is properly affected by them.[28] Therefore, intellectual

---

the real essence of the images (Pl. *R.* VII, 532a). Through this dialectical process, he can eventually give a satisfactory and fully explanatory account of what surrounds him. Only this kind of account constitutes understanding and it offers a revealing new perspective on what the prisoner was confusedly seeing before. In this process of understanding, the error seems not to lie in sense data taken on their own but in how we are able to reason to gain knowledge based on these data: namely, in our ability to use dialectic method correctly (Pl. *R.* VII, 533c7–e2).

21 Arist. *Metaph.* A 1, 980a21–27.

22 Arist. *APo.* I 18, 81a38–b9; I 28, 87a38–b3. On these ideas see among others Sorabji 1980; Burnyeat 1981; Nussbaum 1982; Lear 1988; Barnes 1994 and Tuominen 2007.

23 "Even if the intellectual virtues enable us to discover truths about matter that are recondite and abstract still our increased grasp of truth will serve to broaden and deepen the understanding at the basis of the kind of practical knowledge which is moral virtue" (Annas 2003, p. 22).

24 Pl. *Cri.* 47e–48b; *Symp.* 210d and *Prot.* 356d.

25 Arist. *EN* I 13, 1102a25–1103a10.

26 Arist. *EN* I 6, 1098a1–20.

27 Arist. *EN* III 7, 1135b15–20 see also *MM* I 33, 1195a–b.

28 Arist. *EN* III 2, 1110b18–1111a6. See among others Nussbaum 1978, essay 4; Broadie 1991, pp. 214–219; Annas 1993; Sherman and White 2003.

virtue helps us to make the right kind of decisions but it needs to be combined properly with natural dispositions and adequate habituation. To achieve this balance is difficult and the truly virtuous person is the one who is able to get it right all the time, as it will be discussed at length particularly in Chapter 3 and 5. Practical understanding, therefore, seems apparently to function in a way that is analogous to theoretical understanding: on the basis of a given set of particulars and being affected by certain sensory perceptions, one has to comprehend these elements adequately in order to find out which is the right choice to make.[29] However, by contrast with scientific analysis, the function of ethical understanding is not only to understand things in the right way, but also to be able to act on this understanding to develop an excellent character. It follows that the quality of ethical deliberation does not depend on the outcome being succcessful (this can be affected by variables that do not depend on the agent, such as for instance, chance—as discussed in Chapter 4) but on the quality of the ethical choice itself.

> Moral virtue, then, is a skill in the ancient virtue tradition; it is an expertise, a kind of practical knowledge. Local mundane skills serve as examples of the kind of unified practical understanding, which, if we become virtuous, will order our lives in a unified way based on understanding.[30]

Accordingly, ethics is agent-centred in a manner that is similar to epistemology.[31] We need particular intellectual skills to understand correctly and, finally, in order to to act virtuously.[32] To have ethical virtue means to have developed the best possible disposition to choose to do the right thing in any given situation. As will be discussed in the following chapters, Aristotle's version of this approach has significant points in common with Menander's drama.

---

29 Arist. *EN* III 5, 1112b15–24.

30 Annas 2003, p. 20.

31 The attempt to establish a theory of knowledge based on the model of 'virtue ethics' theory is the main focus of virtue epistemology. Although I cannot pursue this strand of modern theory here, I agree with the general reading of Aristotle that attempts to connect his epistemology and his ethics. See Bloomfield 2000; Annas 2003; Sherman and White 2003 for recent notes on this topic.

32 More recently, with particular emphasis on this point see Russell 2009 and Annas 2011.

2 Understanding, Ethics and Aesthetic Pleasure

When I argue that Menander's comedies engage with issues related to knowledge and ethics, I also mean that the pleasurable experience deriving from his drama is related to these issues. We enjoy characters' misunderstandings and the troubles they go through to achieve finally the full understanding of what happened and the final revelation of their factual and ethical mistakes. At the end of the story, the full comprehension of facts and of people's identity is achieved and we take pleasure from the positive understanding we get from this process. The conclusion that we, as audience, are waiting for is the achievement of a fully explanatory version of the story, namely, a version that frames, and gives sense to, what was supposed by hypothesis before. Also, we wait to know what and who on the stage will make this final comprehension possible: we see the reasoning (or lack of reasoning) by the dramatic figures that leads to (or prevents) this type of understanding. Consequently, at the end of the performance we might say that the understanding of the audience, as well as that of the characters, is improved. One of the aims of this book is to argue that this kind of aesthetic pleasure is comparable with Aristotle ethic and aestehic thought.

Starting with the *Poetics*, it is clear that, according to Aristotle, the pleasure derived from mimetic arts, including drama, depends on the understanding of the logic of the plot: he sees this process of understanding as inherently pleasurable. To imitate (μιμεῖσθαι) is to reproduce a situation similar to the truth, looking at which we learn something about the truth.[33] To understand is a natural desire for human beings and it is the most agreeable activity.[34] "Our pleasure in art is a branch of this pleasure; the poet or the orator or the painter makes us see or understand things that we did not see before, and particularly he points out the relations and similarities between different things that enable us to say, in Aristotle's phrase, this is that".[35]

> τό τε γὰρ μιμεῖσθαι σύμφυτον τοῖς ἀνθρώποις ἐκ παίδων ἐστὶ καὶ τούτῳ διαφέρουσι τῶν ἄλλων ζῴων ὅτι μιμητικώτατόν ἐστι καὶ τὰς μαθήσεις ποιεῖται διὰ μιμήσεως τὰς πρώτας, καὶ τὸ χαίρειν τοῖς μιμήμασι πάντας [...]. αἴτιον δὲ καὶ

33 Arist. *Poet.* 4, 1448b5–9. According to Dosi 1960, Janko 1984 and Fortenbaugh 2005 the relation between imitation (μίμησις) and learning (μάθησις) is seen differently in Theophrastus. Evidence of this is a single testimony in which Theophrastus seems to oppose poetry and truth: the source is Dionysius of Halicarnassus' essay *On Lysias* (*Lys.* 14, 1–4). See also Nesselrath 1990, p. 59 n. 27.

34 Arist. *Rhet.* III 10, 1410b7–12 and see *Metaph.* A 1, 980a21.

35 Hubbard 1972, p. 86.

> τούτου, ὅτι μανθάνειν οὐ μόνον τοῖς φιλοσόφοις ἥδιστον ἀλλὰ καὶ τοῖς ἄλλοις ὁμοίως, ἀλλ' ἐπὶ βραχὺ κοινωνοῦσιν αὐτοῦ. διὰ γὰρ τοῦτο χαίρουσι τὰς εἰκόνας ὁρῶντες, ὅτι συμβαίνει θεωροῦντας μανθάνειν καὶ συλλογίζεσθαι τί ἕκαστον, οἷον ὅτι οὗτος ἐκεῖνος·
>
> To imitate is something natural in men from childhood and in this respect they differ from all other animals: that man is the most imitative creature and learning, [for him], comes through the imitation of what [he has experienced] before; and, the fact that all of them take pleasure in imitations [...]. The reason for this is that to learn is the most pleasant activity not just for philosophers but equally for all the others, they just have a limited share of it. So it is for this that they rejoice when they see the images, because it happens that in beholding [art work] we learn and we infer reasoning syllogistically what each thing is, as [for example] that this person is such and such person.[36]

The pleasure that the audience receives from attending a dramatic representation seems to inhere precisely in this learning process and in the final understanding that this produces. In mimetic arts in general, and drama[37] in particular, what the spectator views is one object—the plot: a story that has, as its content, an imitation of actions, that should be complete in all its parts and fully developed within the space of a beginning, a middle and an end.[38] The plot is formed by the narration of several actions the unitary structure of which is understood progressively by following the performance from the beginning to the end. "The perception of dramatic sequence and structure is comparable to the understanding of a logical or a quasi-logical argument; the audience's sense of intelligible structure is a matching response to the causality within the plot".[39] This is what constitutes the difference between history and poetry:[40] history records particular facts that have not been unified in a

36 Arist. *Poet.* 4, 1448b5–17.

37 Arist. *Poet.* 7, 1450b21–27. This passage refers to the imitation of actions that constitute a tragedy. It is, however, possible to attribute, by symmetry, the same definition to the imitation of actions that constitute a comedy: the imitation should be equally complete in all its parts and should have a beginning, a middle and an end. See Arist. *Poet. II*, fr. IV Janko: "Comedy is an imitation of an action that is absurd and lacking in magnitude, complete" (κωμῳδία ἐστὶ μίμησις πράξεως γελοίας καὶ ἀμοίρου μεγέθους, τελείας).

38 Arist. *Poet.* 7, 1451a30–33.

39 Halliwell 1986, pp. 100–101.

40 On this particular point see de Ste Croix 1992 and Carli 2010.

final version by a poet. The structure of an historical report is not unitary as it is bound to follow circumstances and the random order in which, in the actual historical situation, those circumstances happened to follow one another. This point might also explain why Aristotle dislikes episodic drama:[41] episodes do not form a well-articulated whole and "the scenes follow one another without the inward connection of the 'likely' (εἰκός) or 'necessary' (ἀναγκαῖον)".[42] Mimetic arts, instead, are made to be of this kind;[43] the pleasure that we expect to receive from them depends on the understanding of this general idea, the universal that the poet had in mind while shaping the plot.[44] The understanding of the general idea, the acknowledgement of the real course of events and the definition of the characters' factual and ethical identity is made explicit during the recognition—and this is why recognition, for Aristotle, is a vital element of the plot:[45]

> Only by virtue of the recognition do the truth, the inner coherence and the meaning of the plot [...] become evident to the mind of the spectator.[46]

> Through recognition (*anagnorisis*) the spectator learns to express in an orderly and satisfactory way what is happening on the stage and what is happening in his soul; he passes therefore from unarticulated confusion to articulate knowledge.[47]

---

41 Arist. *Poet.* 9, 1451b33–35.

42 Butcher 1927, p. 282, slightly modified. See also Finkelberg 2006.

43 Arist. *Poet.* 17, 1455b4–7. "The universal of chapters nine and seventeen is built into the plot structure of a drama—into the causal network of actions and events which it comprises [...]. So universals are not inherent in the raw stuff of a tragedy or comedy but become apparent only in and through the shaped mimetic structure of 'action and life' that the poet makes: it is this unified design of the art-work which differentiates poetry, as Aristotle insists, from ordinary events and hence from history. This means that universals are related to causes, reasons, motives and patterns of intelligibility in the action and characters as a whole" (Halliwell 1992, p. 250). See also Butcher 1927 and Yanal 1982.

44 See Arist. *Poet.* 4, 1448b4–19 and also 9, 1451b5–15. See Golden 1992, p. 106: Aristotle's aesthetic theory "explains our attraction to tragedy and comedy on the basis of a deeply felt impulse arising from our very nature as human beings to achieve intellectual insight through that process of learning and inference which represents the essential pleasure and purpose of all artistic *mimesis*".

45 Arist. *Poet.* 9, 1452a11–21.

46 Entralgo 1970 p. 230.

47 Entralgo 1970 p. 233.

Unfortunately, we do not possess a full account of Aristotle's analysis of comedy in the extant text of the *Poetics*.[48] In *Poetics* 5, comedy is briefly defined as an imitation of people that are inferior (μίμησις φαυλοτέρων), "not, however, with respect to every kind of vice, but the laughable is part of what is ugly".[49] Accordingly, the comic error, *hamartēma*, is defined there as an amusing error, that is, a defect that is visibly shameful (αἶσχος), but not to the extent of being painful or destructive.[50] Thus, the error of the comic character, for Aristotle, depends on evident human flaws and visible 'distortions' of the figures on stage. That is to say, watching the comic plot we have a clear understanding of why (inferior) figures make mistakes and which kind of motivations or ethical lapses have produced these mistakes. In comedies, we follow a unitary sequence of events and we laugh at clearly identifiable mistakes done by figures that are evidently less perfect than people ought to be. The kind of aesthetic pleasure provided by Menandrian comedy seems to be in line with this discussion: it is pleasure in understanding the logic of the whole story presented in the plot and pleasure in understanding what went wrong in it and how the mistakes of the characters are finally resolved. This idea will appear more clealy in the course of this book.

Menander seems to have a special interest in leading people in the audience to follow the characters' reasoning and in giving them clear indications when people go wrong and why a given figure, because he or she has a character of a certain kind, made that particular mistake.[51] In Menander's comedy the happy ending arrives when the dramatic figures understand (or are told) what the truth is.[52] In this respect, therefore, our laughter at them is motivated

---

48 The *Tractatus Coislinianus* is however considered, for some, a valid source to reconstruct Aristotle's ideas on Comedy. For the much debated question of the authorship of the *Tractatus Coislinianus* see Bernays 1853; Kayser 1906; Rostagni 1922; Janko 1984. For an extensive summary of the more recent scholarship on the topic see Janko 2001, pp. 52–53. For a general accont of Aristotle's theory of comedy in its social and intellectual context see Hokenson 2006, chapter 1.

49 Arist. *Poet.* 5, 1449a32–37.

50 For a recent and more detailed discussion of the shameful in comedy see Munteanu 2011(a), chapter 4.

51 In this respect, Menander's comedy can be classified as falling within Northrop Frye's fourth kind of fictional mode: "If superior neither to other men nor to his environment, the hero is one of us: we respond to a sense of his common humanity, and demand from the poet the same canons of probability that we find in our own experience. This gives us the hero of the low mimetic mode, of most comedy and of realistic fiction" (Frye 1957, p. 34).

52 See Cave 1988 and his treatment of Donatus-Evanthius's formulation of comic *anagnorisis*

by the fact that we can clearly see from outside the stage, from a detached perspective and well aware of the inevitable happy ending, what is wrong with their reasoning.[53] The happy ending is possible because the relevant characters have understood what they did worng and because the audience is able to see on stage the effects of this improved ethical understading.

in *De Comoedia*, IV 5: "[...] the [comic] 'knot' (*nodus*, from Greek *desis*) is constituted by 'error' and the denouement by a *conversio rerum* (equivalent to peripeteia) which is also a *cognitio gestorum*. The account is clearly analogous to Aristotle's description of the complex plot in tragedy, except that the place of *anagnorisis* is taken by a wider term (*cognitio*) denoting the disclosure to all concerned of 'what has been done'. This is no doubt because the plot of New Comedy is in virtually every case dependent on disguises, secrets, confusions, as well as false identities" (Cave 1988, p. 51).

53 For further discussion of this topic in relation to Menander's comedy, see Halliwell 2008, pp. 400–404.

CHAPTER 2

Degrees of Understanding: Menander and Aristotle on How We Understand

This chapter continues my enquiry into the analogies between the epistemological frameworks that can be identified in the comic plays of Menander and the philosophical writings of Aristotle. I will analyse how Aristotle and Menander present the processes of understanding and the problems involved in reaching understanding. In this chapter, I focus particularly on Menander's *Epitrepontes* and its relationship to Aristotle's epistemology. I argue that Menander's dramatic presentation of the way that characters get to know (or to recognise) something or someone and Aristotle's philosophical treatment of how we gain understanding are similar in certain key respects. In Menander, for instance, recognition-scenes present the achievement of a complete understanding of what has happened following confusion created by ignorance of facts, especially of people's identity and their social roles. The final resolution re-organises the actions into a new and more desirable order:[1] dispersed tokens of recognition find their full meaning at the end of the recognition process. Similarly, for Aristotle, to gain understanding is to locate empirical evidence in a more comprehensive context which involves grasping universal principles that explain the empirical evidence itself.

In the first part of this chapter I start with the analysis of Menander's *Epitrepontes*. The overall structure of this play is an extended recognition the solution of which requires the interaction of several people and a range of different approaches. My reading of this comedy shows that the main focus of this work is on recognition and on the danger of failing to recognise. Firstly, the confusing nexus of events which links all the characters of the plot is built on a multiple *anagnorisis* (recognition): namely, the recognition of the identity of the baby and of his mother and his father. This process is brought to an end after a long process of verification which is organised by one of the characters so as to avoid

1 See Frye 1957, pp. 160–171 and Booker 2004, p. 111. "At the beginning of the play, the obstructing characters are in charge of the play's society, and the audience recognizes that they are usurpers. At the end of the play the device in the plot that brings hero and heroine together causes a new society to crystallize around the hero, and the moment in which this crystallization occurs is the point of resolution of the action, the comic discovery, *anagnorisis* or *cognitio*" (Frye 1957, p. 163).

 DOI: 10.1163/9789004282827_004

false conjectures and to find out the truth of the whole story. Secondly, all the characters on the stage potentially possess all the pieces of information needed to draw correct inferences about what has happened; nevertheless, the final understanding is possible solely thanks to one of them, a female character,[2] who is able to draw the evidence together. Consequently, my analysis of this play will focus specifically on the various steps of the recognition process that extends throughout the plot and on Menander's representation of characters with different intellectual skills who are involved in this process.

To bring out the distinctive character of the Menandrian pattern, I shall discuss a passage of Euripides' *Electra* that features a process of recognition apparently similar to that of the *Epitrepontes*. At first glance, it might seem that Menander adapts rather mechanically in his plays the motifs used by the previous tragic tradition, and, specifically, by Euripides' *Electra*. However, comparison between *Electra* and *Epitrepontes* will suggest that this is not the case: Menander's *Epitrepontes* seems to have a distinctive focus. Menander is interested in themes that are in some ways similar to those treated by fifth-century Attic tragedy but he presents them in an original, distinctive way.

The second part of this chapter will focus on an analysis of philosophical ideas worked out by Aristotle. In examining degrees of knowledge, belief and error in cognition, I offer an example of Aristotle's approach to scientific knowledge or understanding in the *Posterior Analytics*. At the end of the chapter, I aim to show that Menander's comedy and Aristotle's epistemological thought share a focus on a distinct set of topics and treat them in an analogous way. In particular, I believe that they share analogous ideas about the process of getting to know something or someone and about people's differing ability to do so, and also about the danger of not having this ability or having it only to a certain degree. Understanding, for Aristotle and Menander, seems to depend on an accurate evaluation of perceived particulars that includes a comprehensive understanding which gives an account of what has been perceived. Both perceptive insight and intellectual habituation are needed in order to sharpen multiple perceptions according to principles that show how things stand in the world and how situations are to be understood.

---

2 For a broader discussion of the prominent, often dominant, role of female characters in Greek drama see particularly Foley 1981; Zeitlin 1990 and (with specific reference to women in Menandrian comedies) Henry 1985 and Traill 2008. See also pp. 58–59 below where I point out the fact that, in Aristotle, by contrast, given the different aim of his works, women are not even included as possible candidates in the process of acquisition of knowledge.

1 Epitrepontes: Recognition and Understanding

Northrop Frye speaks of the comic *cognitio* as the transition from *pistis* to *gnosis*: the *cognitio* is an epistemological moment in which, as audience, we find the previous misunderstandings, illusions and ignorance explained by a new perspective.[3] I believe that this description suits the plot of Menander's *Epitrepontes* particularly well. The comedy starts with a situation that needs to be clarified (or understood) in order to achieve the restoration of order and the final happy ending. And, as is often the case in Menander, the disclosure of what has happened is provided by recongnition. Goldberg has pointed out the main features of the Menandrian recognition, which he summarises as follows: i) the recognition occurs late but is often foreshadowed; ii) the object of the recognition is often a central character in the play; iii) the recognition makes the happy ending possible.[4] However, the *Epitrepontes* does not follow this pattern: the basic recognition of the exposed child occurs in the second act; the child recognised is not the main character and the first *anagnorisis* is complicated by the mechanism of other scenes which interrupt the unfolding of the play. I will now try to describe in detail the process of recognition and give an interpretation of this process.

At the beginning of the play we have two apparently distinct situations: a young man, Charisios, is currently spending his time in the house of the courtesan Habrotonon because he has discovered that his wife, Pamphile, gave birth and exposed a child that was not his own but was the offspring of a rape. Secondly, Charisios' father-in-law, Smikrines, is called in to be arbiter of a quarrel between two servants: one of them, Daos, has discovered a foundling and given it to the other slave, Syros, while keeping the identifying belongings for himself. Syros is now asking for the child's tokens of recognition (γνωρίσματα) back for the child's sake.[5] From the beginning, it is easy for the audience to imagine how these two situations will eventually be connected: the foundling is discovered to be the child of Pamphile and Charisios and, therefore, Smikrines' grandson. Charisios himself raped his wife, at the festival of the Tauropolia, before their marriage. Nevertheless, for the characters involved, the understanding of this situation is more complex and it is possible to identify various types of reasoning carried out by the characters that take part in the process of recognition.

3 Frye 1957, p. 170.
4 Goldberg 1980, p. 61.
5 On the discussion between Syros and Daos and the delineation of their characters see Iversen 2001.

I am now going to analyse in more detail the main characters, focusing on the role that they have in the process of recognition and pointing out their different approaches to what they experience and what they understand of the situation in which they happen to be. The first attempt at recognition of the foundling comes in Act Two. The recognition could have occurred here during the arbitration scene, when Smikrines sees the tokens of recognition of the foundling. This would represent, according to Aristotle's *Poetics*, the most common kind of recognition in Greek drama: recognition through signs (ἡ διὰ τῶν σημείων).[6] The slaves Daos and Syros enter the stage and ask Smikrines, Charisios' father in law, to be the arbiter of their quarrel about an exposed child.[7] They are fighting for the possession of the child's identifying belongings that Daos, who first found the child, does not want to give back to Syros who is now its adoptive father. The importance that these objects have for retracing the identity of the child is stressed by Syros:

> Συ:—τὰ δέραια καὶ γνωρίσματα
> οὗτός σ' ἀπαιτεῖ Δᾶ'· ἑαυτῶι φησι γὰρ
> ταῦτ' ἐπιτεθῆναι κόσμον, οὐ σοὶ διατροφήν.
>
> SYROS: He [the child] is asking you, Daos, for the necklace and the other tokens of recognition. He says that they have been put in as ornaments for him not as a means of sustenance for you![8]

The passage refers explicitly to these items as 'γνωρίσματα', a term often used in the tragic tradition to indicate tokens of recognition that are, usually, the ornaments of the child's mother.[9] Syros tries to support his argument by giving a few examples that clearly refer to the world of tragedy. Syros' examples are meant to attribute importance to the objects that have been left with the child and, in the tragic tradition, are fundamental to revealing someone's identity.[10]

> Συ: τεθέασαι τραγωιδούς, οἶδ' ὅτι,
> καὶ ταῦτα κατέχεις πάντα. Νηλέα τινὰ

---

6 Arist. *Poet.* 16, 1454b20–21.

7 Men. *Epitr.* 227–229. See Scafuro 1997, p. 156 for the discussion of the legal aspect involved in this process of arbitration.

8 Men. *Epitr.* 303–305.

9 See also Arist. *Phgn.* 806a15 where 'γνωρίσματα' are the signs through which we can identify a certain state of someone's soul and body.

10 See Hurst 1990; see also Scafuro 1997, pp. 156–162.

> Πελίαν τ᾽ ἐκείνους εὗρε πρεσβύτης ἀνὴρ
> αἰπόλος, ἔχων οἵαν ἐγὼ νῦν διφθέραν,
> ὡς δ᾽ ᾔσθετ᾽ αὐτοὺς ὄντας αὐτοῦ κρείττονας,
> λέγει τὸ πρᾶγμ᾽, ὡς εὗρεν, ὡς ἀνείλετο.
> ἔδωκε δ᾽ αὐτοῖς πηρίδιον γνωρισμάτων,
> ἐξ οὗ μαθόντες πάντα τὰ καθ᾽ αὐτοὺς σαφῶς
> ἐγένοντο βασιλεῖς οἱ τότ᾽ ὄντες αἰπόλοι.

> SYROS: You have seen the tragic representations! I know very well, and you indeed understand all these things! An old man, a goatherd, dressed in leather like me, found Neleus and Pelias and when he understood that they were of better origins than him, he told them the whole thing: how he found them, how he collected them. He gave them a bag of tokens from which they learnt clearly everything about themselves; they became kings who before were goatherds.[11]

At the same time, however, the value of these tokens of recognition is played down. The arbiter Smikrines is the actual grandfather of the foundling and yet he is looking at the ornaments belonging to his daughter without recognising what they are when they are shown to him. And we know that he sees them because Syros asks Smikrines to stay to make sure that Daos gives him the child's ornaments one by one.[12] Smikrines' final verdict is in favour of Syros who is claiming the value of the ornaments as indispensable signs of recognition of his foundling; nevertheless, he himself is not paying close attention to them.[13]

To sum up, in the first scene, i) the entrance of the baby close to his grandfather Smikrines ought to lead to the discovery of the identity of the child; ii) the display of the tokens with which the child has been found makes us expect that Smikrines will recognise the child by recognising the ornaments of his daughter. In fact, the inattentive Smikrines goes away quickly as soon as his role of arbiter is ended.[14] The scene is very well constructed so as to make the audience

---

11 Men. *Epitr.* 325–333.

12 Men. *Epitr.* 361–365. According to some scholars, we should see here a reference to Euripides' *Ion* and *Alope*; for Menander's use of metatheatre in this play see Goldberg 1980, p. 67 and Stockert 1997, p. 9. See also Gutzwiller 2000, p. 133 for a more general treatment of this topic.

13 For further reflections on this arbitration scene and Smikrines' character in Epitrepontes see Iversen 1998, especially pp. 121–153.

14 Men. *Epitr.* 366–369.

anticipate consequences that the author will frustrate in the short term[15] and to focus the audience's attention on tokens of recognition that, at this moment, are not bringing about the recognition they are meant to enable.

In the second scene of Act Two, we are once again close to the discovery of the identity of the foundling. In fact, Onesimos, Charisios' slave, unexpectedly, comes out just at the moment at which Syros is showing, and describing in detail to his wife, a peculiar ring he has found among the tokens of the child:

> Συ: ὑπόχρυσος δακτύλιός τις οὑτοσί,
> αὐτὸς σιδηροῦς· γλύμμα ταῦρος ἢ τράγος·
> οὐκ ἂν διαγνοίην· Κλεόστρατος δέ τις
> ἐστὶν ὁ ποήσας, ὡς λέγει τὰ γράμματα.

> SYROS: This is a gold plated ring with iron inside, the seal is a bull or a goat. I would not be able to distinguish which. The one who made it is someone named Kleostratos, as the inscription says.[16]

After this detailed description, we expect that Onesimos will recognise his master's ring; and this is indeed what happens. On the one hand, the accurate description of the ring adds value to its status as a token of recognition; on the other hand, the inference drawn by Onesimos on this basis is shown to be rather superficial. Indeed, as expected, Onesimos quickly infers that Charisios is the father of the child through a process of reasoning that seems not to be very rigorous. Onesimos knows, in fact, that Charisios once lost that ring at the Tauropolia; he therefore guesses that, probably, Charisios raped a girl. He also imagines that she might have got pregnant by him and, consequently, he suggests that, after having given birth to Charisios' child, she might have exposed the baby along with the ring that Charisios lost at the moment of the rape.[17] In any case, we expect the third Act to confirm the still awaited recognition. On the contrary, in Act Three, the recognition of the child through his identifying belongings seems finally to fail. Onesimos is afraid to reveal to his master what he has just discovered and he keeps the ring, being uncertain about what to do next. The entrance of the courtesan Habrotonon will speed up the recognition process. The woman, however, casts doubt on the reliability

15 See Katsouris 1976; Ireland 1983 and Zagagi 1994, especially pp. 83–93.

16 Men. *Epitr.* 386–390.

17 Men. *Epitr.* 446–457.

of the ring as a symbol of recognition and she suggests another way of finding out the truth.[18]

In the *Aspis*, we find another example of a case of recognition based on tokens that turn out not to be trustworthy. There again, tokens are shown to be misleading elements for proving someone's identity. At the beginning of the comedy, a slave, Daos, tells Smikrines (the greedy uncle of Daos' master Kleostratos) that Kleostratos is dead and he gives Smikrines an account of how it happened. However, this account does not seem to be completely trustworthy: Kleostratos is a soldier and he was supposed to have died during an assault made on his camp. Daos declares that, on that occasion, he himself was not physically present in the camp.[19] He has heard (ἤκουον) the story about the assault from others but he has not experienced it directly by seeing his master's death. He has an opinion that was not based on direct sensory evidence.[20] In fact, Smikrines asks Daos whether he has sure evidence to believe that Kleostratos is dead; he asks whether he saw the corpse.

> Σμ: ἐν δὲ τοῖς νεκροῖς
> πεπτωκότ' εἶδες τοῦτον;
>
> SMIKRINES: Did you see him lying among the corpses?[21]

Daos' answer is crucial: he admits that it was not possible to recognise him with any certainty.

> **Δα**: αὐτὸν μὲν σαφῶς
> οὐκ ἦν ἐπιγνῶναι· τετάρτην ἡμέραν
> ἐρριμμένοι γὰρ ἦσαν ἐξῳδηκότες
> τὰ πρόσωπα.
>
> DAOS: It was not possible to recognise him with certainty: their faces were swollen up as [it was] four days [since] they had been thrown there.[22]

18 Men. *Epitr.* 499–510.
19 Men. *Aspis* 50–61.
20 Men. *Aspis* 52–62.
21 Men. *Aspis* 68–69.
22 Men. *Aspis* 70–72. Paduano remarks that, at this point, the text anticipates a remarkable doubt about Kleostratos' death (Paduano 1980, p. 335).

Smikrines, therefore, asks how it is possible then to declare that Kleostratos is dead without having seen him (πῶς οὖν οἶσθα; "But then, how do you know?" asks Smikrines): an exact knowledge of what has happened to Kleostratos seems not to be possible if Daos was not able to see and recognise the corpse as his master's.[23] Smikrines is asking for a verification of Daos' account that is grounded on visual perception; conversely, Daos has said that it has not been possible to verify that Kleostratos was dead by seeing him. Daos has identified Kleostratos' corpse because Kleostratos' shield lay there with him. This implies, for Smikrines as well as for the audience, that he cannot be sure of the fact. Nevertheless, Daos declares that the corpse he saw was his master's and he answers Smikrines' question saying:

> **Δα:** ἔχων τὴν ἀσπίδα
> ἔκειτο·
>
> DAOS: [I know that because] he lay there with his shield.[24]

From this piece of evidence (Kleostratos' shield close to the dead body), Daos infers that his master is dead. However, this recognition through a token (i.e. the shield) is clearly mistaken. Daos does not evaluate rigorously what he has heard and seen: Kleostratos is alive and will soon step on the stage. The shield does not serve as certain token of recognition because it comes as a single piece of sensory evidence without a trustworthy account of its meaning in the context in which it is found. The shield was indeed lying with a corpse that Daos could not identify with certainty as being Kleostratos' corpse. Moreover, the corpse was found by Daos after an assault the details of which he had heard indistinctly from someone else because he was not present at the camp at that moment: the *anagnorisis* that opens the *Aspis* is a false recognition that will be corrected in the course of the comedy.

From the point of view of the staging of the *Epitrepontes*, the failure of the first attempt at recognition through tokens directs our attention to what will follow. Dana Munteanu[25] distinguishes three further kinds of *anagnorisis* performed in this play, which follow Aristotle's divisions in the *Poetics*: *anagnorisis* through memory (διὰ μνήμης), by reasoning (ἐκ συλλογισμοῦ) and by false reasoning (ἐκ παραλογισμοῦ).[26] I will now summarise Onesimos' attempt at

23 Men. *Aspis* 73.

24 Men. *Aspis* 73.

25 Munteanu 2002, pp. 118–119.

26 Arist. *Poet.* 15, 1454b37–1455a14.

recognition and Habrotonon's response to this. As anticipated, Onesimos' first inference about the identity of the child is simple:

> **Ον**: τοιουτονί
> ἐστιν τὸ πρᾶγμ', ἄνθρωπε· τοῦ μὲν δεσπότου
> ἔστ', οἶδ' ἀκριβῶς, οὑτοσὶ Χαρισίου,
> ὀκνῶ δὲ δεῖξαι· πατέρα γὰρ τοῦ παιδίου
> αὐτὸν ποῶ σχεδόν τι τοῦτον προσφέρων
> μεθ' οὗ συνεξέκειτο.
> [...]
> Ταυροπολίοις ἀπώλεσεν τοῦτόν ποτε
> παννυχίδος οὔσης καὶ γυναικῶν. κατὰ λόγον
> ἐστὶν βιασμὸν τοῦτον εἶναι παρθένου·
> ἡ δ' ἔτεκε τοῦτο κἀξέθηκε δηλαδή.
> εἰ μέν τις οὖν εὑρὼν ἐκείνην προσφέροι
> τοῦτον, σαφὲς ἄν τι δεικνύοι τεκμήριον·
> νυνὶ δ' ὑπόνοιαν καὶ ταραχὴν[27] ἔχει.
>
> ONESIMOS: It is like this, man! I know it for sure, it [the ring] belongs to my master Charisios. But I am afraid to show it to him: for I will probably make him the father of the child bringing to him this thing that was exposed with it.
> [...]
> He lost it at the Tauropolia, the women's night-festival! It is reasonable to think that he used violence on a girl: clearly she bore this child and exposed it. If now someone, finding her, would bring her this [ring] he would produce a sure proof, but all there is now is confusion and conjecture.[28]

Habrotonon, who has just arrived on stage, reproaches Onesimos for the fact that he does not want to tell his master what he has just found out. Moreover, she seems to remember an episode of rape at this very same festival of the Tauropolia.[29] Onesimos immediately believes in this second kind of *anagnorisis* (through memory) which confirms his hypothesis: the raped girl about whom Habrotonon speaks is the mother of Charisios' child; thus, it follows logically

---

27 In Plato's *Republic* X, 602c–603b, we have a similar use of the word 'ταραχή' as disorder caused by the appearances provided by perception. See p. 44 below.

28 Men. *Epitr.* 446–457.

29 Men. *Epit.* 471–475.

that Charisios raped her and lost his ring. Onesimos asks her help in finding the girl and showing her the ring as actual proof that her child is Charisios'. On the contrary, the kithara-girl casts doubt on Onesimos' recognition hypothesis because she believes that Onesimos' reconstruction of the facts is not rigorous:

> Ἀβρ: οὐκ ἂν δυναίμην, τὸν ἀδικοῦντα πρὶν [σαφῶς
> τίς ἐστιν εἰδέναι. φοβοῦμαι τοῦτ' ἐγώ,
> μάτην τι μηνύειν[30] πρὸς ἐκείνας ἃς λέγω.
> τίς οἶδεν εἰ καὶ τοῦτον ἐνέχυρον λαβὼν
> τότε τις παρ' αὐτοῦ τῶν παρόντων ἀπέβαλεν
> ἕτερος; κυβεύων τυχὸν ἴσως εἰς συμβολὰς
> ὑπόθημ' ἔδωκ', ἢ συντιθέμενος περί τινος
> περιείλετ', εἶτ' ἔδωκεν· ἕτερα μυρία
> ἐν τοῖς πότοις τοιαῦτα γίνεσθαι φιλεῖ.
> πρὶν εἰδέναι δὲ τὸν ἀδικοῦντ' οὐ βούλομαι
> ζητεῖν ἐκείνην οὐδὲ μηνύειν ἐγὼ
> τοιοῦτον οὐδέν.

> HABROTONON: I couldn't [search for her], before knowing [with certainty] who was the man who used violence on her. I am afraid I would make some declaration in vain to the ladies I mentioned. Who knows, if someone else, among those who were there lost it, after having taken this [ring] from him as a pledge. Maybe, perhaps, he gave it as a pledge into the poll while playing at dice. Or, he was under pressure making an agreement with someone and so he gave it away. Thousands of other things like that happen in these drinking sessions. Before knowing who was guilty for the rape I don't want to search for her or say anything like that.[31]

Charisios, she explains, might not be the child's father and might not have raped that girl: he could simply have lost the ring or pledged it to someone else in making an agreement.[32] She suggests a plan for discovering the truth about the entire story. Her intention now is to find out accurately what happened and to avoid making declarations that are not adequately supported by reasons and reliable evidence. Instead, she suggests a plan for discovering the truth about

---

30 Adele Scafuro pointed out to me that this particular verb (μηνύειν) is often used in forensic rhetoric: Habrotonon is using rhetorical devices to set up an argument that could persuade Onesimos to abandon his hypothesis and follow hers.

31 Men. *Epitr.* 499–509.

32 For more details on this point see Gomme and Sandbach 1973, p. 336.

the identity of the child's father: the courtesan will pretend she is the raped girl wearing Charisios' ring.[33] "This device presupposes an *anagnorisis* through false reasoning as well, because the courtesan will pretend that she is the raped girl".[34] Habrotonon thinks that if Charisios is the one guilty of the rape, he will immediately confirm the story and they can obtain the proof for the recognition of the child: accordingly, Habrotonon suggests here to conduct a further and more reliable attempt at recognition—*anagnorisis* through reasoning, in Aristotle's terms.[35] Once the identity of the child's father is revealed through this scheme, Onesimon and Habrotonon agree that they can search for the child's mother with more calm.[36] What, in conclusion, Habrotonon provides—and what Onesimos does not—is a reasoned verification of what they seem to have discovered by collecting all the pieces of evidence together: this is what the kithara-girl needs in order to make an accusation on the basis of reliable evidence (and, therefore, not at random—μάτην); constructing from the evidence a form of reasoning that makes sense of the evidence.

The last recognition, which brings the definitive reversal and solution of the dramatic not, is made by Habrotonon in the course of Act Four. The recognition is a double *anagnorisis*: Habrotonon recognises Pamphile; Pamphile recognises the child.

> **Ἁβρ:** αὐτή 'στιν [ἣν] ἑό[ρ]ακα· χαῖρε, φιλτάτη.
> **Πα:** τί[ς δ' εἶ] σύ;
> **Ἁβρ:** χεῖρα δεῦρό μοι τὴν σὴν δίδου.
> λέγε μοι, γλυκεῖα, πέρυσιν ἦ[λθες ἐπὶ θέαν
> τοῖς Ταυροπολίοις ε[
> **Πα:** γύναι, πόθεν ἔχεις, εἰπέ μοι, τὸ παιδίον
> λαβοῦσα;
> **Ἁβρ:** ὁρᾷς τι, φιλτάτη, σοι γνώριμον
> ὧν] τοῦτ' ἔχει; μηδέν με δείσῃς, ὦ γύναι.

> HABROTONON: (*aside*) She is the girl, I have seen [her]. (*to Pamphile*) Hello dearest!
> PAMPHILE: Wh[o are] you?
> HABROTONON: Here, give me your hand, tell me sweetheart: did you [come] to the performance at the festival of Tauropolia one year ago?

33 Men. *Epitr.* 511–515.
34 Munteanu 2002, pp. 119.
35 Men. *Epitr.* 516–519.
36 Men. *Epitr.* 536–538.

PAMPHILE: Lady, tell me, where did you find the baby?
HABROTONON: Do you see something, dearest, some symbol of recognition [among the things] that this child has? Do not be afraid of me, lady.[37]

Habrotonon recognises Pamphile and seeks a proof of her identity showing her the child and asking her specific questions: she asks whether Pamphile has recognised something familiar looking at the child Habrotonon is holding. Pamphile, having seen the child and his tokens of recognition, recognises her son and her guess is immediately confirmed by Habrotonon. Both women understand the situation on the basis of signs of recognition (that is, the appearance of the child and its tokens), enquiring into their validity and their place in the part of the story that they have knowledge of. The two accounts complete each other.

Ἀβρ: προσεποιησάμην,
οὐχ ἵν᾽ ἀδικήσω τὴν τεκοῦσαν, ἀλλ᾽ ἵνα
κατὰ σχολὴν εὕροιμι. νῦν δ᾽ εὕρηκα· σὲ
ὁρῶ γάρ, ἣν καὶ τότε.
Πα: τίνος δ᾽ ἐστὶν πατρός;
Ἀβρ: Χαρισίου.
Πα: τοῦτ᾽ οἶσθ᾽ ἀκριβῶς, φιλτάτη;
Ἀβρ: εὖ ο]ἶδ̣᾽ ἔ[γωγ᾽· ἀλλ᾽] οὐ σε τὴν νύμφην ὁρῶ
τὴν ἔνδον οὖσαν;

HABROTONON: I have been pretending [to be his mother] not so as to harm the one who has given birth to him but so that I could find her calmly. Now I have found her, I see you indeed here as I saw you that time.
PAMPHILE: Who is his father?
HABROTONON: [He is] Charisios' [child].
PAMPHILE: Do you know this for sure, my dear?
HABROTONON: [I know this well]! [But] am I not seeing his young wife who was in the house before?[38]

---

37 Men. *Epitr.* 860–866. See Gomme and Sandbach 1973, p. 359, for the forms of address in this scene. See also Trail 2008, pp. 228–230.

38 Men. *Epitr.* 867–873.

This final *anagnorisis* brings the happy ending of the play: everything that has happened finds an explanation, consequently, Charisios and Pamphile are reconciled and the identity of the child is revealed. In Menandrian comedies, "the 'dissolution' almost always involves the conclusion of a dispute, as if 'reconciliation' is the harmonious note on which the playwright must have his players leave the stage: the Aristotelian *lusis* becomes *dialusis*".[39] However, in the specific case of the *Epitrepontes*, the final recognition that allows the *dialusis* of the whole case is only the last of a long series and it occurs because Habrotonon's quick-wittedness helps the recognition. Her behaviour is in contrast to that of the rather slow and suspicious Onesimos.[40] The courtesan remembers the circumstances of the rape at the Tauropolia; but she hesitates to link this fact with Charisios' still hypothetical rape.[41] On the other hand, she quickly thinks of a plan to discover the truth with certainty.[42] Furthermore, she immediately recognises Pamphile and induces her to look at the baby to recognise him[43] giving her additional information that is meant to match and complete Pamphile's account. Therefore, Habrotonon is vital to the plot because: i) "Without her knowledge of Pamphile's rape, the other characters would have only known that the ring had once been Charisios'"[44] and the discovery of the identities of the child and his parents would have not taken place; ii) her lively mind examines pieces of evidence and confirms them with a trustworthy account leading to the true version of the story and reconciliation of Charisios and Pamphile.

The *anagnorisis* of Pamphile's and Charisios' child and the identity of its parents are topics that are presented and discussed throughout the whole play. The process of recognition is broken down into several stages and the final recognition through reasoning (ἐκ συλλογισμοῦ) gives meaning to the first recognition through tokens (διὰ τῶν σημείων). According to Goldberg, the effect of this extended recognition is "to maximise opportunities for expanding their effect upon his characters while maintaining an underlying unity".[45] At the same time, the function of this process is also to exploit the comic effect of

---

39 Scafuro 1997, p. 181.

40 Henry 1985, p. 50. 'When one might have expected a plot solved by the ingenuity of a male slave (e.g. Daos in *Aspis*), it is Habrotonon's intelligence that takes over the task of resolution, leaving Onesimos bemoaning his own ponderous lack of initiative' (Ireland 2010, p. 115). See also Traill 2008, pp. 196–203 and 223–235.

41 Men. *Epitr.* 499–509.

42 Men. *Epitr.* 536–538.

43 Men. *Epitr.* 865–866.

44 Henry 1985, p. 53.

45 Goldberg 1980, p. 71.

recognition leading the audience to focus on the characters' various states of misapprehension and their efforts to find the truth.[46] In conclusion, what is clear is that Menander has built a plot i) on the search for a well-grounded knowledge of truth that can finally explain what happened to the characters and ii) on the different degrees of knowledge or ignorance that characters possess.

Confronted by the tokens of recognition, which constitute empirical evidence, we can see three kinds of cognitive attitude. Smikrines completely ignores the value of the tokens of recognition and fails to understand what is happening around him. Onesimos tries to put the pieces of evidence together; however, he follows a non-rigorous type of reasoning that risks reaching false conclusions. Habrotonon, after having considered all the circumstances, seeks a proof that could validate her reasoning. If my analysis is correct, Menander creates a comic plot by exploiting the interaction between a range of cognitive positions that vary from an inattentive or simplistic approach to empirical evidence to a thoughtful—and consequently successful—analysis of them by a process of reasoning that is able to explain the evidence.[47] What is also interesting is that the whole discovery is completed by a woman, Habrotonon, who is also a courtesan, rather than by the two other male characters involved, Onesimos and Smikrines.[48]

2 Notes on Recognition in Euripides' Electra

If we look at the structure and themes of *Epitrepontes*, it might be possible to argue that Menander is simply reformulating typical tragic *topoi* in a comic style. Indeed, Habrotonon's reply to Onesimos' rather simple line of reasoning may look back to the dialogue between Electra and the Old Man in Euripides' *Electra*, in which the two figures debate about the identity of the people who have come to Agamemnon's grave leaving behind traces of their visit.[49] As in Aeschylus' *Choephoroi*,[50] the Old Man offers Electra three signs to prove that Orestes is the visitor who has come to Agamemnon's grave: the lock of hair matching Electra's hair, the footprints matching those of Electra, and Orestes'

46 Ireland 1983, p. 45.

47 See Goldberg 1980, p. 69 and also Post 1938, pp. 29–33 on Menander's treatment of individuals and characters with variant perspectives on the action.

48 See p. 24 n. 2 above.

49 E. *El.* 527–544.

50 A. *Ch.* 164–234.

clothes that Electra had woven for him. In turn, in what seems to be a pointed response to the *Choephoroi*,[51] Electra engages in a sceptical point-by-point rejection of the Old Man's arguments, making statements such as:

> **Ηλ:** ἔπειτα χαίτης πῶς συνοίσεται πλόκος,
> ὁ μὲν παλαίστραις ἀνδρὸς εὐγενοῦς τραφείς,
> ὁ δὲ κτενισμοῖς θῆλυς; ἀλλ' ἀμήχανον.
> πολλοῖς δ' ἂν εὕροις βοστρύχους ὁμοπτέρους
> καὶ μὴ γεγῶσιν αἵματος ταὐτοῦ, γέρον.
>
> ELECTRA: And then, how can two locks of hair match each other, when one is nurtured in the noble man's wrestling-schools, the other combed and female? No, it's impossible! Anyway, you could find many people with like-coloured locks, even when they are not of the same blood, old man.[52]

Without this piece of dialogue the recognition will be too "simplified and abrupt".[53] Electra's acknowledgment of the fact that her brother is alive, and that he has visited their father's tomb, requires an extended process of recognition to bring out more clearly the emotional tension involved in this process. Thus, Electra here needs to carry out a point-by-point analysis of the Old Man's arguments about the traces that a stranger could have left in paying his visit to Agamemnon and that the Old Man takes promptly as decisive signs of recognition of Orestes. "In insisting on paradox, emotional impact and dramatic irony, even at the cost of some implausibility, Euripides is attending to what conventionally made a 'good' recognition: for Orestes to declare himself directly is too straightforward, and even the old man's simple task can become the vehicle of a *peripeteia* ('turnabout') through Electra's unpreparedness to believe".[54]

When Orestes comes out, his identity is revealed by a scar. However, the scar is another sign of recognition that can be questioned, or at least challenged,

---

51 For discussion on this point, see Lloyd-Jones 1961; Winnington-Ingram 1969(a); Gellie 1981, Solmsen 1982; Kovacs 1989; Davies 1998; Raeburn 2000 and Gallagher 2003.

52 E. *El.* 527–531. All the translations from Euripides' *Electra* are by Cropp 1988 (modified).

53 Cropp 1988, p. 137. On the importance of props in Greek tragedy see Taplin 1978, ch. 6.

54 Cropp 1988, p. 134. See Arnott 1973, p. 63, who explains the extended recognition with Euripides' tendency to tease his audience "by laying false clues, by exploiting conventions of tragedy".

like the others, but this time Electra will trust its validity. On this basis, she also reconsiders the reliability of the signs of recognitions offered by the Old Man and identifies the stanger as Orestes without further ado.[55]

> **Ηλ**: πῶς φήις; ὁρῶ μὲν πτώματος τεκμήριον.
> **Πρ**: ἔπειτα μέλλεις προσπίτνειν τοῖς φιλτάτοις;
> **Ηλ**: ἀλλ' οὐκέτ', ὦ γεραιέ· συμβόλοισι γὰρ
> τοῖς σοῖς πέπεισμαι θυμόν. ὦ χρόνωι φανείς,
> ἔχω σ' ἀέλπτως

> ELECTRA: What do you mean? I do see the sign of a fall ...
> OLD MAN: And then you are slow to embrace your dearest one?
> ELECTRA: No, old man, no longer. My heart is convinced by your signs.
> Oh, at long last you appear; I hold you as I never hoped to.[56]

At this point, the recognition process is successfully concluded but its complexity leaves the audience reflecting on the procedure involved and, perhaps, on the idea that to recognise someone—or to get to know something—is a complicated process that may have no positive outcome and is definitely less instantaneous than what finally happens in the *Electra*. The idea that seems to emerge from this recognition scene is that empirical evidence can be deceptive,[57] empirical signs all have the same worth, what counts is the ability to combine them in order to produce a persuasive explanation for them.[58] The tokens of recognition that the Old Man's shows to Electra will eventually change Electra's mind: the last sign of recognition, on top of the other signs, has finally persuaded her—"πέπεισμαι θυμόν", she says—but we are not fully convinced of the cogency of Electra's reasoning and the empirical evidence by which she is finally persuaded. This impression holds true even though we know from the myth that the recognition between brother and sister will eventually happen one way or another and even though we associate this

55 Indeed Electra at line 577 states that she is eventually persuaded by the signs (σύμβολα) that the old man provided to identify Orestes. "The plural is rather strange here. Perhaps Electra means, somewhat illogically, though naturally, that she is convinced not only by the scar, but by the other signs that she has rejected" (Dennistion 1939, p. 122).

56 E. *El.* 575–579.

57 See in particular Wright 2005, p. 285.

58 On the use of rhetorical techniques in Euripides' *Electra*, with particular reference to the passages quoted here see Goldhill 1986(b); Mossman 2001 and Quijada 2002.

recognition scene with the other famous case of succesful recognition in the *Odissey*.[59]

A comparable line of thought is prompted by another passage from the same play:

> **Ορ**: φεῦ·
> οὐκ ἔστ' ἀκριβὲς οὐδὲν εἰς εὐανδρίαν·
> ἔχουσι γὰρ ταραγμὸν αἱ φύσεις βροτῶν.
> ἤδη γὰρ εἶδον ἄνδρα γενναίου πατρὸς
> τὸ μηδὲν ὄντα, χρηστὰ τ' ἐκ κακῶν τέκνα,
> λιμόν τ' ἐν ἀνδρὸς πλουσίου φρονήματι,
> γνώμην τὲ μεγάλην ἐν πένητι σώματι.
> πῶς οὖν τις αὐτὰ διαλαβὼν ὀρθῶς κρινεῖ;
>
> Orestes: Well! Nothing is clear-cut when it comes to virtue. There is confusion in the nature of men. Before now, I have seen a man of no account sprung from a noble father, and good children from inferior parents; I have seen vacuousness in the thinking of a rich man, and a great mind in the body of a poor one. How then can a man correctly distinguish and rate them?[60]

Orestes says here that there is no accurate (ἀκριβὲς) criterion to determine someone's worth. Wealth, poverty, family relationships are visible signs (σύμβολα) that do not disclose the real situation regarding someone's character and cannot be trusted to correspond to the truth. Orestes seems again to be suggesting here the fallibility of empirical evidence as a way of revealing how things really stand and who someone is by nature.

This passage, when taken with the previous scene, makes it is plausible to argue that, in Orestes' recognition scene in *Electra*, Euripides is reflecting on a famous process of recognition, revising the myth and modifying it to raise new questions, to which he alludes in this other passage:[61] Euripides seems to suggest that pieces of empirical evidence or sensory experience all have the same worth in the context of Orestes' recognition process and as criteria for identi-

---

59 Notably, Euryclea recognising Odisseus from a scar which a boar once inflicted on him (Hom. *Od.* XIX, 386–398).

60 E. *El.* 367–373. At 373 the term 'διαλαμβάνω' identifies a 'method of logical division' Denniston 1939, ad loc.

61 Compare with Goldhill 1986(a), pp. 247–250.

fying someone as having a noble or wicked nature. Thus, it has been argued, Euripides here underlines the difficulty of getting to know something clearly, or, more broadly, raises questions about the relationship between reality and illusion and between ignorance and knowledge.[62] Accordingly, Euripides' references to Aeschylus and his use of metatheatre[63] (or metamythology)[64] may have served the purpose of leading the audience to focus on a certain set of (broadly) epistemological or metaphysical questions.

Accordingly, I suggest that in the *Electra*, despite presenting what seems to be similar material, we can discern significantly different intellectual concerns from those that underlie Menander's *Epitrepontes*.[65] As noted earlier, the process of identification of Orestes and the inquiry into the reliability of the recognition tokens resembles the presentation of the long enquiry carried out by Onesimos and Habrotonon in the *Epitrepontes*. However, in Euripides' *Electra*, pieces of evidence and the reasoning made about them, are not considered as a secure criterion for reconstructing how things really are and who people really are. Menander, in the *Epitrepontes*, underlines a different set of issues. There, the status of empirical evidence is questioned only because characters are not able to interpret this evidence properly and by a rationally rigorous process of reasoning: for instance, the validity of tokens of recognition is not questioned thoroughly by Onesimos and Smikrines. In the *Epitrepontes*, tokens are presented as important pieces of evidence but it is also accentuated that characters must be able to use them adequately to find out the truth. This does not seem to be the issue at the core of Orestes' recognition. In Menander's play, Habrotonon is not questioning the importance of tokens only to replace them with other pieces of evidence that are equally questionable, as happens in Euripides' *Electra*. She is constructing a chain of reasoning to explain those tokens in a more comprehensive and rigorous manner as she knows that there is a true version of the story that needs to be found out. She displays an attitude in constructing a reliable version of the story that can be contrasted with that of Smikrines or Onesimos who do not reason or, rather, are in danger of reasoning inadequately on the basis of empirical evidence. This is what Menander seem

62 For extended discussion of these topics see Wright 2005. See also Reinhardt 2003.

63 As defined by Abel 1963, methatheatre is a conscious self-reference, a dramatic device whereby a play comments on itself, drawing attention to the literal circumstances of its own production, such as the presence of the audience or the fact that the actors are actors, and thus making explicit the literary artifice behind the production.

64 Wright 2005, p. 135.

65 For a dedicated and more detailed account of the relationship between recognition in *Epitrepontes* and antecedent tragic models, see Iversen 1998, chapter 4.

to stress in his extended recognition in the *Epitrepontes* and this emerges more clearly if we compare this scene with the recognition scene in Euripides *Electra*.

3 Aristotle: Grasping the Sense

As discussed in Chapter 1 (section 1), the late fifth century BC introduces some important changes in the history of epistemology. First Socrates, followed by Plato and Aristotle, inaugurate critical and systematic reflection on issues related to knowledge and the scope or limits of human understanding. They start questioning how we acquire the basic contents of our mind, how understanding is possible and what are the starting-points of the knowledge that we have of our world. The general picture conveyed by the Platonic-Aristotelian tradition is that the world has an intelligible structure, and that things are organised in a way that is not random but follows a rational order and human beings have the potentiality to know the truth about it.[66] This process of understanding is not always easy; the steps of the rational reasoning that one should follow to achieve a complete grasp of this order are subject to errors and misunderstandings. Plato and Aristotle also start inquiring into these questions: they start questioning how error or doubt are possible, what are the thought-processes that shape our (right or wrong) understanding; what are the intellectual capacities of our soul and what is their role in the formation of (right or wrong) understanding. Furthermore, as discussed in Chapter 1, in the Platonic-Aristotelian tradition, to know something adequately implies understanding the comprehensive order that explains and makes sense of our beliefs. Seeing, touching, hearsay, inferring, understanding, believing, proving and having an intuition are not seen as being the same thing as knowing.[67] To know is not just to perceive, or to have a belief; it is to understand and reason about what we perceive or believe.[68] We necessarily start our inquiry from the sensible objects available to us. We are provided with senses, perceptions and beliefs arising

66 Tuominen 2007, pp. 155–156. See also Lear 1988 and Everson 1990.

67 Brunschwig 2003, pp. 18–38.

68 "To know is to understand, that is, to bring back together [...] to organise experience according to the structure that belongs to reality, to bring to speech the reason that governs things. To know a single thing is not to know it; taken to the extreme there is no knowledge but total knowledge, and no knowledge but knowledge of everything. [...] Not until Aristotle does the principle of a total science begin to give way to the idea that a science is a structured set of statements bearing on entities that belong to a specific class and to that class alone" (Brunschwig 2003, pp. 29).

from these: the issue is how to evaluate this sensory experience and how to reach a comprehensive understanding of the rational order that explains it.

I will now focus on Aristotle's approach to these questions and analyse his account of how we reach complete understanding. Aristotle's view of the process of getting to know something is broadly similar to what I have attributed to Menander in the first section of this chapter. Earlier I showed that Menander created a type of comic plot in which the characters' perception alone was not enough to make sense of the whole story: a rational account was needed to comprehend what people happened to perceive, and specific skills were necessary to construct this account successfully. In Aristotle we can find a similar set of ideas. My analysis here will focus on two points. First, I will discuss Aristotle's treatment of the role of sensory perception and empirical evidence considered as forming part of a comprehensive understanding. The framework that maintains our understanding is supported by two distinctive starting points. Both of them represent what is more "knowable" (γνωριμώτεραι) in two different and opposite respects that are, nevertheless, necessarily[69] dependent on each other. What we know better, particulars in the world, need to be explained by what we *would have* to know better, if we had complete knowledge of universal principles of the intelligible structure of the world—and of our language—that we can potentially grasp[70] in part through our sensations.[71] Secondly, I will stress the idea that, in Aristotle's account, a successful process of understanding requires a particular attitude or, more precisely, trained intellectual skills, in order to achieve the kind of understanding that can make sense of what is around us. Aristotle's approach to understanding starts from experience but is nevertheless not as gradual as it might seem: understanding requires i) an attitude aiming at recollecting our observational beliefs appropriately and ii) making sense of these in a complete comprehension of our world.

Aristotle describes human access to understanding as a natural and gradual process. First of all, it is a natural process because rational human beings naturally desire to acquire information about things in their world. Indeed, it seems that we love our sensations precisely because they show us things[72] and, therefore, enable us to start getting acquainted (ποιεῖ γνωρίζειν)[73] with them. Moreover, our desire to know is, in principle, not directed to any practical aim: we

69 Sorabji 1980, pp. 85–208.

70 Arist. *APo.* I 1, 71a17–19; Barnes 1994 and Ross 1949 ad loc.

71 Cf. *Top.* I 12, 105a17–18; *Top.* II 7, 113a31–32; *APo.* I 18, 81b5–6; *APo.* I 31, 88a14–15; *APo.* II 19, 99b37–40; *APo.* II 19, 100a4–9; *APo.* II 19, 100b3–4.

72 Arist. *Metaph.* A 1, 980a22.

73 Arist. *Metaph.* A 1, 980a26.

love our sensations also independently of their practical benefits.[74] Secondly, human access to knowledge is gradual. Starting from sensation (αἴσθησις) and moving through memory (μνήμη), experience (ἐμπειρία) and art (τέχνη), a rational being can achieve an overall grasp of all the scattered pieces of information that he receives from the outside world.[75] However, this kind of knowledge is not yet wisdom (σοφία). We exercise wisdom when we understand (ἐπίστασθαι) the causes and principles of what we get to know randomly.[76] Indeed, Aristotle explains further that the sciences (ἐπιστῆμαι) were discovered subsequently to all these disciplines necessary for everyday life. In particular, they were cultivated by people who were free from practical activities and who had time for speculative investigation.[77]

In the *Posterior Analytics*, Aristotle gives a description of what it is to understand something and he also gives some examples of how this process might develop or might go wrong. The *Posterior Analytics* confirms the idea that understanding—that is, *epistēmē*—implies the ability of our mind to collect and recollect acquired beliefs and to sum them up by grasping their significance. The transition from arts to science centres precisely on this ability to grasp, which seems not to be present in everyone. However, even though the results of understanding are epistemologically secure (i.e. true in an objective sense), the process of getting there seems to be neither secure nor guaranteed: we might not understand even though we have the potentiality to do that; we might lack the right understanding of our world even if this understanding is in principle available.

It is worth pointing out that we face comparable features in the field of Aristotle's ethics (as will be discussed in Chapter 3). When, in the *Nicomachean Ethics*, Aristotle defines virtue as a mean, he specifies that the mean varies according to us and according to the particular variables involved in our decision.[78] However, for each circumstance there is a standard of the mean set by those whose judgment is correct and who are virtuous.[79] This is why according to Aristotle it is so difficult to understand what the right mean is in any circumstance and, consequently, act accordingly in the right way.[80] This is why we need time and exercise to sharpen our ethical understanding and

---

74 Arist. *Metaph.* A 1, 980a22.
75 Arist. *Metaph.* A 1, 980b1–981b20.
76 Arist. *Metaph.* A 1, 982a1–3.
77 Arist. *Metaph.* A 1, 981b20–23.
78 Arist. *EN* II 5, 1106a26–b23.
79 For full discussion of this topic see Chappell 2005.
80 Arist. *EN* II 9, 1109b14–26.

character. Analogously, in the field of epistemology, a complete understanding of the principles that organise our world is possible if we make good use of our cognitive abilities: after the arts, the sciences were discovered by those few people who had time for intellectual exercise[81] and grasped the signifiance that the others lacked.

3.1 *Understanding and Missing Understanding*

As specified, in this chapter, I will address issue related to processes of understanding in relation to Aristotle's philosophy. Nevertheless, I believe that Plato's mature works present a set of ideas that is worth considering in this context as they present an understanding of the relationship between perceptions and knowledge that Aristotle will discuss later and, to a certain extent, challenge. In *Republic* book x, we are told that perception presents us with divergent and contrasting appearances.[82] To cope with this disorder (ταραχή), we are equipped with the ability to calculate, measure and assess what the senses suggest. If we exercise this ability, we will be able to judge what things really are. Therefore, it seems that, according to Plato, perception just suggests lines of inquiry that the rational part of the soul must then judge.[83] This treatment of perception is consistent with a comparable passage in the *Theaetetus*.[84] In this dialogue, Socrates and Theaetetus inquire about knowledge and its sources and this particular passage appears as the last argument against the idea, suggested by Theaetetus, that knowledge is perception. Theaetetus has just stated that we perceive something and we judge it to be in a certain way (black and white; sharp or bass) because our sense organs give us an account of what surrounds us: we perceive something because we see, touch and hear things—and that is knowledge. However, the idea suggested by Theaetetus, as Socrates says, generates some difficulties. Perceptions come from various kinds of sources (things that we can hear, touch, see or smell) and they generate different sensations through different sense organs: according to Theaetetus, this is how we perceive (that is, to Theaetetus' mind, how we know). Socrates' objection is that this kind of account is not really plausible and that it does not actually explain how perception works: we do not become aware of what surrounds us by experiencing individual, scattered and diverse sensations.[85] We should

81 On this point see Burnyeat 1981, p. 131.

82 Pl. *R.* x, 602c–603b.

83 Burnyeat 1976, p. 43.

84 Pl. *Tht.* 184d–185d. See Cornford 1935; Cooper 1970 and Burnyeat 1976.

85 Pl. *Tht.* 184d–e.

suppose instead that there is a unitary subject that can collect different sensations coming from different sense organs and judge them: this is presented by Socrates as a more plausible account of how we perceive and assess our perceptions,[86] though it still remains to be determined whether this offers a correct account of what understanding consists in.[87] In any case, the relevant point of this passage is that we perceive through our senses but with the soul that is equipped to use their evidence: in other words, what Socrates shows is that "there is something in us, the soul, which can think and reason about what we perceive".[88] In Plato, this is not yet understanding, it is perception and perception is described as interpretation though one's mind, of diverse sense data.

In Aristotle's account, instead, perception and the soul's ability to interpret sense data are given a larger and more integral role in the process of understanding.

> Φανερὸν δὲ καὶ ὅτι, εἴ τις αἴσθησις ἐκλέλοιπεν, ἀνάγκη καὶ ἐπιστήμην τινὰ ἐκλελοιπέναι, ἣν ἀδύνατον λαβεῖν, εἴπερ μανθάνομεν ἢ ἐπαγωγῇ ἢ ἀποδείξει, ἔστι δ' ἡ μὲν ἀπόδειξις ἐκ τῶν καθόλου, ἡ δ' ἐπαγωγὴ ἐκ τῶν κατὰ μέρος, ἀδύνατον δὲ τὰ καθόλου θεωρῆσαι μὴ δι' ἐπαγωγῆς [...] ἐπαχθῆναι δὲ μὴ ἔχοντας αἴσθησιν ἀδύνατον. τῶν γὰρ καθ' ἕκαστον ἡ αἴσθησις· οὐ γὰρ ἐνδέχεται λαβεῖν αὐτῶν τὴν ἐπιστήμην· οὔτε γὰρ ἐκ τῶν καθόλου ἄνευ ἐπαγωγῆς, οὔτε δι' ἐπαγωγῆς ἄνευ τῆς αἰσθήσεως.

> It is clear too that if some perception is wanting, some understanding must also be wanting—[understanding] which is impossible to get if we learn either by induction or by demonstration, demonstration depend[ing] on universals and induction on particulars; but it is impossible to study universals except through induction [...], and it is impossible to make an induction without having perception (for particulars are grasped by perception). [So] it is not possible to get understanding of these items—either from universals without induction or through induction without perception.[89]

---

86 Cooper 1970, p. 123. See also Cornford 1935.

87 In Pl. *Tht.* 186b–c the argument that perception is knowledge is eventually rejected.

88 Burnyeat 1976, p. 49. See Pl. *Tht.* 184d1–184e1.

89 Arist. *APo.* I 18, 81a38–b9. On this particular passage, see Barnes 1994, p. 168. With reference to the interpretation of these difficult lines, see Mignucci who states that, 'ἔστι', here, as frequently in Aristotle, means 'it is possible'. On the other hand the sentence "ἐπεὶ καὶ τὰ ἐξ ἀφαιρέσεως λεγόμενα ἔσται δι' ἐπαγωγῆς γνώριμα ποιεῖν" (that is omitted in my text), because it is introduced by ἐπεὶ, seems to start the explanation of the sentence "ἀδύνατον

In *Posterior Analytics*, this paragraph follows the discussion of the various possible ways in which ignorance—more specifically, error through deduction—might arise within syllogistic reasoning.[90] According to the lines just quoted, an important factor that influences *epistēmē* is perception: "the whole matter is that sense-perception is the necessary starting point for science".[91] Indeed, universals are only grasped by induction and induction starts from particulars—and sense-perception is about particulars. Therefore, sense-perception provides the basis of *epistēmē* because it is the starting point of induction.[92] The assumption is that we can understand universal principles of *epistēmē* only after passing through a series of empirical experiences from which we should be able to form a systematic and synoptic view.[93] Universal principles of *epistēmē* constitute what is primary, indemonstrable, immediate, causative, and explanatory.

> αἴτιά τε καὶ γνωριμώτερα δεῖ εἶναι καὶ πρότερα, αἴτια μὲν ὅτι τότε ἐπιστάμεθα ὅταν τὴν αἰτίαν εἰδῶμεν, καὶ πρότερα, εἴπερ αἴτια, καὶ προγινωσκόμενα οὐ μόνον τὸν ἕτερον τρόπον τῷ ξυνιέναι, ἀλλὰ καὶ τῷ εἰδέναι ὅτι ἔστιν.

> [The items from which demonstrative understanding proceeds] must be explanatory and more familiar and prior—explanatory because we only understand something when we know its explanation, and, prior, if they are explanatory and we already know them not only in the sense of having insight into them but also of knowing that they are the case.[94]

δὲ τὰ καθόλου θεωρῆσαι μὴ δι' ἐπαγωγῆς". However, it is clear that to say that *it is possible* that τὰ ἐξ ἀφαιρέσεως λεγόμενα are known through induction, does not prove that is *impossible* to get to know the universal principles of science without induction as it is said before "ἀδύνατον δὲ τὰ καθόλου θεωρῆσαι μὴ δι' ἐπαγωγῆς" (Mignucci 1975, p. 384).

90 Arist. *APo.* I 16, 79b23–81a37.

91 Ross 1949, p. 566.

92 See Bolton 1990 who shows a tendency to a more empiricist reading of Aristotle. "Aristotle does not take ordinary perceptual judgments to be in principle or in general unrevisable (*De Anima* III 3, 428b18–25). This is compatible, however, with his general assignment of final epistemic authority in science to perceptual over theoretical beliefs (*De Caelo* III 7, 306a13–17) [...]. It follows from the doctrine that revision must always be made by reference to what is most intelligible to us, together with the doctrine that what is most intelligible to us is always closest to perception. In this respect there is a kind of foundationalist empiricist element in Aristotle's theory of justification both in science and in preirastic dialectic generally" (Bolton 1990, p. 236).

93 Burneyat 1981, p. 112.

94 Arist. *APo.* I 2, 71b29–33.

What is prior and more knowable by nature (γνωριμώτερος φύσει) depends on our perceptions and what is closest to them; that is, what is more knowable to us (γνωριμώτερος πρὸς ἡμᾶς).[95] In this way Aristotle undoubtedly confers an important role on perception and experience. Understanding emerges when we start to take a more global view of objects that we have experienced; this global view needs to be consolidated by understanding of causes and principles.[96] The process seems to be two-fold: in order to understand something, we should move from perception of particulars to universals and from universals to particulars. The aim is to reconstruct an intelligible structure of the world through an understanding of the causes of events in the world.[97]

However, what we can call Aristotle's epistemological 'realism' presents, at this stage, two difficulties. The first problem concerns the possibility of error in interpreting perceptions. In the *De Anima* Aristotle states that perception is never wrong;[98] however, error is possible. This is because the reasoning based on this primary data can lead to wrong conclusions. We find evidence of this also in the *Posterior Analytics* where ignorance is described as the product of error during the process of syllogistic reasoning.

> Ἄγνοια δ' ἡ μὴ κατ' ἀπόφασιν ἀλλὰ κατὰ διάθεσιν λεγομένη ἔστι μὲν ἡ διὰ συλλογισμοῦ γινομένη ἀπάτη.
>
> Ignorance, that is called such not in virtue of a negative state but in virtue of a disposition, is error arising from reasoning.[99]

This is quite an important point if we consider that to reason is the crucial key characteristic of being human. Apparently, then we do not just perceive but we also constantly form opinions about what we perceive.

Moreover, we usually share our reasoning with other members of the community in order to improve our thoughts by mutual interchange: "If the person

---

95 Arist. *APo.* I 2, 71b34–72 a6.

96 See Mansion 1984: "Notre connaissance commence par une saisie globale des objets soumis à notre expérience, saisie qui aura à se *préciser* ensuite en faisant dans la masse confuse des données les distinctions nécessaires" (Mansion 1984, p. 165).

97 See Mansion 1984 and Tuominen 2007.

98 Arist. *DA* III 3, 427b11–14. "Sense organs do not add any contribution of their own to the effects caused by perceptible object. In relation to their objects, senses are never mistaken [...]. Aristotle, however, does not claim that perceptual error is impossible. He only says that perceptions are highly reliable and that typically in the case of perceptual error we can find an explanation why the error occurred" (Tuominen 2007, pp. 173–174).

99 Arist. *APo.* I 16, 79b23–24.

does not speak he ceases to be one of us and we are not required to take account of him. If he does speak, we can urge him to take a close look at his linguistic practices and what they rest on. In doing this we are giving him the *paideia* he lacks, a kind of initiation into the way we do things".[100] This is why the one who possesses more wisdom is the one who has properly understood the causes of what it is and is also able to teach others about it.[101] This implies that fallacious reasoning might have great significance not just for our understanding but for that of the whole community.

As human beings we are provided with tools: reason, perception, memory, a life of experience. Nevertheless, we may fail when we try to attach significance to our perceptions; namely, we may miss the understanding of what is more knowable by nature, namely universals, which is also what we should understand in order to have *epistēmē*.[102] Secondly, perception might just be lacking. We might not have empirical data to start our inquiry. Chance is a potent agent that can hide particulars and this happens also in the realm of ethics: we might not know particulars related to our practical decision-making.[103] In this case we should respond with pity and forgiveness, since we may suppose that the reasoning behind the unfortunate choice could have been, in theory, virtuous. However, a lack of knowledge might lead to the wrong decision and making mistakes.[104] In the same way, according to the passage quoted at the beginning, missing a perception of a single particular can lead to a complete misunderstanding of the nature of things. Going back to Menander, the happy ending following the final understanding of the whole story might not occur if a particular, such as a ring, is missed, or if an hasty reasoning leads to a mistaken recognition.

3.2 *Grasping and Missing the Grasp*

I would now like to discuss how, after having fully grasped sense data, it is still possible to fail in understanding something properly. I would like to analyse this point looking at the verbs that describe this further and final step.

---

100 Nussbaum 1982, p. 285 commenting on Arist. *Metaph.* Γ 4, 1006a13–15. Looking also at the ethical works, in Arist. *Pol.* I 2, 1253a9–15, language (λόγος) is exclusive to man, since only man can use this tool to discuss and define what is good and what is bad, what is virtuous and what is not. I will explore the relevance of this topic to ethics in Chapter 5.

101 Arist. *Metaph.* A 1, 982a12–14.

102 See Taylor 1990, p. 126.

103 Arist. *EN* III 2, 1110b18–1111a2. The relevance of this feature of Aristotle's theory of causation will be explained further in Chapter 4.

104 Arist. *EN* V 10, 1135b12.

> The principal ingredients in Aristotle's vocabulary of knowledge are the three verbs *eidenai*, *gignōskein*, and *epistasthai*, together with the cognate nouns *gnōsis* and *epistēmē*. Aristotle also uses *gnōrizein* (*gnōrimos*, "familiar" […]), *sunienai*, and *echein* (as general as "have" in English, but translated as "grasp" in its epistemological use).[105]

Several studies have been made of the meaning and use of the first three verbs: it seems that, in the *Posterior Analytics*, Aristotle uses them to describe different kinds of knowledge in a way that makes these terms not amenable to substitution by each other.[106] On the other hand, *gnōrizein* has often been discussed with reference to the cognate comparative or superlative adjectives. I shall discuss the meaning of *gnōrizein* after clarifying that of *gignōskein* and *epistasthai*.

In an article published in 1981,[107] Burnyeat clarified the difference between '*gignōskein*' and '*epistasthai*' in the terminology of *Posterior Analytics*. '*Gignōskein*' could be translated as 'to know' whereas, for '*epistasthai*', 'to understand' would be a better translation. With this translation, *gignōskein* would keep its epistemological validity but it is differentiated from *epistasthai*. *Epistasthai* is not just *gignōskein*: it indicates the ability to explain what we get to know and to understand the reasons and principles according to which something is such as we understand it. However, the first difficulty with this account is the fact that Aristotle gives a definition of *epistasthai* by means of the verb *gignōskein*.

> Ἐπίστασθαι δὲ οἰόμεθ' ἕκαστον ἁπλῶς, ἀλλὰ μὴ τὸν σοφιστικὸν τρόπον τὸν κατὰ συμβεβηκός, ὅταν τήν τ' αἰτίαν οἰώμεθα γινώσκειν δι' ἣν τὸ πρᾶγμά ἐστιν, ὅτι ἐκείνου αἰτία ἐστί, καὶ μὴ ἐνδέχεσθαι τοῦτ' ἄλλως ἔχειν. δῆλον τοίνυν ὅτι τοιοῦτόν τι τὸ ἐπίστασθαί ἐστι·
>
> We think we understand (*epistasthai*) something *simpliciter* (and not in the sophistical way, incidentally) when we think we know (*gignōskein*) the cause for which a thing is [as such], that it is its cause, and also that it is not possible for it to be otherwise. It is plain then that to understand is something of this sort.[108]

---

105 Barnes 1994, p. 82.

106 Barnes 1994, p. 82; See also Moravcsik 1974 and Burnyeat 1981. On the use of these verbs in Plato, see Lyons 1963, p. 177.

107 Burnyeat 1981.

108 Arist. *APo.* I 2, 71b9–14.

Barnes recognises that this explanation "would avoid circularity only if 'understand' (*epistasthai*) and 'know' (here *gignōskein*) are kept apart in sense".[109] Burnyeat quotes the same passage as evidence to show the difference in meaning between *epistasthai* and *gignōskein*.[110] However, if the difference in meaning implies a difference between a richer and a more basic concept of knowledge,[111] the quoted passage would mean that *epistēmē* would be possible only through a less complete kind of understanding (that is, *gignōskein*). Consequently, it seems that *epistēmē* is needed to "turn something *which is already knowledge* into that type of knowledge secured by understanding".[112] This remark would explain the distinction between the two senses in which things are more knowable (i.e. for us and by nature) and it implies that Aristotle admits the possibility of, at least, two levels of knowledge that are, nevertheless, both *gnōsis*.

> [...] the celebrated and all-pervasive distinction between what is more knowable or familiar in the order of nature and what is more knowable or familiar to us is intended quite literally. It points not only to a natural order of explanation—an order of explanation which is not relative to the knowledge and needs of particular persons—but also, in view of the remarks about conviction which comes from a grasp of first principles and the man whose conviction must rank as knowledge (*gnōsis*).[113]

This conclusion will help the comprehension of *Posterior Analytics*; however, it does not make our approach to knowledge simple. The world is made to be known: we progress in understanding when we build our knowledge on the senses and we reason about them; this is already *gnōsis* and we can claim to know truly. However, there is also another kind of knowledge, which is more complete—namely *epistēmē*.[114] We might say that *gignōskein* entails having

---

109 Barnes 1994, p. 90.

110 Burnyeat 1981, p. 106.

111 Burnyeat 1981, p. 108.

112 Burnyeat 1981, p. 132 (my emphasis).

113 Burnyeat 1981, pp. 128.

114 In Plato's epistemology, there is only one kind of true knowledge: to be able to see what really is, and what the truth is, is the crucial factor that divides knowledge from mere belief. The empirical world and the sensations connected to it are just starting-points of a process of recollection that is the prerequisite for true knowledge; perceptual knowledge, however, is not knowledge in the proper sense (Tuominen 2007, pp. 172–180; see also Mansion 1984, p. 169).

senses, memory, experience and arts; however, we should know that this is not yet to achieve full understanding. To reach the higher level, that of *epistasthai*, we should not only keep recollecting sensible experiences; we should also have the ability to grasp their overall sense to give an account of them; and, this is a matter of intellectual habituation, time and also luck.

This idea comes out in several passages in the *Posterior Analytics* where the verb *gnōrizein* plays an important role as it describes the final grasp of the principles of our understanding. It is important to understand its meaning by comparison with the verbs already treated—namely, *gignōskein* and *epistasthai*. In Bonitz's *Index Aristotelicus* we find:

> Omnino et significatione et usus ambitu gnorizein et gignoskein vix possunt inter se distingui, ac pro synonimis vel in eodem sententiae contextu vel in iisdem formulis gnorizein, gignoskein, gnosis, [...] eidenai epistasthai leguntur.[115]

Burnyeat also seems to identify a similarity between the use of *gignōskein* and *gnōrizein* but from a different point of view. The starting point for his argument is a passage from *Physics*.

> ἐπειδὴ τὸ εἰδέναι καὶ τὸ ἐπίστασθαι συμβαίνει περὶ πάσας τὰς μεθόδους, ὧν εἰσὶν ἀρχαὶ ἢ αἴτια ἢ στοιχεῖα, ἐκ τοῦ ταῦτα γνωρίζειν (τότε γὰρ οἰόμεθα γιγνώσκειν ἕκαστον, ὅταν τὰ αἴτια γνωρίσωμεν τὰ πρῶτα καὶ τὰς ἀρχὰς τὰς πρώτας καὶ μέχρι τῶν στοιχείων), δῆλον ὅτι καὶ τῆς περὶ φύσεως ἐπιστήμης πειρατέον διορίσασθαι πρῶτον τὰ περὶ τὰς ἀρχάς.
>
> Since knowing and understanding (*epistasthai*) in every inquiry concerned with things having principles or causes or elements results from the knowledge (*gnōrizein*) of these (for we think that we know (*gignōskein*) each thing when we think that we know (*gnōrisōmen*) the first causes and the first principles and have reached the elements), clearly, in the science of nature too we should first try to determine what is the case with regard to the principles.[116]

He compares this passage with *Posterior Analytics* I 2, 71b9–14 and he argues that here between *gignōskein* and *gnōrizein* occurs the same relationship that occurs between *gignōskein* and *epistasthai*. He then concludes:

---

115 Bonitz 1955, *s. v.*

116 Arist. *Ph.* I 1, 184a10–14.

> In both passages, the definition of *epistasthai* in the *Posterior Analytics* and the definition of *gignōskein* in the *Physics*, our verb 'know' is needed in the analysans not in the analysandum. Aristotle is analysing a cognitive state which is achieved by knowing explanations, and whether he is currently calling it *epistasthai* or *gignōskein* the corresponding term for that state in philosophical English is 'understand'.[117]

Consequently, the translation of *gnōrizein* as 'to know' serves again the purpose of clarifying the translation of *gignōskein* as 'to understand'. However, this translation lacks a particular nuance of *gnōrizein* which is: 'grasp', 'gain knowledge of', 'make something known',[118] recollecting pieces of knowledge or signs to get to know something. For instance, in *Prior Analytics*, *gnōrizein* is used to say that: "we shall *identify* (γνωριοῦμεν) the figure of the syllogism by the position of the middle term".[119] *'gnōrisma'* is usually used to mean 'that for which a thing is made known'.[120] *'Gnōrismata'* is the name given to tokens of recognition that serve to recollect the identity of an exposed child.[121] And also in the *Posterior Analytics* we find that:

> Ἔστι δὲ γνωρίζειν τὰ μὲν πρότερον γνωρίσαντα, τῶν δὲ καὶ ἅμα λαμβάνοντα τὴν γνῶσιν, οἷον ὅσα τυγχάνει ὄντα ὑπὸ τὸ καθόλου οὗ ἔχει τὴν γνῶσιν.
>
> To 'grasp' (*gnōrizein*) is when one has grasped some items earlier and gained knowledge of the other items at the very same time (e.g. items which in fact fall under the universal of which you possess knowledge).[122]

Therefore, this sense of *gnōrizein* should be taken into account particularly in Aristotle's *Posterior Analytics*, as it has interesting epistemological implications. The original meaning of this verb implies an interpretative effort that needs to be made on the data starting from which we gain understanding of something. Thus, in the light of this sense of *gnōrizein*, to understand something is not only to recollect particulars that are more knowable to us; one should

117 Burnyeat 1981, p. 106.
118 A. *Pr.* 487.
119 Arist. *APr.* I 32, 47b14.
120 LSJ *s. v.*; See X. *Cyr.* 2.1.27; Arist. *Phgn.* 806a15 and Plu. 2.885b.
121 Men. *Epitr.* 303; Plu. *Thes.* 4.
122 Arist. *APo.* I 2, 71a17–19.

also have readiness of mind[123] and be able to evaluate this correctly in order to grasp an understanding of what is more knowable by nature. To some extent, the possibility of getting the process of understanding right is therefore *person-based.*[124] As noted in Chapter 1 (section 1), according to Aristotle, to be able to grasp understanding we need to exercise our intellectual skills and perfect them until we achieve excellence in reasoning and in finding the truth about things in every circumstance; to cultivate this kind of excellence is, to a great extent, up to us and how we decide to engage with our cognitive skills.

If my reading is correct, it would be important to take into account all the passages in which *gnōrizein* is used to describe the way we get to understand universals. Indeed, this usage is found in several passages of *Posterior Analytics*: I 2, 72a39; I 3, 72b25; I 18, 81b3; I 31, 87b39; II 8, 93a18; II 19, 99b18; II 19, 99b29 and II 19, 100b4. Maintaining the original sense of the verb *gnōrizein* in these contexts will produce interesting results: these passages will confirm the idea that understanding is possible through grasping. Grasping premises is much more than making a generalization on the basis of scattered fragments of empirical evidence; it constitutes an interpretation of them in the light of their principles and causes. These latter make scientific discourse possible; they form the necessary truths that we should get to know to understand the nature of things properly.

However, premises are known immediately (ἄμεσον) by induction: that is, they cannot be proved syllogistically by means of a middle term.[125] Indeed, in the final paragraph of the book we find that *epistasthai*[126] (understanding the premises) in some ways needs perceptions, particulars, empirical elements. But then, *nous* needs to work on it to attempt to achieve *gnōrizein*, that is,

123 Ἡ δ' ἀγχίνοιά ἐστιν εὐστοχία τις ἐν ἀσκέπτῳ χρόνῳ τοῦ μέσου; "readiness of mind is a talent for hitting upon the middle term in an imperceptible time" (Arist. *APo.* I 34, 89b10–12).

124 See Chapter 1, pp. 14–15. In virtue epistemology, this may imply that the agent has also an epistemic responsibility and he should be motivated to get the process of understanding right, finding the truth and avoiding error. "The simplest way to describe the motivational basis of the intellectual virtues is to say that they are all based in the motivation for knowledge. They are all forms of the motivation to have cognitive contact with reality, where this includes more than what is usually expressed by saying that people desire the truth. [...] Understanding is also a form of cognitive contact with reality, one that has been considered a component of the knowing state in some period of philosophical history. [...] Understanding [...] is a state that includes the comprehension of abstract structures of reality apart from the propositional" (Zagzebski 1996, p. 167).

125 LSJ, *s. v.*

126 Arist. *APo.* I 3, 72b30; II 5, 91b 34.

the final explanatory grasp. It seems that, even after a correct recollection of empirical data (things that are more knowable to us) our knowledge is still not complete.[127] A more complete knowledge, that is *epistēmē*, depends on our individual ability to grasp things (ἡ γνωρίζουσα ἕξις)[128] and on a specific faculty, *nous*.[129] We sharpen this kind of ability through a process of habituation and through engaging within this kind of epistemic exercises. In the next chapters, we will see that this kind of exercise is also necessary to achieve a higher level of ethical understanding.

> Rather than regarding intellectual excellences as the competences or traits or affects by which we are best positioned to pursue the truth, he [Aristotle] views them as states that mark an intellectual grasp of the truth, in the sense of having arrived at scientific understanding, or wisdom of various sorts, or a grasp of foundational first principles. The emphasis on achievement underscores basic Aristotelian points about virtue, namely, that virtue is a cultivated and acquired state. Intellectual excellences will depend on natural powers, faculties, and receptivities as moral virtue does.[130]

This reading sheds light also on other fields of Aristotle's thought: his treatment of dramatic recognition in the *Poetics*, for instance, acquires new significance if read in the light of these observations. Aristotle seems to dislike dramatic recognitions that are brought about by the mere use of tokens. He states that recognition through signs is the simplest kind of recognition and the least suitable in terms of poetic art.[131] Indeed, it is quite evident that this kind of discovery does not require the characters to exercise much reasoning: sometimes, in drama, a necklace or a scar can identify someone quickly without further need

127 Taylor 1990, p. 122.

128 Arist. *APo.* II 19, 99b18.

129 Arist. *APo.* II 19, 100b12. See Irwin 1988 for a slightly different account of the role of *nous* in grasping the first principles: "Experience and familiarity with appearances are useful to us as a way of approaching the first principles: they might be psychologically indispensable as a way to form right intuitions. But they form no part of the justification of the first principles. When we come to have the right intuition we are aware of the principles as self evident, with no external justification [...]. The acquisition of *nous* is not meant to be magical, entirely independent of inquiry. Nor however, it is simply a summary of the inquiry or a conclusion that depends on the inquiry for its warrant" (Irwin 1988, p. 136).

130 Sherman and White 2003, pp. 38–39.

131 Arist. *Poet.* 16, 1454b20–21.

of reasoning on these tokens of recognition. The recognition of the best kind is the one that proceeds from the circumstances of the action (ἡ ἐξ αὐτῶν τῶν πραγμάτων) and the one that proceeds from the characters' reasoning about the circumstances they find themselves involved in (ἡ ἐκ συλλογισμοῦ).[132] What I have said with respect to the *Posterior Analytics* can help us to understand why this is the case.

In Aristotle's epistemology, mere perception of sensible objects does not, by itself, constitute complete understanding: in the first place, mere perception might be misleading if it is not accompanied by adequate reasoning and, secondly, to reason about our perception is a crucial exercise that we need to undertake to sharpen our intellectual skills and achieve complete understanding. My suggestion is that, analogously, in drama, to say that someone has been recognised through signs or tokens does not constitute a good type of recognition because it is not truly convincing and the process is not supported by adequate explanation of the evidence that has been found. The example of Menander's *Epitrepontes* can clarify the point made by Aristotle. As Habrotonon explains, Charisios' ring is not a good token of recognition of the child's identity because the ring might have been lost or stolen by someone who then raped Pamphile: consequently, Charisios cannot be identified with certainty as the child's father.

Secondly, it might be argued that recognitions through tokens take place too quickly: spectators find themselves at the end of the recognition process without having engaged in any sort of reasoning. That is to say, a recognition through tokens does not engage the audience's intellectual skills in the same way as a recognition that involves some kind of reasoning on the basis of pieces of evidence in order to find out the truth of what happened. As an audience, we want to be shown each step of the reasoning that brings about the solution of a plot; the more complex the recognition is, the more we will pay attention to how characters will find the solution to it, as we want to be sure that they find the right one and that their reasoning is secure and rigorous. A recognition that proceeds through reasoning succeeds better than the others in leading the audience's understanding through the causal network of evidence, actions and events that comprises a recognition process.[133] That is why this kind of recognition is of the best kind according to Aristotle; namely, because it engages the characters and the audience in a process of understanding that is rigorous

---

132 Arist. *Poet.* 16, 1455a15–21.

133 See Halliwell 1992, pp. 249–250. For scholarship on Aristotle's treatment of recognition and cognitivist readings of Aristotle's *Poetics*, see Chapter 1, section 2.

and that implies a good deal of intellectual involvement from the audience providing a greater pleasure in the final moment of discovery.

I will now summarise the main points of Aristotle's approach to understanding and, in the conclusion of this chapter, I will link these ideas to Menander's *Epitrepontes*. In the first part of this section, the distinction between the two senses of 'being more knowable' has been shown to be important. Both particulars and universals are needed in order to make up complete knowledge: particulars seem to be a necessary starting-point that needs to be framed in a wider theoretical explanation that necessarily includes principles and causes. Nevertheless, in this dual movement from universal to particulars and particulars to universal, I have distinguished two main risks that seem to have parallels in Aristotle's ethical works and that might apply as well to Menander's plots. Firstly, it is possible to fail in the process of reasoning about the data of our experience and to miss the significance of what we have been recollecting. Secondly, experience might just be lacking and ignorance of the smallest particular might invalidate our reasoning. As a third point, I have also shown that interpersonal debate about relevant topics is important for the intellectual enhancement of the whole community: the more we talk about things, the more we understand them. This will be shown to be particularly relevant also in matters of ethical understanding because, as shown in Chapter 5, we understand better the right way to live by engaging in discussion with people that care about us and that we care about.

In the second part of this section, I have analysed in more detail the movement from knowledge to understanding, from what is more knowable to us to what is more knowable by nature. Indeed, in drawing this distinction between the two senses of knowable, Aristotle also suggests the possibility of two levels of knowledge. As explained in *Metaphysics A*, we might acquire art (τέχνη) as we are able to take advantage of senses, memories, experiences, in order to know the general principles that form the basis of those arts. However, to understand is a completely different matter. It also implies an ability that develops with intellectual habituation:[134] *epistēmē* needs time and cultivation and a *nous* from which time and cultivation can produce some epistemologically valuable results. The problem is that a perfect combination of these components may not actually exist in everyone. Consequently, the transition to a superior degree of knowledge might not happen: therefore, the process of getting there is neither easy not guaranteed. In *Metaphysics A* the movement from art to *epistēmē* undergoes variation precisely because to make this passage an ability to grasp

134 Burnyeat 1981, p. 139.

(γνωρίζειν) is required and this, unfortunately, is not common. At the same time, understanding does not need scientific deductive reasoning.[135] To understand causes and principles it is necessary to grasp them and to develop a certain ability in doing so. I have also hinted that this idea has its counterpart in Aristotle's ethics and aesthetics.

4 Conclusions

In the preceding discussion I have not attempted to answer conclusively certain much debated questions regarding Aristotle's epistemology or about the structure and functioning of scientific reasoning. My aim has been to stress some relevant features that are interestingly connected with a kind of drama that is sensitive to these issues. Menander is highly interested in recognitions, lack of knowledge, and in different attempts to gain a clear understanding of what the character's story is.[136] Could it just be a coincidence that his drama is preceded by an intellectual discussion that deals with analogous topics in a comparable manner? My guess is that this is not the case, because Aristotle's and Menander's points of view and framework of ideas on this topic seem to be comparable to a great extent. I think that my analysis so far has shown that Menander and Aristotle provide an interpretation of the process of understanding and making factual mistakes that is analogous in many important respects.

Aristotle and Menander both stress the importance of the achievement of a stable, complete understanding. This understanding does not consist in a simple acquaintance with people or facts: to have a happy ending all the evidence should be included in an explanatory account. To produce this account, perceptual insight and intellectual ability are necessary; what might create a problem is not having this ability or having it only to a certain degree. It seems, therefore, that whether we are Aristotelian philosophers or Menandrian figures, what we mean by understanding is the achievement of a fully explanatory version of the story; namely, a recognition, recollection or understanding of a system that frames, and makes sense of, what we experience at a particular level.

In this respect, I believe that the analysis of Aristotle's treatment of recognition through tokens associated with the analysis of Menander's *Epitrepontes*

135 Arist. *APo.* I 3, 72b19–22; I 9, 76a16–22; II 19, 99b20–41.

136 See Greimas and Courtés 1989 where New Comedy seems to be included in a particular kind of narrative discourse which has knowledge as its narrative pivot.

has produced positive results. In section 3.2 of this chapter, I suggested a possible solution for Aristotle's negative view of recognition through signs (a view whose rationale is not obvious). On the basis of what we learn from the *Posterior Analytics*, recognition through tokens does not appear to be convincing as often the evidence provided by tokens is not supported by adequate reasoning. In Menander, we find an analogous idea: in the *Epitrepontes*, Menander avoids a quick resolution of the process of discovery of Charisios' and Pamphile's child. We will discover that Onesimos is right to believe that Charisios is the father of the child solely on the basis of the evidence of the ring; nevertheless, at first, we are not completely convinced of his reasoning. As Habrotonon suggests, a complete understanding of the story is not possible without a reasoned evaluation of what the empirical evidence suggests. Furthermore, in the case of the *Aspis*, we learn that Kleostratos' recognition (his identification with the corpse lying with the shield) is completely mistaken because the sign of recognition (Kleostratos' shield) was not appropriately supported by a trustworthy account of the circumstances.

More importantly, I hope to have shown that it is not just Aristotle's treatment of recognition in *Poetics* that is analogous to Menander's use of recognition in the *Epitrepontes*. The way in which Menander presents his character's reasoning on stage seems to be analogous to Aristotle's version of the thought-processes through which we get to know something, as discussed with reference to *Posterior Analytics*. It is true that the kind of speculative, theoretical understanding with which Aristotle is concerned in the *Posterior Analytics* is not the factual understanding with which Menander's characters are dealing. However, despite this difference, their ideas about the steps of the reasoning that lead to the final understanding of something (scientific principles or the story behind the plot) are comparable and analogous in many respects.

Menander builds plots based on problems caused by lack of proper knowledge of what circumstances or people are. As we have seen, these plots ended happily after some clever person had enabled the full understanding of what had happened and who the people involved were. It is relevant to point out, that the figures who, in comedy, bring about the final understanding (very often being slaves and courtesans)[137] do not correspond to the class of the people that, in Aristotle's opinion, had the privilege of gaining understanding (that is, people who had time for intellectual exercise and speculative research).[138] Nev-

137 For a recent account of Menander's presentation of geneder relationships see Traill 2008 and Lape 2010.

138 At the same time, assuming that what is required to get to know something are intellectual

ertheless, in both Aristotle and Menander, the ones who are successful in the process of understanding and that make the final recognition possible, reason in a specific way: they start from sensory experience to build up a kind of a reasoning that can explain why these things are as we see them. Perception, that is, mere sensory evidence, in Aristotle and Menander, is not enough to guarantee that something has been fully understood or that a recognition has been completed. The transition from perception to understanding needs to be supported by adequate reasoning. Concluding, the long recognition process in Menander's *Epitrepontes* acquires new significance when looked at from the perspective of Aristotle's theory of understanding. Thus, my inquiry suggests that the way in which Menander builds dramatic recognitions has various original aspects and is not a mere adaptation of tragic themes into a comic plot.

---

skills and a life-time of habituation in dealing with certain topics, courtesans and slaves, as depicted in New Comedy and Roman Comedy, are certainly good candidates for possession of these qualities and this can be seen as part of the subversive message at the core of the comic genre. For discussion on this topic see Silk 1988; see also p. 24 n. 2 above.

CHAPTER 3

The Misleading Power of Perceptions and Emotions

In the previous chapter, I have considered the analogies between Menander and Aristotle focusing on what understanding means to them and what its preconditions are. The overall result of my inquiry is that, in both Aristotle and Menander, understanding depends on an accurate evaluation of perceived particulars which includes a comprehensive grasp of what has been perceived. Both perceptive insight and intellectual exercise are needed in order to organise multiple perceptions under principles that show how things stand in the world and how situations are to be understood. The argument of this chapter is that this kind of understanding is also implied in Menander's and Aristotle's ethical thinking. Correct ethical choice, in fact, is seen as dependent on the context of the action, on how this context affects the agent and on the agent's ability to reason about this context so as to perform the ethically right action. As a consequence, practical life also depends on how we perceive particular situations, how well we can understand them and how we recognise what is the appropriate response to them. Thus, correct ethical choice involves i) understanding which are the particulars involved in our choice, ii) feeling correct emotions as well as iii) performing right actions. Consequently, the ability to interpret multiple perceptions properly so as to give a correct account of what surrounds us seems to be crucial also in the fields of ethics because it is on this basis that we make right or wrong ethical choices.

At the same time, the rational process that leads to correct ethical choice might go wrong in various ways: for instance, the perception of actual particulars can unleash emotions that we are not able to control or we might not be able to reconstruct the context of our action, thereby misjudging people and facts. Situation of this kind are often at the core of Menandrian comedies and, to my mind, the way in which Menander describes his characters and their processes of decision-making, is again analogous to Aristotle's thinking on comparable topics. To illustrate this point I shall compare the plot and characters of Menander's *Samia* and Aristotle's works on ethics and psychology.[1]

In the first part, I will consider Menander's *Samia*, focusing on the characters of Demeas and Moschion, Demeas' adopted son. Scholars have often presented their relationship as the main focus of the plot;[2] however, here, I focus mainly

1 Cf. Cinaglia 2012 for a preliminary study of Menander's *Samia* in view of this topic.

2 See Wehrli 1936; Barigazzi 1965; Treu 1969; Keuls 1973 and Grant 1986.

 | DOI: 10.1163/9789004282827_005

on the problems that prevent this relationship from remaining untroubled during the dramatic action. Before introducing the topics related to this particular text, I will provide a short outline of the plot. The whole situation is explained by Moschion at the beginning of the play, in a monologue which makes the audience aware of some important pieces of information needed to understand the facts that follow. Moschion informs the audience that, during the festival of Adonis, he raped a girl, namely, the daughter of their neighbour Nikeratos. The girl got pregnant and, at the moment of the action, she has just given birth to his child. Moschion wants to marry her and he must ask Demeas about this. However, the young man is ashamed and would like to keep secret from his father the fact that he now has a baby by the girl, which is the product of the rape: accordingly, he decides to leave Demeas' *hetaira*, Chrysis, nursing the child, pretending it was the child of her and Demeas. Demeas wrongly believes that the child is that of Moschion and Chrysis and he drives Chrysis out from his house.

What I am interested in seeing here is, first, how Demeas forms his incorrect belief. This misunderstanding is due to lack of knowledge but also due to a) wrong conclusions inferred from his sensory perceptions and b) his altered state of mind in reacting to these perceptions. His misconception of what really happened leads him to act wrongly and to misjudge Chrysis and Moschion. In addition, I will analyse Moschion's behaviour in order to determine why, in his case, despite his correct knowledge of the facts he fails to behave properly. In every circumstance he knows, in theory, what the right thing to do is and he is aware of the particulars involved in the action; however, when facing the specific situation he fails to act as he should. Thus, Demeas fails to manage perceptions and emotions in the act of understanding what has happened; he then misunderstands everything and acts wrongly. On the other hand, Moschion has a clear understanding of how things stand but he fails to control perceptions and emotions in deciding what it is best to do in a given circumstance. The two of them are presented as characters who would normally know what it is right to do and, at the end of the comedy, their regret confirms this; however, faced with the specific circumstances involved they fail to do so.

In the second part, I will take into account how Aristotle conceives the same topic. The relevant issue that I will consider is how error is possible in judging practical circumstances and what is the role that emotions play in this process. In order to explain this, I will start with the *De Anima* in considering how, in general, it is possible to go wrong in drawing inferences from sensory evidence. On the basis of specific passages from Aristotle's works on psychology, it will become clear that the correct analysis of sense data is a process internal to the agent and, therefore, the successful outcome of this process depends on the agent's state of mind.

Having clarified this, I will explain how this analysis relates to practical life. In Aristotle, choice is sometimes described as a process in which the agent, having specific desires and being in a specific situation, tries to find out, on this basis, what is the right action to perform in order to obtain his desired end,[3] which, in the virtuous person, coincides with what is ethically correct in this situation.[4] Deliberation is activated by desires and emotions stimulated by a specific circumstance, but it also requires calculation and reasoning to be finally carried out. Aristotle sometimes summarises this process schematically in the form of a syllogism:[5] the first premise of the syllogism is an opinion that relates to what an agent desires to do; the second premise relates to the particular circumstances of the action to which the first premise applies; the conclusion follows as the result of a process of calculation that takes into account both these premises.

The right (ethical) choice, therefore, should follow from reasoning of the following kind: the agent considers what is universally considered good to do (and what one should desire to do if one is a truly virtuous agent) and the particular context of the action; the result is that he makes the right choice, and calculates the best possible way to achieve his desired end. This process is, therefore, context-dependent and also affected by the agent's state of mind. On this basis, the effective completion of the ethical syllogism can be perverted in two ways. It is possible to be mistaken at the level of the first premise: i.e., the agent may not recognise what would be generally considered good to do in a specific type of situation. For instance, particular situations can overpower his better judgement and lead him to make a mistake in considering the major relevant premise. Secondly, the ethical reasoning can be perverted at the level of the second premise: i.e., the agent might miss the understanding of what the particulars of the actions are in the kind of situation in which he finds himself acting. For instance, the emotion felt at the perception of a given particular may hinder the correct understanding of the context of the agent's action. Thus, as we will see in more detail later, an incorrect management of the agent's emotions may influence the agent's insight considerably and it may affect the content both of the first and the second premises of his practical reasoning. This can happen also to people who are normally considered to be of good character but whose judgement, at a crucial moment, is somehow clouded so that they fail to act in the right way.

3 Arist. *EN* III 4, 1112a15–16 and III 5, 1112b11–24.

4 Arist. *EN* III 6, 1113a29–b2.

5 See Arist. *EN* VII 5, 1147a25–35 and *MA* 7, 701a32–36. See also Gill 1996, pp. 52–53 and section 2.2 below for further discussion and relevant bibliography.

I need to clarify here that, in this part, I am not considering cases in which the ethically good choice is made, because of bad luck, in circumstances that could not have been grasped properly by the agent;[6] this will be the topic of Chapter 4. On the contrary, I will analyse here cases in which the right ethical choice is prevented by other factors internal to the agent, cases in which the successful working of practical reasoning is affected by i) inattentive processing of sensory perceptive experience, which leads to an incorrect evaluation of the particulars involved in the action; and ii), an emotionally altered state of mind that leads to the wrong choice of what the action should be.

1 "Is This Plausible?" (Men. *Sam.* 216)

1.1 *Demeas*

The fact that Moschion, at the beginning of *Samia*, decides to conceal the truth about the baby, causes a series of misunderstandings among which that of Demeas is the most complex and interesting. Demeas is, in fact, the figure with the lowest level of information and the one who is in most urgent need of having a clear understanding of what happened in his household while he was away. In the third act of *Samia*, after Moschion's monologue has informed the audience of the events, Demeas comes out in a state of desperation and explains why he is in this state.[7] He says that he has just i) heard a nurse referring to the child (which he thought was that of Chrysis and himself) as Moschion's; and ii) that he has seen Chrysis nursing and feeding the child. On the basis of these two separate pieces of perceptible evidence he rapidly concludes that the child is that of Moschion and Chrysis. His inference could

6 Annas 2003 defines clearly the complexity of the concept of success in relation to virtue: "[…] a virtuous person can succeed in achieving the overall aim of living virtuously by performing a virtuous act, even if, through no fault of her own, she fails to achieve the immediate target. […] It is crucial, therefore, in examining a virtuous act, to ask what kind of success is in question—success in achieving the overall goal or success in achieving the immediate target. For achieving the overall goal is a matter of having the right motivation […], and this is up to the agent. But success in achieving the immediate target may not be in this way up to the agent, and may depend on various kind of moral luck" (Annas 2003, pp. 24–25).

7 "Demeas comes out of his house and in a long monologue confides in the audience that as all seemed set fair, he had been struck out of the blue by a catastrophe. By a brilliant piece of writing the hearer is kept waiting for some 40 lines before he learns the nature of the blow, which is revealed, when it comes, as unexpectedly as it had hit Demeas" (Gomme and Sandbach 1973, p. 564).

be partly justified as, at the beginning of the comedy, we know that Demeas has been informed that Chrysis gave birth to a child of which he was said to be the father. It is true that Moschion's distortion of the story provides Demeas with a version that plausibly matches the interpretation of what he has heard and seen. However, when Demeas attempts to investigate the matter further, he is clearly in a confused state of mind, caused by what he has just experienced and he is not able to reconstruct adequately the circumstances he witnesses. I am now going to examine Demeas' reconstruction of what has happened as he describes his impressions to the audience.

In a first attempt to analyse carefully what he had just experienced, Demeas asks the audience to examine the credibility of what he has seen and inferred. He is not sure that he has seen things in the right way, but he has the impression that something really bad has happened to him. He does not know whether he has inferred a plausible version of the story through correct reasoning or whether he is in a state of rage that may have influenced his conclusions about the whole situation.

> **Δη**: οὐδ' εἰ βλέπω, μὰ τὴν Ἀθηνᾶν, οἶδ[α νῦν
> καλῶς ἔτ'· οὔκ, ἀλλ' εἰς τὸ πρόσθεν π̣[ροάγομαι,
> πληγ]ήν τιν' ἀνυπέρβλητον ἐ̣ξ[αίφνης λαβών.
> ἦ 'στ[ὶ] πιθανόν; σκέψασθε πότερο[ν εὖ φρονῶ
> ἢ μαίνομ', οὐδέν τ' εἰς ἀκρίβειαν [τότε
> λαβὼν ἐπάγομαι μέγ' ἀτύχημα.
>
> Demeas: I don't know if I am seeing straight, by Athena! But I am [coming here] at the front, having received a [sudden] exceptional [blow]. Is this plausible? Please consider whether [I am sane] or mad! Am I bringing a great misfortune on myself by interpreting nothing accurately?[8]

He then explains how he formed his belief about the present case. As we will see in the following pages, his reasoning seems not to be stringent and the audience is invited by Demeas himself to be the silent judge of his misleading reasoning, at the end of which, he decides to drive Chrysis out of his house with the accusation of having betrayed him by having an affair with his son. As Scafuro notes,[9] Demeas, like most Menandrian characters, displays his reasoning to the

8 Men. *Sam.* 213–218. See Bain 1983, p. 117 who comments at line 213 ("I don't know if I am seeing straight"): "This is explained later when he tells us how he saw Chrysis nursing the baby".

9 Scafuro 1997 and 2003.

audience in a discourse that includes proofs and arguments as if he was settling a lawsuit. However, as often happens in a law-court, the aim of his address is not to find out the truth of what has happened but to convince the audience, and, maybe, also himself, of his version of the story.[10] The structure and purpose of this kind of discourse have analogues in the contemporary intellectual and philosophical context.

> Menander's preoccupation with 'proving' has both a philosophical basis and a foundation in the tradition of rhetoric. While it cannot be proven with certainty that Menander is reproducing Peripatetic ideas, it can be shown that his intellectual framework for proving and argumentation shares a common background with that school.[11]

In particular, the reasoning that Demeas develops in his speech has a structure that is similar to what Aristotle calls an *enthymeme*. This is a particular kind of syllogism used in rhetorical speeches: in the case of an enthymeme the conjunction of the first premise with the second produces a conclusion that is persuasive but may not be logically correct:

> ἐπεὶ δ' ἐστὶν ὀλίγα μὲν τῶν ἀναγκαίων ἐξ ὧν οἱ ῥητορικοὶ συλλογισμοί εἰσι [...] τὰ δ' ὡς ἐπὶ τὸ πολὺ συμβαίνοντα καὶ ἐνδεχόμενα ἐκ τοιούτων ἀνάγκη ἑτέρων συλλογίζεσθαι, τὰ δ' ἀναγκαῖα ἐξ ἀναγκαίων, [...] φανερὸν ὅτι ἐξ ὧν τὰ ἐνθυμήματα λέγεται, τὰ μὲν ἀναγκαῖα ἔσται, τὰ δὲ πλεῖστα ὡς ἐπὶ τὸ πολύ.

> Since few of the premises from which rhetorical syllogism are constituted are necessary [...] and since things that happen for the most part and are possible must be reasoned on the basis of other such things, and necessary actions from necessities, [...] it is evident that those [premises] by which the *enthymemes* are spoken sometimes are necessarily true and most of the time [they are true only] for the most part.[12]

---

10 According to Traill, in this speech, Demeas is convincing himself that Chrysis has betrayed him. Demeas' subsequent accusation of Chrysis is made relying on the assumption of what people of her status usually do; therefore, he needs little evidence to condemn her and convince himself of this: "Menander counted on his audience to recognise when characters use arguments intended for winning a lawsuit in order to fool themselves" (Traill 2008, p. 85).

11 Scafuro 2003, p. 114. See also Munteanu 2002.

12 Arist. *Rhet.* I 2, 1357a22–33. "Aristotle is speaking here about the kind of statement which is possible in *enthymemes*. In what it infers, any syllogism differs according to the character

An *enthymeme* gives scope, therefore, for a kind of reasoning that is plausible and convincing because it appears in the form of a logically rigorous argument, even if, at times, this is not really the case. In some cases, *enthymemes* have necessary premises, but, in other cases, it is possible that an *enthymeme* is based on principles that are valid only for the most part and not necessarily, and, therefore, they do not constitute a valid premise for a logically consistent conclusion. These two cases—of *enthymemes* based on necessary premises or premises valid only for the most part—relate to what Aristotle describes as *enthymemes* built on 'necessary signs', *tekmēria*, or 'signs', *sēmeia*.[13]

> τὰ ἐνθυμήματα λέγεται ἐκ τεττάρων, τὰ δὲ τέτταρα ταῦτ' ἐστίν, εἰκὸς παράδειγμα τεκμήριον σημεῖον, ἔστι δὲ τὰ μὲν ἐκ τῶν ὡς ἐπὶ τὸ πολὺ ἢ ὄντων ἢ δοκούντων συνηγμένα ἐνθυμήματα ἐκ τῶν εἰκότων, τὰ δὲ δι' ἐπαγωγῆς ἐκ τοῦ ὁμοίου, ἢ ἑνὸς ἢ πλειόνων, ὅταν λαβὼν τὸ καθόλου εἶτα συλλογίσηται τὰ κατὰ μέρος, διὰ παραδείγματος, τὰ δὲ διὰ ἀναγκαίου καὶ ἀεὶ ὄντος διὰ τεκμηρίου, τὰ δὲ διὰ τοῦ καθόλου ἢ τοῦ ἐν μέρει ὄντος, ἐάν τε ὂν ἐάν τε μή, διὰ σημείων.
>
> *Enthymemes* are drawn from four sources and these four are what is probable, an example, a necessary sign (*tekmērion*) and a sign (*sēmeion*). *Enthymemes* from probability are drawn from things that either are, or seem from the most part [to be] true; those from example are drawn from induction from a similar case, whether one case or more, whenever a general statement is made and then is supported by particular instances; those drawn from necessity and what is always the case, from a necessary sing; those drown from what it is generally or in part true, existing or non existing, from signs.[14]

In Scafuro's opinion, the reasoning that Demeas discloses to the audience is not based exclusively on necessary signs: consequently, Demeas' version of the story is persuasive but not logically correct. My argument builds on this point and aims to take it further. It can be asked, in fact, why Demeas is offering to the audience and to himself misleading arguments and how they eventually affect his ethical choice.

---

of its premises. For example, if the modality of the premises is necessary, the syllogism asserts necessary relations; if the modality is contingent, it asserts contingent or possible relationships" (Grimaldi 1980(a), p. 60). See also Burnyeat 1994.

13 For further discussion on this distinction see Grimaldi 1980(b).

14 Arist. *Rhet.* II 25, 1402b12–20.

In order to do this, I would like to examine closely the structure of Demeas' discourse. Demeas tells the audience that, in the storeroom, he has heard the nurse taking care of the child and addressing him as "son of Moschion".[15] After that, Demeas says that he came out from the storeroom in a completely calm state:

> Δη: κἀγὼ προήιειν τοῦτον ὅνπερ ἐνθάδε
> τρόπον ἀρτίως ἐξῆλθον, ἡσυχῆι πάνυ,
> ὡς οὔτ' ἀκούσας οὐδὲν οὔτ' ἠισθημένος.

> DEMEAS: and I went in exactly in the same way I came out, being absolutely calm, as if I did not hear and perceive anything.[16]

Considering that he had already been told that Chrysis was th e child's mother, the revelation that Moschion was the child's father should have created in Demeas an angry reaction. On the contrary, it seems that the nurse's statement leaves him calm and, maybe, willing to investigate further on the matter of the child's paternity. However, after having heard the nurse, coming out from where he was, he says that he has seen (ὁρῶ) Chrysis nursing the child.[17] Therefore, he infers that it is definite, knowable (γνώριμον)[18] that the child is Chrysis' and Moschion's child.[19] It is at this point that his state of mind changes completely and he speeds up his inquiry hastily: this critical moment comes precisely when he sees Chrysis holding the child close to her breast. However, at this point he receives confirmation (or so he believes) of what he was told by Moschion at the beginning of the play and before hearing the nurse's words: namely, the fact that Chrysis was the child's mother. Demeas would still need to verify the validiy of what he has heard from the nurse and Moschion and what he has seen with his eyes. But when Demeas links the last vivid perception of Chrysis to what he has heard before from the nurse, he is completely driven out of his mind.[20] This state of confusion causes his false inference and diverts him from inquiring further to discover what has really happened. Menander seems here

15 Men. *Sam.* 245–254.
16 Men. *Sam.* 262–264.
17 Men. *Sam.* 265–266.
18 "Here Demeas means 'that this is her child is something that can be *known*', as opposed to the mere hypothesis about paternity. It is comic irony that he is mistaken on the one point he believes to be certain" (Gomme and Sandbach 1973, p. 569).
19 Men. *Sam.* 267.
20 Men. *Sam.* 279.

to be concerned to present Demeas as someone that is not just misled by others, but rather someone whose own temper complicates the situation and thus produces a situation in which Demeas relies solely on his own judgement, deaf to any doubt and not making any sustained attempt to investigate, building up his anger against a non-existent enemy.

If we look at his reasoning more closely, we realise that, from the first piece of audible evidence, Demeas learns that he is not the father of the child, as he has been told, and that the child is Moschion's. However, Demeas seems to be keen to inquire further about this point. After that, when Demeas sees Chrysis with the child, he infers that the child is also Chrysis's and that the two of them have betrayed his trust while he was away. However, the piece of evidence that Demeas uses to draw his final conclusion and to complete the reconstruction of the whole story, appears to be not that reliable. I will now explain why.

> **Δη:** αὐτὴν δ' ἔχουσαν αὐτὸ τὴν Σαμίαν ὁρῶ
> ἔξω καθ' αὑτὴν ⟨καὶ⟩ διδοῦσαν τιτθίον·
> ὥσθ' ὅτι μὲν αὐτῆς ἐστι τοῦτο γνώριμον
> εἶναι, πατρὸς δ' ὅτου ποτ' ἐστίν, εἴτ' ἐμὸν
> εἴτ'—
>
> DEMEAS: Outside, I see her, the Samian woman, holding him close to her ⟨and⟩ giving him her breast. So now the fact that this is her child is well-known, but from which father could he possibly be, either me or—?[21]

In the passage just quoted, Demeas concludes that, because he saw Chrysis feeding the child, that child must have been hers and, as he has just learned, Moschion's. However, it is possible to argue that this inference might be challenged: the fact that Demeas says that Chrysis was nursing the child does not necessary imply that she is its mother.

It is true that, according to the ancient medical tradition, a woman feeding a child is clearly a sign that the woman had recently given birth. This kind of example was reported in rhetorical treatises as an example of infallible proof: a woman having milk must be or must have been recently pregnant.[22] However, it is not necessarily true that a woman has given birth to the same child that she feeds with her milk. Accordingly, the first problem in Demeas' reasoning

---

21 Men. *Sam.* 265–269. This case is another example of recognition through false reasoning according to Munteanu 2002, pp. 123–125.

22 See Arist. *APr.* II 27, 70a11–b6. See Scafuro 2003 pp. 117–118 for a detailed explanation.

is that he declares that he saw Chrysis holding the child and giving it the breast (διδοῦσαν τιτθίον)[23] and, he believes that this is the proof that Chrysis has recently given birth to the same infant that she is now nursing and that he has discovered to be son of Moschion. However, the fact that Chrysis gives her breast to a child does not imply that she has actually given birth *to the child to whom she is giving her breast.* Demeas is wrong in believing that her doing so is a confirmation that she is the child's mother.

Scafuro reconstructs Demeas' reasoning in this way:[24]

I premise: Women feeding a child have given birth to the infant to whom they are giving their breast
II premise: Chrysis is giving her breast to a child

Conclusion: Chrysis has given birth to the infant to whom she is giving her breast

Demeas is, therefore, misleading himself and the audience in formulating the first premise of this reasoning.[25] Also, the piece of empirical evidence on which he is building his reasoning is, actually, not very reliable. In fact, towards the end of the play, when Nikeratos comes out saying that he saw his daughter offering her breast to the child, Demeas, in a calmer state of mind, replies that she could just have been playing with him.[26] It is true that, in this context, Demeas' reply is meant to be a clumsy attempt to calm Nikeratos down. However, it is arguable that, when Demeas saw Chrysis holding the child, he was in a confused state of mind similar to that of Nikeratos later:[27] Demeas recognises here that seeing a woman holding a child close to her breast does not entail that she is its mother.

23 Men. *Sam.* 266.

24 Scafuro 2003, p. 128.

25 Moreover, it is plausible to think that Demeas also gets the second premise of his reasoning wrong. In fact, the fact that Demeas tells the audience that Chrysis was διδοῦσαν τιτθίον might also not imply that Chrysis was actually feeding the child: she might just have held him close to her breast and Demeas could have been misled by this image. We know that, at the beginning of this third Act, when Demeas comes out from his house, he states that he is not sure how to see things straight any more (Men. *Sam.* 213).

26 Men. *Sam.* 540–543.

27 "Menander has formulated the eyewitness testimony of both Demeas and Nikeratos with ambiguous phraseology: both report they have witnessed a woman διδοῦσαν τιτθίον to the infant [...] but neither man precisely says the infant actually received nourishment thereby" (Scafuro 2003, p. 129).

All things considered, the second piece of evidence which forms the minor premise of Demeas' *enthymeme* is not an infallible proof but a fallible one, and this corresponds to the way in which Aristotle defines a *sēmeion*.[28] And, as Aristotle suggests, an *enthymeme* based on a *sēmeion* can be easily refuted because no fallible sign can enter into a strictly logical proof.[29]

In conclusion, it is arguable that Demeas' reasoning took the following form:

I premise: Moschion *might be* the child's father because the nurse said so

II premise: Chrysis *is undoubtedly* the child's mother as *I saw* her feeding it (and *I was told* she was).

Conclusion: Moschion and Chrysis are the child's parents and Chrysis was the one who seduced Moschion.[30]

As we can see, Demeas makes use of several conjectures that are not properly verified as being true. A possible explanation is that Demeas is in love with Chrysis[31] and, when he sees her, the possibility that she could be breast-feeding Moschion's child and that that child could have been the result of a relationship with his son, makes him so angry as to prevent a rigorous inquiry. Indeed, when Demeas comes out from the house, he is in an evident state of confusion and he is not sure any more if he can see and reason properly.[32] The apparent possibility that Chrysis had a child with Moschion has a devastating effect on

---

28 As opposed to an 'infallible sign' (τεκμήριον). See p. 66.

29 "λύεται δὲ καὶ τὰ σημεῖα καὶ τὰ διὰ σημείου ἐνθυμήματα εἰρημένα, κἂν ᾖ ὑπάρχοντα, ὥσπερ ἐλέχθη ἐν τοῖς πρώτοις· ὅτι γὰρ ἀσυλλόγιστόν ἐστιν πᾶν σημεῖον." Translation: "*sēmeia* and *enthymemes* that draw conclusion through a *sēmeion* are refutable even if true, as was said in the first lecture, for the fact that any *sēmeion* is non-syllogistic" (Arist. *Rhet.* II 25, 1403a2–4).

"τὰ δὲ τεκμήρια καὶ τεκμηριώδη ἐνθυμήματα κατὰ μὲν τὸ ἀσυλλόγιστον οὐκ ἔσται λῦσαι [...], λείπεται δ' ὡς οὐχ ὑπάρχει τὸ λεγόμενον δεικνύναι. εἰ δὲ φανερὸν καὶ ὅτι ὑπάρχει καὶ ὅτι τεκμήριον, ἄλυτον ἤδη γίγνεται τοῦτο." Translation: "But *tekmēria* and *enthymemes* with *tekmēria* cannot be refuted as non syllogistic [...], and what is left to show is that the alleged fact is not true. If it is evident that it is true and that it is a *tekmērion*, the argument is irrefutable" (Arist. *Rhet.* II 25, 1403a10–15). For further discussion about these passages and the distinction between fallible and non-fallible signs see Grimaldi 1980(b).

30 Demeas formulates this accusation explicitly at Men. *Sam.* 333–342.

31 Men. *Sam.* 80–85.

32 See Men. *Sam.* 213–216. See Sander 2014, pp. 158–160 for a more detailed discussion of the kind of emotions at work in Demea's case.

Demeas and prevents him from inquiring thoroughly about the identity of the child's father, which he seemed determined to discover before seeing Chrysis with the child.

We realise this point if we continue to examine Demeas' monologue. After having established in his mind that the child was Chrysis', he laments that the whole thing is unbelievable: Moschion has always been an affectionate child and he couldn't have done something like that. However, when Demeas looks back again in his mind at those images and those words and he considers them again, dwelling on the memories that they have left in him, he is completely driven out of mind. And, as we will see from the following scene, this will lead him to complete his wrong version of the story.

> Δη: οὐχ ὑπονοῶ, τὸ πρᾶγμα δ' εἰς μέσον φέρω
> ἅ τ' ἀκήκο' αὐτός, οὐκ ἀγανακτῶν οὐδέπω.
> σύνοιδα γὰρ τῶι μειρακίωι, νὴ τοὺς θεούς,
> καὶ κοσμίωι τὸν πρότερον ὄντι χρόνον ἀεὶ
> καὶ περὶ ἔμ' ὡς ἔνεστιν εὐσεβεστάτωι.
> πάλιν δ', ἐπειδὰν τὴν λέγουσαν καταμάθω
> τίτθην ἐκείνου πρῶτον οὖσαν, εἶτ' ἐμοῦ
> λάθραι λέγουσαν, εἶτ' ἀποβλέψω πάλιν
> εἰς τὴν ἀγαπῶσαν αὐτὸ καὶ βεβιασμένην
> ἐμοῦ τρέφειν ἄκοντος, ἐξέστηχ' ὅλως.
>
> DEMEAS: I am not just making a conjecture, I am bringing the facts before you, and what I have myself heard, I am not yet angry. I know the young boy, I really do, and he has always been moderate before and always as dutiful to me as he could be. But whenever I consider once more that the nurse who was talking was once his own, and she was talking secretly, and whenever I look again at her [Chrysis] who adores it [the child] and who forced me to raise it when I did not want to, I am out of my mind.[33]

On one hand, Demeas considers that what he has just experienced seems to be incredible; on the other hand, the repeated images of the nurse and Chrysis only confirm his doubts. In particular, he cannot stop looking in his mind at the sight of the woman he loved with the child. Accordingly, having been impressed and confused by all these circumstances, Demeas just accepts a persuasive (but wrong) version of the story that appears to his mind right at the moment that he

33 Men. *Sam.* 270–279.

interprets the perceptive data. This conclusion, in fact, is drawn while Demeas, in an evidently excited state of mind, recapitulates what he has seen and heard, having been powerfully impressed by those images and those words.

A further passage may serve as evidence of the fact that the state of mind in which Demeas is drawing inferences is not suitable for carrying on a rational inquiry about what he has seen and heard. Immediately after his first monologue, when Demeas attempts to interrogate Parmenon in order to be sure of his assumption about Chrysis, the child and Moschion, he is again prevented from discovering the truth by his excited state of mind. In front of Parmenon Demeas claims that he is not just guessing (οὐ γὰρ εἰκάζων λέγω),[34] but he knows with certainty what happened (εἰδότα γ' ἀκριβῶς): Moschion is the father of the child that Chrysis is nursing and he just wants confirmation of this.

Δη: εἰδότα γ' ἀκριβῶς πάντα καὶ πεπυσμένον
ὅτι Μοσχίωνός ἐστιν, ὅτι σύνοισθα σύ,
ὅτι δι' ἐκεῖνον αὐτὸ νῦν αὕτη τρέφει.
Πα: τίς φησι;
Δη: πάντες. ἀλλ' ἀπόκριναι τοῦτό μοι·
ταῦτ' ἐστίν;
Πα: ἔστι, δέσποτ', ἀλλὰ λανθάνειν—
Δη: τί "λανθάνειν"; ἱμάντα παίδων τις δότω
ἐπὶ τουτονί μοι τὸν ἀσεβῆ.

Demeas: I know everything accurately and I have found out that [the child] is Moschion's, that you also know about that and that she [Chrysis] is nursing it now for him.
Parmenon: Who says?
Demeas: Everyone! But now answer this question for me: is that true?
Parmenon: It is sir, but you are missing something ...
Demeas: what [is this] "you are missing something"? Some one among you slaves, give me a leather strap for this sacrilegious man![35]

---

34 Men. *Sam.* 310.

35 Men. *Sam.* 316–323. "Demeas proceeds quite in the wrong way in his interrogation of Parmenon and ends by having his own misconception confirmed as the truth:
Q. Who is the baby's mother? A. Chrysis (Parmenon sticking to the story)
Q. Who is the father? A. You, she says
When Demeas then goes on to say that he knows the truth, Parmenon would undoubtedly, if questioned correctly, have revealed the true state of affairs. Demeas, however, by saying only that he knows that Moschion is the father and not enquiring further about the mother

Demeas makes an interesting choice of words in order to explain what he has grasped: talking with Parmenon, Demeas seems to have acquired, apparently, a clearer view of the situation. He tells Parmenon what he has concluded from the facts that he has just witnessed but, when talking with him, he does not present them in the distorted version of the story that he offered just a moment before meeting him. He says that he knows that Moschion is the father of the child and that Chrysis is nursing it for him. But he does not actually state that he thinks that Chrysis is also the mother of the child. Thus, Demeas asks Parmenon to confirm what is in fact the true version of the story (the child is Moschion's and Chrysis is nursing it for him)—though Demeas has not recognised the truth of this version. Demeas' phrasing leaves open the possibility that Moschion actually is the child's father and that, when he saw her, Chrysis was nursing a child that might not have been her own. However, his grasp of the situation is only apparent as, at the end of the dialogue, Demeas refuses to listen to what Parmenon has to tell him and is still convinced that the child is that of Moschion and Chrysis.

On the other hand, Parmenon tries to let him know that something escaped Demeas' notice. Parmenon says that Demeas is missing something in the reconstruction that Demeas has just asked to confirm. That is, something has not been clearly detected by Demeas and so he fails to understand what has really happened. Demeas, instead, misunderstands Parmenon's expression and infers that he has missed something because someone has actively concealed the fact that Chrysis and Moschion are the child's parents. Parmenon tries to tell Demeas that what escaped his notice are the real facts: namely, that Moschion is the father's child but that Nikeratos' daughter, whom he now wants to marry, is its mother, not Chrysis. However, Demeas refuses to listen; hence, his attempt at inquiry will fail and the misunderstanding will continue.

This scene recalls in certain respects the first episode of the *Oedipus Tyrannos*. At the end of that episode, Oedipus is having a lively debate with Tiresias who is trying to explain to him who is the cause of the plague that is afflicting Thebes and, therefore, who Oedipus is and what he has done.[36] Oedipus does not understand the final revelatory sentence that Tiresias pronounces, as he still cannot imagine why Tiresias is accusing him of killing Laius. He goes

---

leaves himself open to misunderstanding. Parmenon assumes that if Demeas knows that Moschion is the father he must also know that Plangon is the mother. All that he is actually asked to agree to is Moschion's share in the matter and this simply confirms to Demeas that he has been cuckolded" (Bain 1983, pp. 118–119).

36 S. *OT.* 449–462.

away full of anger, threatening Tiresias and accusing him and Creon of being authors of a plot to overthrow his kingship.[37] Oedipus subsequently discovers the truth by carrying on his inquiry alone, collecting relevant information that he missed before. Thus, apparently, both Demeas and Oedipus seem to have a disposition to draw inferences quickly which have the effect of extending the initial misunderstanding.[38] On the other hand, what we have in *Oedipus Tyrannos* is a rational process of inquiry and a progressive discovery that requires boldness and steady resolution on the part of the main character to find the truth to be solved.[39] In Demeas' case, the character is highly influenced by his state of mind: anger and deception prevent rigorous reasoning and lead him to construct a parallel fictional scenario in which he struggles on alone.[40]

There is another passage that supports this reading of Demea's character: in the fourth Act, Demeas will behave similarly while speaking with Moschion. There, he claims to know everything because he has heard the truth from Parmenon.

> **Δη**: ἀλλ' ἐγώ. τὸ παιδίον σόν ἐστιν. οἶδ',[41] ἀκήκοα
> τοῦ συνειδότος τὰ κρυπτὰ Παρμένοντος· ὥστε μὴ
> πρὸς ἐμὲ παῖζε.
>
> DEMEAS: Then I [will tell you]! The child is yours, I know. I have heard from Parmenon who shares knowledge of these secrets; and so, do not make fun of me.[42]

However, as shown in the first section, just to hear or to see something—that is, to have bare sensory evidence—is not a warrant of certain knowledge,

37 S. *OT.* 446. See Konstan 2006(b), p. 38. On this much-debated passage see Carrière, 1956; Taplin 1978, pp. 43–45; Knox 1980.

38 For a dedicated reading of Demeas' anger in the context of the previous dramatic tradition see Iversen 1998, chapter 5.

39 See esp. Bowra 1944; Knox 1957; Diano 1968; Golden 1978; Giangrande 1983; Segal C. 2001; Longo 2006 and Greenspan 2008.

40 See Scafuro 2003 and Traill 2008, pp. 86–92. Groton 1987 declares that Demeas' anger is contagious and that, in particular, Nikeratos will be affected by it. In Groton's opinion the arousing of the characters one after another does not only generate humour but also serves the function of organising, energising and unifying the plot.

41 Where οἶδα is emphatic and not parenthetic as when it is parenthetic it is normally joined with σαφῶς (Gomme and Sandbach 1973 ad loc.).

42 Men. *Sam.* 477–479.

especially if the person who is having the sensory evidence is as enraged as Demeas was while talking to Parmenon. In reality, Parmenon did not have the opportunity to tell Demeas the whole truth and, consequently, Demeas did not have the chance to listen to the whole story. Menander insists on Demeas' lack of knowledge, caused partly by his angry temper, and on the difficulty, because of his angry temper, of informing him about his erroneous inferences. We will find a verification of this at the end of the comedy. In Act Five, Demeas will explain his own error with a significant series of verbs the presence of which is strongly accentuated by asyndeton.

> **Δη:** οὐ δικαίως ᾐτιασάμην τί σε·
> ἠγνόησ', ἥμαρτον, ἐμάνην.

> DEMEAS: I accused you wrongly; I did not know, I made a mistake, I was out of my mind.[43]

He wrongly accused his son—and Chrysis—because he did not understand the situation; he formulated a false belief about the circumstances[44] and made a mistake. He recognises now that he behaved like a mad man. He now sees clearly that when he came out from the house (right a the beginning of the plot) and told the audience what he had witnessed, he did not reason correctly (εὖ φρονῶ), but he understood things wrongly as he was angry (μαίνομαι) at what he had seen.[45] Accordingly, Demeas' state of knowledge and lack of accuracy in making the right judgment about the situation leads him to a complete misunderstanding of people and of what he saw and heard. Consequently, absence of knowledge is not the only reason for his misguided response; misinterpretation of his perceptions is also a remarkably important element and his bad temper contributes to extending this misunderstanding for a considerable part of the action.

---

43 Men. *Sam.* 702–703. "Thus the *agnoia*, i.e. unawareness of the real state of affairs, is supposed to clear him of his error. On the other hand, Demeas is aware of his rash action and therefore he explains his *hamartia* also as a result of temporary madness (*mania*)" (Dworacki 1977, p. 21).

44 Gomme and Sandbach 1973 ad loc. "ἠγνόησα is more than 'I did not know'; it means I had a false belief". See Men. *Sam.* 705.

45 See Men. *Sam.* 216. Perception of a certain situation creates a certain emotion that, in its turn, influences the agents' beliefs about that situation. I will come back to the dynamic of this process when discussing Aristotle (see section 2.1 below).

Demeas' perceptions are not adequately evaluated and connected in a rigorous line of inquiry. Between perception and knowledge there is the possibility of wrong belief: all perceptual awareness seems to be subject to error and this is affected by the perceptive subject's state of mind. Demeas does not consider sufficiently this possibility, as he is evidently angry, and he does not check the reliability of what he has perceived. The false belief affects Demeas' understanding of who the characters are—or what they have done—and sets the action in motion. According to my analysis, the potential scope for error, in Demeas evaluation of the circumstances, lies in the reasoning that constitutes the transition between acquisition of perceptions and certain knowledge.

At this point, it is relevant to recall that the contrast between the beliefs of dramatic characters and the reality of the situation is also a recurrent topic in tragedy. For instance, the opposition between opinion (δόξα) and knowledge gained after a process of verification (ἐπιστήμη) is one of the core themes of Sophocles' *Trachiniae*.[46] The play mainly centres on the two versions of this contrast: namely, one in which an opinion is verified in order to gain understanding; and, one in which it is not.[47] In the play, Deianeira believes that Heracles has betrayed her with Iole, daughter of Eurytus, who entered Deianeira's house as Heracles' slave. Before accusing her husband, Deianeira enquires scrupulously in order to discover the real identity of Iole. She asks the Messenger and Lichas many times to explain clearly what happened and to tell her the whole truth.[48] Once certain knowledge about Iole is achieved, Deianeira plans to use the charm that the centaur Nessos gave her to win back Heracles' heart. However, in this case, she does not make an inquiry about the real power of the charm: she has never done an experiment (πεῖρα) to test the effectiveness of Nessos' suggestion. Nevertheless, she acknowledges that knowledge based only on opinion does not provide ground for confidence (πίστις).

> Δη: Οὕτως ἔχει γ' ἡ πίστις, ὡς τὸ μὲν δοκεῖν
> ἔνεστι, πείρᾳ δ' οὐ προσωμίλησά πω.

> DEIANEIRA: Indeed, to tell the truth, my ground of confidence lies only in having personal opinion, I have not yet confirmed it with experience.[49]

46 This is explicitly set out by the Chorus at S. *Tr.* 588–593. See Lawrence 1978.

47 Papadimitriopulos 2006 argues that *Trachiniae* is divided into four parts, each part presenting conflicting versions of the truth and each part contributing to the transition from ignorance to knowledge.

48 S. *Tr.* 349–350; 398; 400; 437; 453. See Di Benedetto 1983, p. 148.

49 S. *Tr.* 590–591.

However, because she needs urgently to restore her house's welfare, she resolve to test the charm on Heracles himself. Thus, she acts on the basis of her belief about the charm but without having verified whether her belief is right or not.[50] Accordingly, she achieves a clear understanding of the situation[51] only after having sent the robe, smeared with Nessos' deadly blood, to Heracles.[52] In Deianira's case, what leads her into error is the fact that she fails to seek empirical experience to verify what Nessos tells her about the power of the charm. Thus, Deianeira's error does not lie in the incorrect working out of empirical evidence but in the tragic lack of empirical evidence itself.

Similar issues related to knowledge *versus* opinion and truth *versus* deception arise in the *Helen* of Euripides. In the *Helen*, at the moment of the recognition scene between Helen and Menelaus, Helen tries to convince Menelaus that she is the real Helen and that she should not be blamed for actions that she did not perform. The Helen for whom Menelaus fought at Troy is just a phantom (εἴδωλον).[53] The real Helen asks him to look (σκέψαι) at her as nothing better than Menelaus' eyes could produce evidence for what she is saying. Menelaus admits that the woman in front of him has Helen's appearance but he does not trust his eyes which seem to be failing him.[54] However, Menelaus will promptly trust the servant's words when the latter enters on stage and declares that the Helen brought back from Troy has suddenly disappeared in the sky as a phantom.[55] Thus, in the context of this recognition scene, sensory evidence seems to be of no worth for the purpose of producing a clear understanding of what people and facts really are. What is perceived with our senses (be it the

---

50 S. *Tr.* 588–593.

51 S. *Tr.* 711.

52 See Whitman's thesis about the "late learning" of Deianeira (Whitman 1951, pp. 105–116).

53 E. *Hel.* 582. "Ironically Helen herself appeals to the very source of 'knowledge' which her circumstances show to be wholly unreliable as a guide to reality. Thus, given Menelaus' belief in the phantom, Helen's argument is self-refuting and Menelaus rejects the visual 'proof' [...] of her identity on the evidence [...] of his own eyes" (Allan 2008, p. 211).

54 τὸ δ'ὄμμα μου νοσεῖ E. *Hel.* 575. "These lines ring the changes of the appearance/reality antithesis. Menelaus first wonders whether his eyes rather than his mind are deceiving him; the implicit contrast is between the hallucinations just pondered, which would be a sign of god-sent madness, and the possibility of simple mistaken identity. The latter is figured, however, as a different form of ill-health [...]. Helen responds with the language of appearance and when Menelaus admits that she seems to be Helen, she presses the point, urging him to accept the evidence of his own eyes. Menelaus' response shows that he has decided that it is precisely his eyes (i.e. her appearance) that he cannot trust" (Burian 2007, p. 226).

55 E. *Hel.* 605.

real Helen or her phantom) may be deceiving. The words of the servant are, eventually, the element that persuades Menelaus.[56]

Accordingly, from what I have observed so far, in the *Trachiniae* and the *Helen* the scope for misunderstanding seems to lie in the sphere of external evidence. In the case of Deianeira, what is stressed is the importance of sensory evidence and the tragic consequences that its absence produces. In the second case, the power of sensory evidence is denied and replaced by the power of words. Thus, by contrast with Demeas' case, the error in judging a situation is not produced by the subject's internal reflection on sensory evidence but by the lack or worthlessness of this kind of evidence itself. If we consider Demeas' misunderstanding, we find that the problem is not simply the fatal lack of sufficient knowledge, as in Deianeira's case, or the impossibility of recognising someone by his perceptible appearance, as in the *Helen*. In Demeas' case, what is stressed is Demeas' struggle to draw correct inferences from empirical evidence in order to understand the sequence of actions. This may be the reason why Menander gives Demeas two long monologues:[57] this is so that the playwright can make clear what Demeas has misunderstood—and why he did so—and so that he can present Demeas' misleading reasoning to the audience. Menander is interested in pointing out that Demeas fails to carry out a correct process of inference from sensory evidence already observed and this failure indicates a degree of ethical failure in his state of mind or character. This representation, I believe, is strikingly analogous to Aristotle's analysis, as explained in the next sections.

In Menander's extant works, there is another similar case in which a figure, because of being emotionally involved in the situation, completely misunderstands it: this is that of Sostratos in the *Dis Exapaton*. The comedy is largely fragmentary, but it is possible to reconstruct the plot on the basis of Plautus' *Bacchides*, which is most probably the Roman version of the Menandrian comedy.[58] Sostratos, a young Athenian, meets Bacchis, a *hetaira*, in Ephesos and falls in love with her. Immediately after their meeting, Bacchis must leave Ephesos for Athens as she has sold herself to a soldier who is living there. Sostratos asks his friend Moschos, who is in Athens, to find the girl: Sostratos would have provided the money for taking the girl back on his return from Ephesos. However, Bacchis has a sister in Athens: she is a *hetaira* and she is using the same

56 See Wright 2005, pp. 267–278 for a detailed discussion of these topics in the *Helen*.

57 Men. *Sam.* 207–282 and 324–356.

58 See Handley 1968; Questa 1970; Del Corno 1975, Bain 1979; Barsby 1986; Lefèvre 2001(b) and Paduano 2008.

professional name as her sister. When Moschos finds the two girls he falls in love with Bacchis' sister.

When Menander's fragment starts, Sostratos has probably just been told that his friend Moschos is involved in an affair with a courtesan, Bacchis: Moschos' tutor (*paedagogus*) begs Sostratos to scold his friend for his relationship with her.[59] Sostratos suddenly infers that Moschos' Bacchis is the same one he is in love with. Thus, as soon as he is alone on the stage, he starts his monologue already convinced of the culpability of Bacchis: she has betrayed him with his friend; the courtesan, he says, is reckless, everything is clear to him.[60]

Sostratos then starts to formulate his strategy:[61] he will give the money that he received to buy Bacchis back to his father and the greedy *hetaira* will be left with nothing; her seductive words will have no power on him any more.[62]

> If the emotional language and hints of ambivalence in these speeches warn us not to trust them, so too do the obvious elements of fantasy. We are not allowed to forget that the speakers' assertions spring from their imagination as they sketch the unmistakably hypothetical scenarios.[63]

While Sostratos is forming these resolutions and making these accusations building a case on his own, he does not check the reliability of his hypothesis either with Bacchis or with Moschos. His emotional involvement does not allow him to enquire further; he is sure of the conclusions drawn on the basis of what he has heard and he is angry as result. In Act Four, we find that Sostratos has not made progress in his understanding or his resolutions;[64] he declares that he is angry at his friend and he is still accusing the charming Bacchis of being the cause of what he thinks they have done to him:

---

59 Men. *Dis Ex.* 15–17.

60 Men. *Dis. Ex.* 20–21.

61 See Batstone 2005, p. 18.

62 Men. *Dis Ex.* 29–30.

63 Traill 2008, p. 101. As usually happens in this sort of speeches, "il momento fantastico e associativo, prevale fino a quasi escludere quello logico, discorsivo" (Del Corno 1975, p. 207).

64 "Per quello che si riesce a vedere, Menandro esprime con vivacità e duttilità di stile ed abilità scenica l'incoerenza dei pensieri dell'innamorato deluso che oscilla, prima e dopo aver restituito il denaro al padre, tra la stizza nei suoi propri confronti, l'ira per la creduta fedigrafa, la delusione nei confronti di Moscho-Pistoclero, anch'esso creduto traditore" (Questa 1970, p. 195).

> Σω: αὕτη δ' ἱκανῶς, καλῶς ποοῦσά γ', εὑρέθη
> οἵα(ν) ποτ' ᾤμην οὖσα, τὸν δ' ἀβέλτερον
> Μόσχον ἐ.ε..· καὶ τὰ μὲν ἔγωγ' ὀργίζομαι,
> τὰ δ' οὐκ ἐκεῖνον τοῦ γεγονότος αἴτιον
> ἀδικήματος νενόμικα, τὴν δ' ἰταμωτάτην
> πασῶν ἐκείνην.
>
> SOSTRATOS: She has revealed herself enough (and she did well) to be as once I thought. Silly Moschos ... and indeed I am enraged, but I think that that one [Moschos] is not the cause of the mistake that was made but she, the most reckless woman of all.[65]

Immediately after this, Moschos enters. He does not understand why Sostratos is accusing him of having offended his friend.[66] He asks for an explanation,[67] and, perhaps, the misunderstanding will be clarified. Summing up, Sostratos has heard something that is true: in fact, Moschos is in love with a courtesan named Bacchis. On the sole basis of this auditory knowledge he infers something wrong: that Moschos is in love with *the same Bacchis* that he is in love with. Like Demeas, he does not make any further inquiry to support his inference with a larger set of proofs: love for the courtesan and anger towards her and his friend prevent any inquiry.

1.2 *Moschion*

In Samia, there is also another character, Moschion, for whom emotions play an important role in matters of ethical choice. In Moschion's case it is not possible to talk about misunderstanding or partial knowledge with respect to particulars or circumstances involved in his action. Nevertheless, even if Moschion seems to have a clear understanding of the circumstances in which he is acting, he fails to act correctly on at least two occasions. At the beginning

---

65 Men *Dis. Ex.* 97–102. "The self-congratulatory pity, framed from the perspective of the experienced ex-lover, is designed to console Sostratos with the fantasy that poor Moschos will be betrayed. Then for a moment we hear the truth: 'yes, in a way, I am angry', a truth carefully worded to protect Moschos from its consequences [...]. Then just as quickly the anger at Moschos is hidden in the conventional insults directed at the *hetaira*. This moment of revealed suppression allows us to see something that was hiding in Sostratos' 'strategy of the self' and in the rhetorical organisation of his earlier speech: Sostratos is faking it" (Batstone 2005, pp. 22–23).

66 Men. *Dis. Ex.* 108–112.

67 Men. *Dis. Ex.* 112.

of the play, Moschion decides not to tell Demeas the truth about the child he had by Nikeratos' daughter: the process by which he made this choice merits detailed study.

Menander describes his relationship with his adoptive father Demeas as close and as allowing frank discussion.[68] He knows he does not have to be ashamed to talk to him about what he has done; however, he decides to conceal the truth. Moschion's shame prevents him from understanding Demeas' character properly and forming a correct judgement about what he should do in the present situation.[69]

> **Πα:** ἀλλ' ὅπως ἔσει
> ἀνδρεῖος εὐθύς τ' ἐμβαλεῖς περὶ τοῦ γάμου
> λόγον.
> **Μο:** τίνα τρόπον; δειλὸς ἤδη γίνομαι
> ὡς πλησίον τὸ πρᾶγμα γέγονε.
> **Πα:** πῶς λέγεις;
> **Μο:** αἰσχύνομαι τὸν πατέρα.

> PARMENON: But act like a man and get straight to the matter of the wedding.
> MOSCHION: How? I am a coward now that the matter has come close.
> PARMENON: How do you mean?
> MOSCHION: I am ashamed before my father.[70]

Shame and its objects are clearly defined in Aristotle's *Rhetoric*. I will quote the passage here to spell out the kind of feeling that Menander's Moschion may have in mind in speaking of his shame before his father. In the *Rhetoric* Aristotle describes what sort of things people are ashamed of and we find what Moschion has done included there.

> ἔστω δὴ αἰσχύνη λύπη τις ἢ ταραχὴ περὶ τὰ εἰς ἀδοξίαν φαινόμενα φέρειν τῶν κακῶν, ἢ παρόντων ἢ γεγονότων ἢ μελλόντων [...], ἀνάγκη αἰσχύνεσθαι ἐπὶ

---

68 Men. *Sam.* 16–22. In addition to that, Moschion's fear that Demeas would have not given his consent to a union between him and Plangon, is hardly justified. Nikeratos and Demeas seem to be in good terms. In Act 1, they enter on stage discussing amicably as they return in Athens from a trip they made together in Byzantium and the Pontos (Blume 1974, pp. 54–55).

69 See Blume 1974, pp. 12–15; Goldberg 1980, p. 94 and Dutsch and Konstan 2011.

70 Men. *Sam.* 63–67. For the discussion on this passage see Wehrli 1936 and Jäkel 1982.

> τοῖς τοιούτοις τῶν κακῶν ὅσα αἰσχρὰ δοκεῖ εἶναι ἢ αὐτῷ ἢ ὧν φροντίζει [...], τὸ συγγενέσθαι αἷς οὐ δεῖ ἢ οὗ οὐ δεῖ ἢ ὅτε οὐ δεῖ.
>
> Let shame be [defined as] a sort of pain or agitation concerning the class of evils, whether present, past or future, that seems to bring a person in disrespect [...]. By necessity being ashamed applies to such evils as seem [in the eyes of the others] to be disgraceful to a person or one about whom one cares. [...] And [such is] having sexual relations with those with whom one should not or where one should not or when one should not.[71]

Shame, which is a sort of pain or emotion characteristic of young people, as Aristotle defines it in the *Nicomachean Ethics*,[72] powerfully affects the state of mind of Moschion who has done something of which, he knows very well, he is now ashamed. We can suppose that the possibility that his act will bring on him the disapproval of his adoptive father, whom he holds in the greatest respect, affects his reasoning: he decides not to tell the truth, but this will cause an even worse misunderstanding.

This is not the only case in which emotions overpower Moschion's rational reasoning and lead him to make mistakes. The young man, in fact, seems to have found himself in a similar state of mind at the moment of the young girl's rape, though the kind of dominating *pathos* involved was different. To analyse this point, it is worth recalling Moschion's confession of his error during his monologue at the beginning of the play. There, he plainly confesses to the audience that he has made a mistake (ἡμάρτηκα γάρ),[73] as he says, referring to the rape of Nikeratos' daughter. Moschion's error lies in the fact that he knows clearly the circumstances in which he find himself acting; he knows the identity of the girl that he approaches at the festival of Adonis[74] and he also knows very well that he should not approach her and, least of all, rape her.

> **Mo:** ἐξ ἀγροῦ δὴ καταδραμὼν
> ὡς ἔτυ]χ̣[έ] γ' εἰς Ἀδώνι' αὐτὰς κατέλαβον
> συνηγμένας ἐνθάδε πρὸς ἡμᾶς μετά τινων
> ἄλλω]ν γυναικῶν· τῆς δ' ἑορτῆς παιδιὰν
> πολλὴ]ν ἐχούσης οἷον εἰκός, συμπαρὼν

71 Arist. *Rhet.* II 6, 1383b12–23.

72 Arist. *EN* IV 15, 1128b10–21.

73 Men. *Sam.* 3.

74 See Detienne 1979.

> ἐγινόμην οἶμαι θεατής·
> [...]
> ὀκνῶ λέγειν τὰ λοίπ', ἴσως δ' αἰσχύνομαι
> οἷς] οὐδὲν ὄφελός ἐσθ'· ὅμως αἰσχύνομαι.
>
> MOSCHION: One day, hastening down from the country, it happened that I found them inside our house all together with other women to celebrate the festival of Adonis. As you might imagine, since the feasting was bringing a lot of fun, being present there I became, I think, a spectator. [...] I hesitate to say what followed, perhaps I am ashamed and it is not at all useful [to be ashamed] of that, but all the same, I am ashamed.[75]

What has happened to Moschion is that, led by the sudden passion for the girl, he could not restrain his erotic desire and he made a mistake in raping the girl. Moschion was clearly overwhelmed by the circumstances he found himself in. He says that, from being a spectator of the festival of Adonis, he became one of the protagonists of the festival, raping, eventually, one of them. He now feels shame because he now regrets that he approached sexually someone he should not have approached. It seems that, in this kind of situation, the vulnerable state of mind of a young man such as Moschion, powerfully affected by the whole festive atmosphere, quickly led him to lose grip of himself and to make a mistake, acting against his better judgment. Once the deed has been done, Moschion knows that he does not have any plausible justification for his behaviour and, as he says, he is ashamed of what he has done. Thus, at the beginning of the play, Moschion, recovering his senses, gives a clear account of his mistake and he takes responsibility for it. Clearly, erotic desire influenced his thoughts about what should have been done at that present moment in the same way as shame influences his choice about how to deal with his adoptive father.

Overall, then, Moschion, like Demeas, represents a case in which perceptions and emotions affect clear insight about what the right course of action is. In Demeas' case, the character's understanding of the situation is influenced by his overwhelming emotional reaction at what Demeas has perceived. Demeas would be right to be angry at Chrysis and Moschion if they actually had an affair, however, this is not the case. This is also what creates a comic situation for the audience: Demeas believes he is in a tragic situation;[76] but he is not and the audience knows this. Demeas attaches importance to his relationship with

75 Men. *Sam.* 38–48. See Gomme and Sandbach 1973 ad loc.

76 See Men. *Sam.* 324–336.

his adoptive son and his courtesan and he is clearly vulnerable to the emotional intensity that this involves. A few scattered pieces of information make him angry and unable to conduct a rigorous analysis of what really happened. Moschion's example is different: like any young man of his age, the emotions aroused by the sight of the girl or his adoptive father eclipse any ethically good reason he might have thought of in deciding what has to be done.

Menander seems to be interested in constructing two characters that the audience can recognise as clearly mistaken. The errors they make depend on their inability to control their emotions when responding to situations and this is what triggers the chain of events leading to a happy ending. Furthermore, Moschion and Demeas confess openly to the audience their (wrong) thought-processes, the deceptive reasoning that leads them to making a wrong choice. In this way, the audience is able to spot their flaws and to laugh at their mistakes, being aware of the happy ending and understanding exactly how and why they make wrong decisions and, therefore, what it is that makes events unfold in a certain way.

2 Aristotle on the Vulnerability of Correct (Ethical) Reasoning

If we turn now to Aristotle, we realise that he is interested in dealing with a very similar analysis of human motivations. The description that Aristotle gives of the psychological and ethical process we experience when we form opinions from perceptions and respond emotionally to circumstances, matches, and can help to explain, what happens to Moschion and Demeas on the stage. Generally speaking, in Aristotle we find that the difference between ethically right and wrong choice depends on how we perceive[77] the particular facts on which we act. The success of this process of evaluation relies significantly on the subject's ability to understand the various aspects of his situation in order to respond adequately to this understanding.[78] This relates to a point made in Chapter 2:[79] for Aristotle, what seems to be essential, in theoretical understanding as in practical actions, is the ability to grasp salient features of the various situations

77 I am using here the verb 'to perceive' in the sense of 'to apprehend what is not present to observation; to see through', Onions 1983, *s. v.*

78 The principles of practical understanding are not universal but context-dependent (Nussbaum 1986(b), pp. 298–306). This does not mean that Aristotle is a relativist; action is concerned with particulars and these are relative to the specific situation (see further Chappell 2005).

79 See Chapter 2, section 3.

that we experience in a lifetime.[80] This ability should provide i) theoretical knowledge with the acquisition of first principles that explain the phenomenal world; and ii) practical knowledge with the completion of the final decision of what the ethically good action should be in a particular circumstance.

> καὶ ὁ νοῦς τῶν ἐσχάτων ἐπ' ἀμφότερα· καὶ γὰρ τῶν πρώτων ὅρων καὶ τῶν ἐσχάτων νοῦς ἐστὶ καὶ οὐ λόγος, καὶ ὁ μὲν κατὰ τὰς ἀποδείξεις τῶν ἀκινήτων ὅρων καὶ πρώτων, ὁ δ' ἐν ταῖς πρακτικαῖς τοῦ ἐσχάτου καὶ ἐνδεχομένου καὶ τῆς ἑτέρας προτάσεως· ἀρχαὶ γὰρ τοῦ οὗ ἕνεκα αὗται· ἐκ τῶν καθ' ἕκαστα γὰρ τὰ καθόλου· τούτων οὖν ἔχειν δεῖ αἴσθησιν, αὕτη δ' ἐστὶ νοῦς.

> And insight, too, is of ultimates, and in both directions, for of both the primary terms and the ultimate particulars there is insight and not reasoning; and insight with respect to demonstrations is of immovable terms and of that which is primary; but, in practical [reasoning, intuition] is of the ultimate and variable objects and of the other [i.e., minor] premises, since these are principle of the final cause; for it is from particulars that we come to universals. Accordingly, we should have perception of these particulars, and this is insight.[81]

It is worth reporting here Sarha Broadie's and Christopher Rowe's clear commentary of this passage:

> On the theoretical level, to see an object of the first kind (it might be a fact) as made up of its elements is to have an explanation (systematic knowledge) of why it is as it is. The practical analogue is: seeing the general aim of pushing some desired objective in terms of a decision that reflects an analysis of the particular circumstances, thereby making the general aim into something that a good person in those circumstances can bring to realisation.[82]

To restate this line of thought: universal practical principles differ from universal principles of understanding. They are not universal in the sense that they form the basis of an unchangeable deductive system of knowledge or that they are the explanatory causes of our understanding of facts and ideas. Principles

---

80 Nussbaum 1986(b), p. 305; See also Wiggins 1981(a) and Miller 1984.

81 Arist. *EN* VI 12, 1143a35–b5. On this passage see Sorabji 1973; Irwin 1978; Woods 1986 and Walsh 1999.

82 Broadie and Rowe 2002, pp. 378 on Arist. *EN* VI 12, 1143a35–b5.

of practical reasoning are universal in the sense that they are chosen as objectively best by an ongoing reasoned ethical inquiry. On the basis of a shared idea of human nature, its aims and inclinations, this enquiry selects guidelines that each human being should be able to apply to the specific circumstance in which he finds himself acting. The reciprocal sharing and understanding of these objective practical principles provides benefits for everyone.[83] The ability to apply to specific situations universal ethical principles that can guide the agent's choice requires a certain education and a developed state of ethical character.

I have already analysed, in Chapter 2, how an analogous kind of ability is necessary also in theoretical understanding and the way in which it functions there.[84] Here, I consider how this kind of skill is also necessary in practical understanding and I focus on the steps of the practical decision and the way that perceptions and emotions might influence the agent's practical insight in this process. According to Aristotle's description of practical deliberation, it seems that in order to act virtuously the agent must i) understand exactly the circumstances in which he finds himself acting; and ii) consider what would generally be considered good to do in these circumstances. In order to choose virtuously what has to be done, it is important that the agent handles his emotions correctly at both these stages. To analyse this process, I will consider, first, the thought-processes that, in general, Aristotle ascribes to someone who draws together pieces of evidence: this process has not only epistemological relevance but also has ethical implications. In fact, in considering a practical situation, the correct working out of this process shapes the agent's understanding of the situation in which his action is involved. Secondly, I will discuss why an accurate management of the agent's emotions is fundamental in this process: in fact, to understand correctly the particulars involved in the practical action is sometimes not enough to produce right actions.

2.1 *Thinking about One's Own Perceptions*

In Aristotle, inference from perceptions is a complex procedure that, in order to be correct, needs the accurate evaluation of pieces of evidence and the way they are connected. We find a good explanation of how this process of infer-

83 For what he calls an 'objective-participant' conception of the functioning of ethical reflection see Gill 1996, pp. 342–343 where he sees it as pervasive in Classical Greek culture. See also Gill 2005 on the relationship between universality and objectivity in ancient Greek ethics. See Nussbaum 1978, essay 4, on the difference between the principles of practical and theoretical reasoning.

84 See Chapter 2, section 3.2.

ence from perception works in the third book of *De Anima*. There, Aristotle considers that perception, in human beings, implies thinking (νοεῖν) and judging (φρονεῖν): thinking and judging what is in front of us are, in fact, a sort of perceiving (αἴσθησις) since the soul, in both of these states, forms a judgement and becomes acquainted with something existent.

> Ἐπεὶ δὲ δύο διαφοραῖς ὁρίζονται μάλιστα τὴν ψυχήν, κινήσει τε τῇ κατὰ τόπον καὶ τῷ νοεῖν καὶ φρονεῖν καὶ αἰσθάνεσθαι, δοκεῖ δὲ καὶ τὸ νοεῖν καὶ τὸ φρονεῖν ὥσπερ αἰσθάνεσθαί τι εἶναι (ἐν ἀμφοτέροις γὰρ τούτοις κρίνει τι ἡ ψυχὴ καὶ γνωρίζει τῶν ὄντων).
>
> There are two different characteristics by which the soul is mainly defined. i) Movement in space and ii) thinking, judging and perceiving. To think and to judge are thought to be a sort of perceiving (since the soul, in both of these states, forms a judgement and becomes acquainted with something existent).[85]

However, perceiving differs from thinking. Indeed, the perception *per se* is always true and is found in all animals, whereas it is possible to think falsely also, and thinking is found in no animal in which there is not also reason (λόγος). Thus, once sense data have been perceived we can still make mistakes in interpreting them, that is, we can construct wrong reasoning on the basis of mere perceptions. This is why Aristotle distinguishes between sound judgement (φρόνησις), understanding (ἐπιστήμη), true opinion (δόξα ἀληθής) and perception (αἴσθησις). Sound judgement, understanding, true opinion and mere perceiving are not the same because the first three are always right; that is to say, they already imply right thinking and the ability to make the right kind of reasoning. Mere perceiving, however, can give scope for false thinking (μὴ ὀρθῶς νοεῖν) and, consequently, false belief (μὴ ὀρθῶς δοξάζειν).

> ὅτι μὲν οὖν οὐ ταὐτόν ἐστι τὸ αἰσθάνεσθαι καὶ τὸ φρονεῖν, φανερόν· τοῦ μὲν γὰρ πᾶσι μέτεστι, τοῦ δὲ ὀλίγοις τῶν ζῴων. ἀλλ' οὐδὲ τὸ νοεῖν, ἐν ᾧ ἐστι τὸ ὀρθῶς καὶ τὸ μὴ ὀρθῶς, τὸ μὲν ὀρθῶς φρόνησις καὶ ἐπιστήμη καὶ δόξα ἀληθής, τὸ δὲ μὴ ὀρθῶς τἀναντία τούτων—οὐδὲ τοῦτό ἐστι ταὐτὸ τῷ αἰσθάνεσθαι· ἡ μὲν γὰρ αἴσθησις τῶν ἰδίων ἀεὶ ἀληθής, καὶ πᾶσιν ὑπάρχει τοῖς ζῴοις, διανοεῖσθαι δ' ἐνδέχεται καὶ ψευδῶς, καὶ οὐδενὶ ὑπάρχει ᾧ μὴ καὶ λόγος.

---

85 Arist. *DA* III 3, 427a17–21. Here I suggest for 'τὸ φρονεῖν' the translation 'to judge' as it fits this more general case.

> It is indeed clear that to perceive and to judge are not the same thing: for all animals have a share of the one, but few of the other. Neither is thinking [the same as perceiving], in which is included right thinking and not right thinking: right thinking being sound judgement, understanding and true opinion, and not right thinking the opposites of these—and this is not the same as perception. Indeed perception of proper objects of specific senses is always true and it belongs to all animals, while thinking can be [true or] false and it belongs to no one that does not have also reason.[86]

It seems that, for Aristotle, in all these processes, which involve the movement from sense-perception to thinking or belief, the possibility of cognitive failure arises in the reasoning that accompanies perceptions, which is internal to the subject and dependent on how he interprets sense data. Thinking and believing can be right or wrong and human beings have the capacity to reason on the basis of their perceptions. This is why sound judgement and understanding are always true—as they imply an already successful completion of the process of understanding. These differ fundamentally from thinking, (νοεῖν) and belief (δόξα) which can also be false[87] as they have not yet achieved the exactness of a comprehensive understanding.[88] Having said that, it would, therefore, be interesting to look more closely at the thought-process of belief-formation as presented by Aristotle and to discuss the way in which it is possible for the subject to form a wrong opinion, after having perceived something.

According to *De Anima*, to form an opinion it is necessary to be convinced of it. Thus, opinion seems to require that one reasons about sensations and about the rationality of one's own reasoning.

> [...] γίνεται γὰρ δόξα καὶ ἀληθὴς καὶ ψευδής, ἀλλὰ δόξῃ μὲν ἕπεται πίστις (οὐκ ἐνδέχεται γὰρ δοξάζοντα οἷς δοκεῖ μὴ πιστεύειν), τῶν δὲ θηρίων οὐθενὶ ὑπάρχει πίστις, φαντασία δὲ πολλοῖς.

> [...] opinion may be true or false. But opinion is attended by conviction, for it is impossible to hold opinions without being convinced of them: but no brute is ever convinced, though many have imagination.[89]

86 Arist. *DA* III 3, 427b6–16.

87 We find evidence of this also in the *Posterior Analytics* where ignorance is described as error during the process of syllogistic reasoning (Arist. *APo.* I 16, 79b23–24 and Chapter 2, p. 47).

88 See Chapter 2, section 3.2 for further discussion on this point.

89 Arist. *DA* III 3, 428a19–22. See Hicks 1907: 'πίστις' (conviction) as defined in *Ind. Ar.* 595

Accordingly, it seems that the state of mind of someone who is in the process of forming an opinion about something is crucial as this process involves reasoning about perceptions and convincing oneself of what one has understood from them. Persuasion and reasoning, in fact, also depend on the individual state of mind and this is made clear in *Rhetoric*. There, Aristotle explains that in order to produce persuasion, the speaker must understand the character of the audience and frame his discourse to produce the right kind of emotions that might convince the audience of the orator's argument.[90] Aristotle explains this problem in these terms:

> οὐ γὰρ ταὐτὰ φαίνεται φιλοῦσι καὶ μισοῦσιν, οὐδ' ὀργιζομένοις καὶ πράως ἔχουσιν, ἀλλ' ἢ τὸ παράπαν ἕτερα ἢ κατὰ μέγεθος ἕτερα·
>
> The same thing does not appear the same to men when they are friendly and when they hate, nor when they are angry and when they are in gentle mood; [but the same thing will appear] either wholly different in kind, or different with respect to magnitude.[91]

The idea is that, in an ideal setting, anyone would be able to reason correctly; however, it is possible that situations, emotions and desires influence how things appear to us.[92] One of the reason why we form false opinion about perceived particulars is because we not only perceive things passively but we interpret them actively according to our states of mind, inclinations and affections:

---

b 8sq. is "persuasionis firmitas, sive ea ex argumentis et rationibus, sive ex sensu et experientia orta est, atque eae res quae ad efficiendam eam persuasionem conferunt". Here the word has the former subjective meaning 'persuasionis firmitas' and the 'belief' is 'derived from reasoning' (Hicks 1907, p. 464).

90 Arist. *Rhet.* II 1, 1377b20–28.

91 Arist. *Rhet.* II 1, 1377b31–1378a1. Grimaldi emphasises 'τὸ παράπαν', which he takes as meaning "absolutely different" (Grimaldi 1988, ad loc.). See Rorty 1994: "The psychology of the *Rhetoric* hardly qualifies as explanatory scientific knowledge. [...] Like the pre-theoretical biology of which it is a branch, pre-scientific psychology is qualified in many different kinds of contingent variables. But psychology is even further from being rigorous than biology. The range of variables that affect our psychology is 'up to us' to an astonishing degree. Indeed rhetoric, politics, and poetry would have virtually no place if it were not so" (Rorty 1994, pp. 55–56).

92 Rorty 1994, p. 74. See also Konstan 2006(b): "The role of evaluation in emotion is thus not merely constitutive but dynamic: a belief enters into the formation of an emotion that in turn contributes to modifying some other belief or, perhaps, intensifying the original one" (Konstan 2006(b), p. 37).

we can recollect with our mind images of things that we have experienced.[93] We do not have just passive sensations but we retain perceptions, ascribing them specific meanings and actively interpreting them in our minds; Aristotle associates this process with *phantasia*.[94]

Accordingly, the reasoned reconstruction of various experiences, in the form of belief, might be affected negatively by the agent's emotions because sense-perception itself might be vitiated by the individual's state of mind in interpreting, or recalling through memory, what has been perceived. This is one of the reasons why belief can be false.[95] This constitutes a problem when the agent's opinion about a certain situation underlies his ethical choice. The content of sense-perception itself, in fact, might be affected by this kind of *phatos* which is characterised by Aristotle as *phantasia*, and things might appear in some way differently from what they really are.[96] This is because *phantasia* is not separable from, but interdependent with sensation, and whatever appears to someone is bound up with his or her particular history, prejudices, feelings and needs.[97]

> εἶτα αἱ μὲν ἀληθεῖς ἀεί, αἱ δὲ φαντασίαι γίνονται αἱ πλείους ψευδεῖς. ἔπειτα οὐδὲ λέγομεν, ὅταν ἐνεργῶμεν ἀκριβῶς περὶ τὸ αἰσθητόν, ὅτι φαίνεται τοῦτο ἡμῖν ἄνθρωπος, ἀλλὰ μᾶλλον ὅταν μὴ ἐναργῶς αἰσθανώμεθα πότερον ἀληθὴς ἢ ψευδής. καὶ ὅπερ δὴ ἐλέγομεν πρότερον, φαίνεται καὶ μύουσιν ὁράματα.
>
> Moreover, sensations are always true, but *phantasiai* prove for the most part false. Further, it is not when we direct our energies accurately to the

93 Arist. *DA* III 3, 427b17–20.

94 "Aristotle's theory of *phantasia* attempts to deal with a large range of problems. [...] The basic insight underlying the theory is the important one that perceptual perception is inseparable from interpretation" (Nussbaum 1978, p. 268).

95 See Arist. *DA* III 3, 427b15–429b20 and see Schofield 1979 and Frede 1995 on the distinction between the concepts of sense-perception, *phantasia*, conjecture (ὑπόληψις), belief and thinking.

96 On *phantasia* see also Hankinson 1990: "Perception is [...] rich enough to include judgment: but judgment only in relation to the objects of the sense considered as those objects. [...] but to imagine that your lover's eyes are the blue of cornflowers or that she has the body of Venus de Milo (just in a better state of preservation); or to think that your creditor has a complexion like a jaundice sufferer's or that he looks just like a gorilla: all of these require some further mental effort, one of which involves comparisons" (Hankinson 1990, p. 49).

97 Nussbaum 1978, pp. 261. See Price 1952; Nussbaum 1978 essay 5; Schofield 1979, pp. 111–113; Frede 1995, p. 289.

> sensible object, that we say that this object appears to us to be a man, but rather when we do not distinctively perceive it then the term true or false is applied. And, as we said before, visions present themselves even if we have our eyes closed.[98]

Consequently, a wrong judgment about how things really are in front of us, can easily lead one to act wrongly: indeed, for Aristotle, in order to perform an ethically good action, we need to know what context we are acting in. A clear judgment of this kind is difficult for human beings whose perceptions are easily affected by particular memories, prejudices and emotions; and Aristotle has a special interest in cases of this kind.

2.2 *Acting on the Basis of One's Own Perceptions*

Having discussed the possible ways in which, from sense-perception, one might build up false beliefs, I would now like to explore in more detail, how this kind of misunderstanding might affect ethical reasoning and ethical life in general. Aristotle explains animal practical activity by reference to the psychological process that motivates our actions: when stimulated by sense-perception, human beings (like other animals) are sometimes presented as going through a process of reasoning, articulated in the form of syllogism, which results in the action or the decision to act in a certain way.[99] Whether we consider the practical syllogism as the actual reasoning undertaken by the agent or as an explanation of human action that specifies all the relevant factors that might influence motivation, human beings, for Aristotle, mostly act following some kind of reasoning and the practical syllogism sets out this reasoning.[100] The practical syllogism represents the reasoning that, all circumstances and facts considered, helps to explain practical judgment and activity. The major, general, premise of this syllogism is an opinion relating to the good;[101] the second premise represents the particular situation or object with which we have to deal in our processs of decision making.[102] These particulars are those to which we should be able to apply the universal statement of the first premise in order to bring the syllogism to a successful conclusion. Thus, in any practical action,

98 Arist. *DA* III 3, 428a11–16.

99 Arist. *MA* 6, 701a3–5.

100 See Nussbaum 1978, pp. 165–222; Kenny 1979; Charles 1984, pp. 86–149; Dahl 1984; Broadie 1991, pp. 214–219; Annas 1993, pp. 87–91 and Sherman 1997, pp. 255–283.

101 Wiggins 1981(b), p. 248. A "universal action-guiding principle" (Nussbaum 1978, p. 204).

102 Arist. *EN* VII 5, 1147a25–26.

the process involved must deal, in the minor premise, with a particular. And, particulars are a matter where sensation is critical.

> ὅτι δ' ἡ φρόνησις οὐκ ἐπιστήμη, φανερόν· τοῦ γὰρ ἐσχάτου ἐστίν, [...] ἧ δὲ τοῦ ἐσχάτου, οὗ οὐκ ἔστιν ἐπιστήμη ἀλλ' αἴσθησις, οὐχ ἡ τῶν ἰδίων, ἀλλ' οἵᾳ αἰσθανόμεθα ὅτι τὸ [ἐν τοῖς μαθηματικοῖς] ἔσχατον τρίγωνον· στήσεται γὰρ κἀκεῖ. ἀλλ' αὕτη μᾶλλον αἴσθησις ἢ φρόνησις.
>
> It is evident, then, that judgment [in matter of ethical choice] is not knowledge; for it is concerned with the particular [...]. And the ultimate particular is not the object of knowledge but of sensation, not the sensation of proper sensibles, but like that by which we sense that the ultimate particular [in mathematics] is a triangle, and this kind of sensation is more similar to perception than to judgment [in matter of ethical choice].[103]

Accordingly, assuming that the agent knows, in theory, how he should act, he might still fail to evaluate adequately the particular circumstances he is in. As explained before, with reference to the *De Anima*,[104] one might, for instance, form a false opinion in interpreting sense data or uncontrolled emotions, unleashed by a given perception, might influence one's decision. Nevertheless, in order to act appropriately, the particular situation has to be clearly recognised and the agent has to be in a state of mind that enables him to understand it correctly; and errors may arise in either respects. I will first analyse the first type of situation: namely, someone who forms a false belief about the situation and, consequently acts wrongly.

In Aristotle's account, animals, including humans, are motivated by desire (ὄρεξις), when some alteration has taken place in accordance with sense-perception or *phantasia*. However, even if desire is necessary to motivate action, in human beings this is shaped by (rational) beliefs and is amenable to

---

103 Arist. *EN* VI 9, 1142a23–30. See also Arist. *EN* II 9, 1109b21–23. "There is such a thing as neutral cleverness, but the virtuous person does not have this *plus* having the right ends; rather he makes the judgement because his feelings and emotions guide him the right way and make him sensitive to the right factors, and because he is able intelligently to discern what in the situation is the morally right factor. Intelligence, *phrōnesis*, requires that in the agent the affective and the intellectual aspects of virtue have developed together in a mutually reinforcing way" (Annas 1993, p. 87).

104 See above pp. 87–90.

rational control.[105] Emotions are subset of desires, they are informed by our beliefs and they are a mode of registering and communicating the value we attribute to things or events.[106] Thus, they are key elements in motivating our actions. However, like desires, emotions should be brought in conformity with reason. I will now explain more clearly this point. In the *Eudemian Ethics*, Aristotle lists three kinds of desires: namely wish (βούλησις), anger or temper (θυμός), and appetite (ἐπιθυμία).[107] The first, 'wish', is described as a rational desire: it constitutes the kind of emotional responsiveness that enables a reasoned decision.[108] 'Anger' or 'temper' and 'appetite' are described as *non*-rational desires that are more difficult to handle in accordance with reason.[109] I will now consider the case of temper, aiming to connect these ideas with my interpretation of the *Samia*.

In the *Nicomachean Ethics* we learn that the action stimulated by temper that is not fully controlled by reason represents a case of 'lack of self-controll (*akrasia*) regarding anger' (ἀκρασία τοῦ θυμοῦ). The person who does not control his temper adequately is someone who displays a rushed and uncontrolled angry reaction to the perception of an offence. In this respect, temper might be said to follow reason partially. It is, in fact, right to feel anger, desire of revenge, in the right circumstance with the right person and in the right way. However, uncontrolled anger immediately leads to revenge without paying enough attention to what an accurate evaluation of the circumstances would suggest.

> ἔοικε γὰρ ὁ θυμὸς ἀκούειν μέν τι τοῦ λόγου, παρακούειν δέ, καθάπερ οἱ ταχεῖς τῶν διακόνων, οἳ πρὶν ἀκοῦσαι πᾶν τὸ λεγόμενον ἐκθέουσιν, εἶτα ἁμαρτάνουσι τῆς προστάξεως, καὶ οἱ κύνες, πρὶν σκέψασθαι εἰ φίλος, ἂν μόνον ψοφήσῃ, ὑλακτοῦσιν· οὕτως ὁ θυμὸς διὰ θερμότητα καὶ ταχυτῆτα τῆς φύσεως ἀκούσας μέν, οὐκ ἐπίταγμα δ' ἀκούσας, ὁρμᾷ πρὸς τὴν τιμωρίαν. ὁ μὲν γὰρ λόγος ἢ ἡ φαντασία ὅτι ὕβρις ἢ ὀλιγωρία ἐδήλωσεν, ὃ δ' ὥσπερ συλλογισάμενος ὅτι δεῖ τῷ τοιούτῳ πολεμεῖν χαλεπαίνει δὴ εὐθύς·
>
> For temper seems to listen to reason to some extent, but inattentively, like hasty servants who take off before having heard all that was said and then fail to carry out the right order, or like dogs who bark when they hear the sound of a man approaching without looking to see whether is

105 See Broadie 1991, p. 217.

106 Sherman 1997, p. 28.

107 Arist. *EE* II 7, 1223a26–28.

108 Arist. *EE* II 10, 1226b9.

109 See also Arist. *Rhet.* I 10, 1369a1–4.

> a friend; so although temper listens, it does not, because of its excited and hasty nature, hear the order but rushes to take vengeance. Reason or imagination indicates to us insult or slight, [and temper] as *if* reasoning that it is necessary to fight something like this, boils up straightaway.[110]

It seems, therefore, that the person who lack self control as regards anger or temper (ἀκρατὴς τοῦ θυμοῦ) acts wrongly because he does not discern correctly the content of the second premise of the practical syllogism; namely, the particular circumstance with which he is dealing. Often, at the mere appearance of an offence, anger concludes, 'as if reasoning', that the person has to take revenge immediately. More precisely, in these cases, the agent applies the first universal premise that he knows (e.g. "it is right to feel anger and desire of revenge at a given offence")[111] to a particular situation ("this is an offence"). However, he does not acknowledge fully that excessive temper has interfered with his judgment, preventing a thorough examination: the result is that he acts wrongly. Therefore, the person who is in this state runs the risk of going wrong as regards discerning whether the particular circumstance with which he is dealing requires such an angry reaction. Aspasius' commentary on the *Nicomachean Ethics* explains this concept in a particularly clear way.

> Although reason has in no way said nor has there occurred an impression that it must take revenge, one's temper leaps to it, as thought it has been ordered to take revenge. It does not reason syllogistically (for to reason syllogistically pertains to rational things), but it experiences something similar to one who has reasoned syllogistically that he must fight this man. For reason, as has been said, only says: so-and-so insulted me; but one's temper, as though the universal premise had been posited that one

110 Arist. *EN* VII 7, 1149a25–34. "When men are angered, they are not victims of some totally irrational force. Rather they are responding in accordance with the thought of an unjust insult. Their belief might be erroneous and their anger unreasonable, but their behaviour is intelligent and cognitive in the sense that it is grounded upon a belief which might be criticised and even altered by argumentation" (Fortenbaugh 1975, p. 17).

111 "Anger for Aristotle, then, is anything but a reflex to pain or harm, even when the cause is intentional. Aristotle envisages a world in which self-esteem depends on social interaction: the moment someone's negative opinion of your worth is actualized publicly in the form of a slight, you have lost credit, and the only recourse is a compensatory act that restores your social position. Anger is precisely the desire to adjust the record in this way" (Konstan 2006(b), pp. 74–75).

> must fight with those who have insulted one, and also the conclusion 'therefore I must fight this man', immediately grows angry and rushes off. So this is what temper is like.[112]

If we now consider the *Samia* with these reflections in minds, we can find some striking analogies between Menander's and Aristotle's treatment of these topics. Demeas can serve as an excellent example of this phenomenon. He is convinced by his beliefs about the other charachters on the basis of an inaccurate interpretation of his perceptions. What he has seen and heard is not adequately examined and probably not adequately perceived: the sight of Chrysis, from a distance, holding the child close to her breast gives him the impression that she is nursing the child and feeding an infant that it is hers and Moschion's. He places his trust in these misleading appearances without further inquiry. Moreover, when he goes back in memory over what he has seen and heard, he gets angrier and more convinced of what those appearances have suggested to him. In this way, moved by *phantasia* and desire, in the form of temper, Demeas hastly formulates an accusation that is not based on rigorous reasoning but is convincing for himself and presented persuasively to the audience. He would be right to be angry with Chrysis and Moschion if what he had thought he understood was true; however it is not. Moreover, when he tries to make further inquiry, he is again prevented by anger from hearing the truth when expressed by Parmenon. In this way he fails to achieve a more certain degree of knowledge about the circumstances in which he finds himself acting and he acts wrongly with respect to Chrysis and Moschion. Anger and love for Chrysis disturb his judgment and lead him to false conclusions.

As suggested earlier,[113] in Aristotle, the agent's judgment can be altered also at another level: that of the first universal premise. Suppose the agent knows exactly the particulars of his action: that is, he knows with whom he is dealing and under which circumstance, he still needs to decide what would be better to do, given these particulars. At the level of the practical syllogism, knowing exactly the particulars of the actions (that is, the content of the second premise), does not exclude the possibility of being wrong in figuring out which is the right choice to make. This might happen, for instance, when the agent does not give "the right genuinely pertinent concern to the major premise".[114]

112 Asp. *in EN*, 127.11–18 translation by Konstan 2006(a).

113 See above pp. 91–92.

114 Wiggins 1981(a), p. 234.

That is, he replaces the judgment about what would be universally considered good to do in his case with the judgment about what it is good for him at that moment, because he is affected by emotions and desires that a given situation might arouse.[115]

> ὅταν οὖν ἡ [δόξα] μὲν καθόλου ἐνῇ κωλύουσα γεύεσθαι, ἡ δέ, ὅτι πᾶν γλυκὺ ἡδύ, τουτὶ δὲ γλυκύ (αὕτη δὲ ἐνεργεῖ), τύχῃ δ' ἐπιθυμία ἐνοῦσα, ἡ μὲν οὖν λέγει φεύγειν τοῦτο, ἡ δ' ἐπιθυμία ἄγει.
>
> Accordingly, if there is a universal belief which forbids us to taste sweet and another belief, namely, 'everything sweet is pleasant', and if there is also before us a particular x which is sweet (and this is activated) and a desire in us to taste what is sweet, then the former belief tells us to avoid tasting x but desire bids us to taste x.[116]

In these circumstances, the attractiveness of the content of the second premise is so strong for the agent that his reasoning is controlled by his emotional reaction to the given situation, and this is what produces the final decision and the resulting action. This is what happens in cases of '*akrasia* because of appetite' (ἀκρασία τῶν ἐπιθυμιῶν). The kind of desire that leads to the action is, in this case, appetite. Appetite promotes the action of pursuing pleasure:[117] by contrast with temper, it does not follow reason but only pleasure.[118]

This is why Aristotle states that emotions alter our judgment in the same way that sleep, madness or drunkenness can.[119] When we judge the circumstances in which we happen to be, our state of mind is particularly relevant. Indeed it is on the basis of the appreciation of these particular circumstances that we should form our ethical choice. It is clear that, for Aristotle, people that are

---

115 Wiggins 1981(b).

116 Arist. *EN* VII 5, 1147a31–34.

117 Arist. *EN* VII 7, 1149a35.

118 "When it bursts out even against one's better judgment, this is lack of self-control of temper. But the uncontrolled reaction is fuelled by something rational and reflective, since the evaluation it embodies can be unpacked as the thought that one's own worth is to be preserved by asserting itself against anything that denies it. This general evaluation functions as a premiss from which the particular response follows as conclusion. Appetite, by contrast, is a simple tendency to move, with no sense that the move is fitting, towards or away from an object as soon as it is realised that the object is pleasant or painful". (Broadie and Rowe 2002, p. 56, commenting on the above quoted passage).

119 Arist. *EN* VII 5, 1147a11–15.

under the influence of emotion are not able to do this and, therefore, they are unable to apply their potential knowledge to present circumstances.

> ἔτι τὸ ἔχειν τὴν ἐπιστήμην ἄλλον τρόπον τῶν νῦν ῥηθέντων ὑπάρχει τοῖς ἀνθρώποις· ἐν τῷ γὰρ ἔχειν μὲν μὴ χρῆσθαι δὲ διαφέρουσαν ὁρῶμεν τὴν ἕξιν, ὥστε καὶ ἔχειν πως καὶ μὴ ἔχειν, οἷον τὸν καθεύδοντα καὶ μαινόμενον καὶ οἰνωμένον. ἀλλὰ μὴν οὕτω διατίθενται οἵ γε ἐν τοῖς πάθεσιν ὄντες.
>
> Again, the possession of knowledge may belong to men in a manner distinct from those just stated; for in having but not using that knowledge we observe a difference in state of mind, so that in one sense he has and in another he does not have knowledge, as someone who is asleep or mad or drunk. And indeed this is the disposition of those who are under the influence of emotions.[120]

The *akratēs* is someone who potentially acts according to the right evaluation of the circumstances; however, he sometimes fails to do so. Although he is able to recognise the truth of the major (universal) premise and sometimes also that of the minor (particular) one, he fails to act appropriately as regards the latter; thus, he fails to apply the knowledge that he potentially has to the specific circumstances.[121]

Moschion's case provides a good example of the second kind of *akrasia* that I have discussed (*akrasia* because of appetite). Moschion knew who Plangon was and he knew what he should have been doing. A correct form of reasoning in this situation should have been:

120 Arist. *EN* VII 5, 1147a10–15. "There is nothing absurd in *acting* against one's *knowledge* if the agent is not using all the knowledge required for his *action*; but it would seem strange if he were using all that knowledge but acted in violation of it. Perhaps it is assumed here that only knowledge determines an action; for *desire* too may determine an action, and if both *knowledge* and *desire* are present then the stronger of the two prevails" (Apostle 1975, p. 301).

121 See Davidson 1980 who sees *akrasia* extending to a broader domain of actions: cases of incontinence are not limited to cases in which an action is performed against what it is suggested by the correct application of a prescriptive universal judgment on a particular case. 'Incontinence' also applies to cases in which the subject acts in a certain way while he holds some available course of action to be "better" than the one he takes, and, what the agent considers "better" is not necessarily a universal prescriptive judgment.

I premise: To approach an attractive citizen woman who is not one's own wife is wrong
II premise: This woman who is a citizen and is not my own wife is attractive

---

Conclusion: To approach this woman is wrong

However, the desire for the girl and the sight of her stimulates Moschion's appetite. Thus, his appetite hinders his reasoning replacing the correct universal premise with the premise that is more desirable in that circumstance for the subject. Therefore, Moschion's reasoning takes the following form:

I premise: I find it pleasant to approach an attractive woman
II premise: This woman who is a citizen and is not my own wife is attractive

---

Conclusion: I will approach this woman.[122]

According to David Charles, in cases of *akrasia* regarding appetite, the agent does not formulate any kind of syllogism but simply follows what perception suggests without engaging in a rational assessment of the means through which he can achieve his desired end.[123] Similarly, John Cooper suggests that the practical syllogism does not, in such cases, enter the agent's deliberation because the actual sight of the object itself, or the way the agent represents it to himself, forms a link in a "psychological chain leading from decision through perception on to action". That is to say, in general, every agent, without calculation and without stopping to think about the relevant minor premise, infers that a given action is in order.[124] Even so, if we suppose that Moschion does not actually work out the latter type of syllogism in order to decide what

122 "Et incontinens habet quidam scientiam quoniam malum est fornicari, non operatur autem circa ipsam ut recedat ab hoc; et si scientiam habet quidem, non operatur tamen, nihil est inconveniens si attractus a concupiscentia fornicetur" (Heylbut 1892, p. 418, 25–28, commentary on *EN* VII 5, 1146b31–1147a5; Latin translation by Mercken 1973).

123 "There is no necessity to attribute such agents calculation or practical reasoning. In their cases there is a sequence involving perceptions and desires in which the final desire arises through perception (*MA* 7, 701a35–36) without the agent reasoning about what to do. For Aristotle there can be intentional action without the agent reasoning or going through a practical syllogism" (Charles 1984, p. 96).

124 Cooper 1975, pp. 52–53.

to do, we can still attribute a fundamental significance to the crucial moment in which Moschion sees the object of his desires: the sight of the girl arouses the desire to approach her and, eventually, it is this desire that overpowers Moschion's better judgment. When he sees her, Moschion no longer thinks that to approach an attractive citizen girl who is not one's own wife is wrong. On the contrary, he thinks that this is a very pleasant activity and that Plangon is actually a good candidate to fulfill his desire to engage in it. Whether or not we accept the interpretation of Charles or Cooper, it seems that the initial cause of the action of the *akratēs* is the actual perception, or appearence, of some object that is relevant to the agent. I believe, however, that some kind of reasoning of the kind represented in the practical syllogism is needed to make full sense of the process going on in the mind of the *akratēs*.

In fact, I believe that we need to presume different levels of response by different kinds of agent. Some agents, those who are completely virtuous and those who are not virtuous at all, respond readily to perceptions according to what their (good or bad) character suggests. It is, therefore, possible that, in these cases, virtually no reasoning (right or wrong) is involved in the process of deliberation and consequent action. On the other hand, some other kinds of agents, such as Moschion, who do not have perfect virtue but do have some degree of virtue, feel the need to consider alternative courses of action and to reason about them. This is because their disposition to be properly affected by circumstances and to respond to them in the right way has not yet become second nature for them as it has in the case of the truly virtuous person.[125] However, at the same time, because they are, to some degree, good people, they do not immediately go after what pleasure suggests but reason about what has to be done and whether it should be done. Moschion and Demeas are not bad persons but they are not perfectly virtuous characters either: their decisions require some kind of (right or wrong) reasoning in order to compare alternatives and decide which kind of action is in order.

In conclusion, I have pointed out in Aristotle two possible cases in which practical choice is affected by the agent's perceptions and emotional reactions in a given situation. First of all, emotions that are not adequately managed can lead to a wrong understanding of people and facts: accordingly, scattered pieces of evidence can deceive if they are not interpreted appropriately by the subject. In this respect, I have stressed that having an appropriate insight about the particulars involved in the action is fundamental in order to determine how it would be best to deal with them. Second, given a clear understanding of

---

125 Arist. *EN* X 10, 1179b20–32.

the circumstances, the emotions aroused by the perception of facts or persons involved can still influence a character's ethical choice; problems arise when the kind and level of emotion is not ethically appropriate to the situation.[126]

3 Conclusions

This discussion clarifies Aristotle's approach to emotions and how they can affect people's actions. I do not want to link these passages of the *Nicomachean Ethics* with *Samia* too closely; I do not want to claim that Menander reproduces on stage what he has read in Aristotle's work. As explained in the introduction,[127] this hypothesis would be very hard to prove. It seems, however, that the views held by Aristotle and Menander about the effects that emotions and perceptions have on people are highly comparable and this suggests that they share a common framework of thought. Aristotle identifies a crucial point when emotions get involved in the rational process that leads to ethical choice. Indeed, in this process it is the sensation of a specific particular that controls our decision and this is often altered by specific emotions that we feel in this context. It seems again that between particulars and right rational choice, there is a gap left for error; and this error is highly conditioned by the way we feel about the particular circumstances that we are experiencing. Aristotle compares people who are affected by anger and erotic desire to those who are asleep, mad or drunk: anger and erotic desire affect their bodies and minds and, consequently, such people fail to apply the ethical understanding that they potentially have to respond adequately to situations.[128] The examples of Demeas and Moschion in Menander's *Samia* seem to reflect ethical and psychological processes of the same kind. Indeed, Menander's depiction of characters and situations shows a special focus on the way that perceptions and emotions can interfere in people's rational reasoning and ethical behaviour.

Specifically, in the first part, I have presented the consequences produced by Demeas' uncritical approach to perceptions. Although Demeas makes an effort to assemble the pieces of evidence he encounters, he does so hastily and forms a mistaken set of conclusions. Aristotle provides a theoretical framework that analyses and explains this kind of erroneous reasoning. Menander seems to have constructed his presentation of Demeas with a view of human reasoning

126 Gill 1997, pp. 5–6.

127 See pp. 1–2.

128 Arist. *EN* VII 5, 1147a10–17.

and of misguided inference that is similar to that presented in Aristotle. In fact, Demeas is shown as not being able to manage his anger appropriately and this leads him to misjudge Moschion and Chrysis: his understanding of what happened is thus completely mistaken. Moschion presents a further example of how an agent can go wrong in deciding how to act. When Moschion raped Nikeratos' daughter and when he decided to lie to Demeas, his choice was altered by erotic desire in the first case and by shame in the second.

Aristotle appears to describe a very similar process in his *Ethics*, as illustrated in the second section of this chapter. In many cases, simply having knowledge of what we should do does not mean that we will necessarily act accordingly. Perceptions and emotions have great power over our cognitive faculties and thus, in turn, determine how we represent facts to ourselves. Our thought-processes affect and are affected by our perception of particular things or circumstances on which our ethical choice is based. Thus, emotion and perceptions can lead agents to overvalue desires and feelings in a way that is inappropriate to the specifics of the situation. Reading Aristotle improves considerably our understanding of Menander's characters and the reasons behind their choices. Accordingly, my interpretation of *Samia* contributes further in supporting the general hypothesis that Menander and Aristotle apply similar approaches to problems related to ethical choice.

CHAPTER 4

Chance, Ignorance and Human Agency

In the next two chapters, I continue to focus on the ethical theory of Menander and Aristotle, considering further some issues relating to practical action that have been raised by my previous analysis. In the previous chapters, I have discussed the way in which, according to Aristotle and Menander, emotions and states of mind can influence people's theoretical and practical understanding. More broadly, I have discussed how correct intellectual and ethical education helps to give a clearer insight into how things stand and how we should act. I have focused on cases in which the performing of right and wrong actions or the achievement of understanding depends clearly on the agents' ability to act, think and feel in a way appropriate to the situation. For instance, in Chapter 2, I have shown how, in the *Epitrepontes*, Habrotonon's careful analysis of the situation brings together hypothesis, evidence and proofs and concludes the process of recognition successfully. In Chapter 3, with respect to the *Samia*, I have analysed how Demeas' anger and Moschion's shame and lust, by contrast, prevented correct insight into ethical decisions and created the situation around which the complications of the plot unfolded. Accordingly, the comic cases discussed so far, and the parallel discussion of philosophical material, has offered the basis for a comparative study of Menander's and Aristotle's treatment of the individual ability to reason and deliberate on the basis of one's own intellectual and ethical skills.

In this chapter, I consider a different topic: namely, the role of chance and accidental ignorance in people's lives and choices, and the way this is treated by Menander and Aristotle.[1] In these cases, the cause of the agent's factual or ethical ignorance does not consist solely in the agent's ability to handle emotions, for instance in reasoning and understanding correctly. Rather, it depends on something external, as the agent is affected by chance events or accidental ignorance. In this type of situation, the agent is not in a position to achieve an exact knowledge of the particulars of the relevant action, and he finds himself in the middle of a series of unexpected circumstances. Situations of this kind

1 See also Casanova 2014 and Cinaglia 2014 for a discussion of the topic of luck and ignorance in Menander and Aristotle, their analogies and the implications that these analogies have for the understanding of Menander in its intellectual, social and ideological context. My reflections on the topic are here reconsidered with a different focus and in the context of the broader analogies found between Aristotle and Menander.

 DOI: 10.1163/9789004282827_006

are treated by both Menander and Aristotle and the way in which they are presented raises analogous questions: first, what is the role of the agent in these cases; which kind of challenge do chance and accidental ignorance present to the agent's reasoning and understanding, and how does the importance of the agent's intellectual and ethical ability differ in these cases in comparison with cases of *akrasia* as analysed in Chapter 3.[2] Secondly, there is the question whether, with respect to the action, the agent's intellectual and ethical virtues are presented as a constitutively significant factor in the process of dealing with chance events. Do these virtues determine the agent's choice and lead to an ethically successful outcome despite chance events that might lead to a different result?

Menander and Aristotle seem to raise the question whether accidental events are to be understood as an inevitable product of fate that determines people's life or as events that agents can significantly affect by a choice (προαίρεσις) that makes a difference to what the event means for the agents themselves and their ethical life. My overall view is that, from the perspective of Aristotle and Menander, the way in which people respond to and handle accidental events is important and forms a significant part of the presentation of the person as an ethical agent. Accordingly, for both Aristotle and Menander, chance events and cases of accidental ignorance turn out to be indispensable ingredients of the human condition because they challenge human rationality and are significant elements in the evaluation of an agent's intentions and choices. An accidental event does not have meaning *per se*: it only acquires significance when we consider how the people concerned respond to the accident. I will start with the analysis of some Menandrian material that is particularly suitable for this kind of inquiry. In particular, I will consider two comedies of Menander, *Perikeiromene* and *Aspis*, in which chance and accidental ignorance play a prominent role in the unfolding of the plot. I will then explore these examples together with Aristotle's treatment of chance and involuntary actions caused by chance and ignorance.

The two comedies I have mentioned contain prologues stated by two peculiar goddess: Tychē (Chance) and Agnoia (Ignorance). My view is that, even though these two figures are presented as divinities shaping the action and controlling the characters on stage, manipulating their state of ignorance or surprising them with unexpected events, in the play itself there are evident signs that point in a different direction. These two divine prologue speakers offer an outside perspective on the figures' actions: they explain to the audience what is

2 See Chapter 3, section 2.2.

happening and why they made it happen. They set the plot in motion and they say they wish to achieve a certain result. However, the prologue-speaker does not force the characters into (wrong) involuntary actions and, in their turn, characters can only be partly excused for the mistakes they make as a consequence of unexpected events or unknown situations. Once the circumstances have been created by these two divine-type figures, characters perform good or bad actions voluntarily and are judged accordingly; they are what we can call 'significant agents' because they determine, by their choices, the good or bad quality of their actions. Moreover, it is through characters' choices and actions that the prologue speakers bring about the end they desire and fulfil their plan.

In Aristotle, we can see an analogous treatment of comparable issues. In the *Physics*, in particular, Aristotle makes it clear that the meaning of chance events is significantly affected by the agents' choice in response to the specific event. Human beings, in particular, are able to make use of circumstances of this kind in a way that is different from animals and inanimate beings. In fact, we find that all accidental events, for Aristotle, are given a name according to the subject they affect. Irrational beings can only be subject to natural accidents that might or might not produce significant outcomes.[3] On the other hand, rational beings are able to see the accident as a matter of chance (τύχη) to which they have to respond in one way or other.[4] In this context, he argues, it is not easy to establish which is the primary cause of the action and, therefore, it is difficult to draw a distinction between voluntary and involuntary actions: specifically, it is difficult to say whether the action is determined by chance or is dependent on the agent's choice. It is clear, however, that there is a range of responses that the agent can give to accidental events and, depending on these responses, the agent can affect the ethical quality of his choice and the meaning of the event itself within the context of his life—independently of the more or less successful result the agent produces by this choice. Accordingly, in the *Nicomachean Ethics* we find that, depending on the quality of the agent's ethical choices, accidental events can be transformed by the agent into injustice (ἀδίκημα), error (ἁμάρτημα) or misfortune (ἀτύχημα): the question of which category is relevant to describe a certain action depends on how the agent confronts the action and responds to it.[5] Therefore, even in circumstances that we cannot entirely control as rational beings, we are not passive subjects but significant agents and our choices in some way always

3 Arist. *Ph.* II 6, 197b20–31.

4 Arist. *Ph.* II 5, 197a1–9.

5 Arist. *EN* V 10, 1135b11–25.

affect the quality of our action no matter how fortunate or unfortunate we might be.

1 A Play of Chance / A Chance to Play

In this section, I will explore the plots of *Perikeiromene* and *Aspis* with a particular focus on the way in which characters face the unclear or unexpected circumstances in which they find themselves acting. The prologues of the two plays seem to invite us to interpret them as plays of destiny in which the characters on stage act according to what they are made to do by the figures in the prologue, that is Tychē and Agnoia. I will argue, instead, that the focus of these comedies is not on the working of these two external forces but rather on the various ways in which characters choose to face them. Menander introduces at least two perspectives on the figures' actions. From an external perspective, the goddess explains why certain events will happen on the stage and which results they will produce. From a human perspective, Menander presents characters in a way that makes it clear to the audience what their own errors or weakness are in responding to the set of circumstances that the goddesses create for them. Thus, the unfolding of the dramatic action and its conclusion, in the *Perikeiromene* and *Aspis*, do not represent an involuntary outcome of fortunate or unfortunate events. The characters themselves collaborate in achieving a happy ending on the basis of their own deliberations and, on this same basis, they identify themselves as ethical agents of a certain kind.

1.1 *Perikeiromene*

The first surviving part of the play starts in the middle of the prologue given by Agnoia. The figure on stage explains what has happened in the opening lost scenes of the comedy.[6] We are told by the prologue speaker that an Old Corinthian woman once found two exposed siblings, Glykera and Moschion: the woman decided to keep the girl with her and to give the boy to Myrrhine, a wealthy woman who was her neighbour. Before dying, the Old Corinthian let Polemon (a soldier in love with Glykera) have the girl and revealed to her the story of her adoption and the identity of her brother, giving the girl the old clothes that were in her cradle. We are also told that Moschion, seeing Glykera every day and not knowing that she was his sister, has fallen in love with her,

6 It is debated which of the characters appear before the prologue. See Gomme and Sandbach 1973, pp. 467–468; Mastromarco 1985 and Arnott 1988.

and, once, passing by Polemon's house, has hugged and kissed her: the girl did not react as she knew he was her brother. But, Polemon's slave, Sosias, saw the scene and reported everything to Polemon. The soldier, driven by anger, and not knowing that Moschion was the girl's brother, cut off her hair. At the moment at which the surviving part of the play starts, Glykera has already left Polemon's house and is now settled in Myrrhine's place. Pataikos (an old man, Polemon's friend) tries to convince her to go back to Polemon, who now regrets his actions; but Glykera begs Pataikos to bring back from Polemon's house her belongings, including the clothes she wore when she was exposed with her brother. When Glykera and Pataikos examine them, they discover that they are daughter and father. Moschion, overhearing their conversation, reconstructs his origins and, once all the identities are revealed, Glykera and Polemon get married with the blessing of Pataikos.

The plot has a complex structure and raises various interpretative questions. I will concentrate here mainly on issues related to its structure and characters: in particular, I will consider how the story told by the divine-like figure in the prologue has to be understood. Then, I will focus on two characters, Polemon and Moschion: these two figures are less well-informed than others in the play but, by contrast to Demeas in the *Samia*, it appears as they are not expected to discover the truth at any point of the play as they do not have enough evidence to understand clearly what they are experiencing and the real state of affairs. Nevertheless, as with Demeas, their reactions can only be partly excused by accidental ignorance: the temper of the first and the hasty lust of the second lead them to act in a way that is not appropriate to any kind of situation, whatever their state of knowledge at the beginning of their action. Consequently, their errors can be considered non-voluntary only in certain respects and, in fact, their actions are presented as wrong to the audience.

1.1.1 The Prologue of Agnoia

The personified figure of Agnoia appears for the first time, in extant Greek literature, in this prologue. As regards visual representations, we have two definite images of Agnoia. In one of them, she is a female figure seen from the front and the picture is probably part of an illustrated edition of the *Perikeiromene*.[7] In the other, she is presiding at the murder of Laius and, in this scene, she is represented as turning her face away from the crime that Oedipus is about to perform.[8] The possible analogy between the two figures lies in the context in

7 LIMC, s. v. (Papyrus. *Oxford, P.Oxy. 2652*. Oxyrhynchos).

8 LIMC, s. v. (*Painting from Hermopolis*. Cairo, Museum JE 63609; Lehmann tavv. 9,1; 10,1).

which they are represented: both figures representing Agnoia witness incidents caused by absence of knowledge of family ties leading to incest or parricide. However, Agnoia is neither a mythological figure nor an Olympian god and there are no traces of a priest or temple devoted to her. The fact that in the *Perikeiromene* she claims power over the events that she is outlining is not supported by any evidence of cult that could entitle her to do so.[9] It is true that often, in the ancient world, natural phenomena, places, divisions of time, states of the body and emotions appear to be represented in human, often female, form. In some cases, they become deities and are honoured as Olympian gods,[10] but this is not the case with Agnoia. Nevertheless, her role as a prologue speaker draws our attention to a topic that Menander has treated in the comedies I have analysed in the previous chapters: namely, human misunderstanding, lack of knowledge and the effects that these have on people's actions and character.

In choosing Agnoia as the prologue speaker in the *Perikeiromene*, Menander draws attention to these topics from the outset; this figure initiates the action and she knows what the consequences will be. Her role seems to be close to that of *tychē* in human affairs. She represents the fact that people canot predict what will happen to them and in some cases they do not know, or at least they do not fully understand, what happened to them in the past. In the *Perikeiromene*, the responses of the characters on stage seem to be psychologically motivated and intelligible also without Agnoia as prologue-speaker. However, her presence draws attention to the fact that everyone can be liable to a state of ignorance regarding their own lives. The figures involved in the plot are not (or at least not necessarily) responsible for this ignorance, even if they are responsible for other aspects of their lives. Here, the figures are assigned by Menander the level of knowledge that Agnoia wants them to possess; and they handle this in different specific ways according to their character: this forms the basis of the plot of the *Perikeiromene*. I will now discuss this aspect conducting a closer analysis of the text of Agnoia's prologue.

At the beginning of the play, we are told that the Old Corinthian who took care of Glykera is the only one who knows the whole truth. Agnoia does not seem to have a direct effect on her but rather an indirect one: the Old Corinthian tries to oppose the effects of Agnoia when the latter decides to change Glykera's state of knowledge. In fact, she is afraid that Agnoia might

9 See Stafford 2002 who claims that evidence of cult is a crucial factor for establishing a figure's claim to divine power. "Any figures to whom sacrifice are made must be deemed capable of acknowledging the fact, since those who are making sacrifices are hoping for a response" (Stafford 2002, p. 2).

10 Stafford and Herrin 2005, pp. xix.

get Glykera in an awkward situation and, therefore, she decides to prevent the potential effects of the goddess's action by revealing the whole truth to her.

> **Ἄγνοια:** τὸν ἀγνοούμενόν τ' ἀδελφὸν τῆι φύσει
> φράζει, προνοουμένη τι τῶν ἀνθρωπίνων,
> εἴ ποτε δεηθείη βοηθείας τινός,
> ὁρῶσα τοῦτον ὄντ' ἀναγκαῖον μόνον
> αὐτῆι, φυλακήν τε λαμβάνουσα μή ποτε
> δι' ἐμέ τι τὴν Ἄγνοιαν αὐτοῖς συμπέσηι
> ἀκούσιον.
>
> IGNORANCE: She told her about her unknown brother by birth, as she foresaw some [possible] mischance of the kind that happens to human beings; she knew that he was the only relative of that girl in case the girl ever needed help, and this way, she took precautions against something unintended ever happening to them through me—Ignorance.[11]

Thus, the motive that lies behind the Old Corinthian woman's revelation is that she knows that, because of ignorance, the human condition is liable to lead to unintended actions. Therefore, she decides to change Glykera's state of knowledge.[12] The Corinthian makes sure that Glykera has appropriate knowledge of who she is so as to avoid some misfortune happening involving her and her brother.[13]

Having acquired knowledge of the truth from the Old Corinthian, Glykera decides to withhold it from her brother as she wishes him to continue his life untroubled by this knowledge. In this way, Glykera contributes to the continuing effect of Agnoia. In fact, she says, Moschion happens to have the chance of leading a contented life and Glykera decides not to change his state of ignorance for the sake of his happiness.

---

11 Men. *Pk.* 136–142.

12 The Old Corinthian's πρόνοια (prevision) imply γνῶσις (knowledge) and it is contrary to ἄγνοια (*agnoia*; ignorance). "La natura stessa di queste azioni (pre-visione e pre-occupazione, intesa qui in senso etimologico) necessita di un possesso di nozioni che implica e sottintende una γνῶσις" (Lamagna 1994, ad loc.).

13 These sorts of accidents are a recurrent theme in tragedy. Aristotle, in particular, recommends tragic plots that involve dealings between those who are bonded by kinship or friendship (Arist. *Poet.* 14, 1453b11–22; see Belfiore 1992, pp. 366–368 and 2000) and in which the prospect of an immediate tragedy is averted and the characters' fortune changes from bad to good (Arist. *Poet.* 1454a4–9; see Halliwell 1986, pp. 224–226; Belfiore 2000, pp. 21–38), these are almost like Menandrian happy endings.

Ἄγνοια: ἐν γειτόνων δ' οἰκοῦσα τἀδελφοῦ τὸ μὲν
πρᾶγμ' οὐ μεμήνυκ' οὐδ' ἐκεῖνον βούλεται
εἶναι δοκοῦντα λαμπρὸν εἰς μεταλλαγὴν
ἀγαγεῖν, ὄνασθαι δ' ὧν δέδωκεν ἡ τύχη.

IGNORANCE: The girl lives now close to her brother but she has not revealed the fact. He seems to be an admirable person and she does not want to bring about any change [in his life]; she wants him to enjoy the gifts that fortune has given to him.[14]

Having been assigned a certain degree of knowledge, the Old Corinthian and Glykera are the ones who decide who must share their knowledge or who must remain in ignorance of the truth. The female characters[15] are the only ones who possess a clear understanding of the situation and who use the knowledge they have; on the other hand, all the other characters are in danger of doing something wrong as they do not know what has happened and are kept in ignorance of the truth.

The prologue continues and the focus now moves to the other characters who do not know how things really stand. The divine-like figure tells us that the insolent (θρασύς) Moschion, in love with Glykera and always hanging around Polemon's house with intentions,[16] decides to kiss her. At this moment, Sosias, Polemon's slave, happens to pass by the house: he sees them hugging and kissing and he tells everything to Polemon. It is at this point that Agnoia says:

Ἄγνοια: πάντα δ' ἐξεκάετο
ταῦθ' ἕνεκα τοῦ μέλλοντος, εἰς ὀργήν θ' ἵνα
οὗτος ἀφίκητ'—ἐγὼ γὰρ ἦγον οὐ φύσει
τοιοῦτον ὄντα τοῦτον, ἀρχὴν δ' ἵνα λάβηι
μηνύσεως τὰ λοιπά—τούς θ' αὑτῶν ποτε
εὕροιεν.

IGNORANCE: All this flared up for the sake of what had to come, so that he might get angry (I brought him to this as he is not like this by nature, and so as to set the beginning of all the remaining things to be revealed) and so that they finally discover their families.[17]

---

14 Men. *Pk.* 147–150.

15 See Chapter 2 p. 24 n. 2 and 58 n. 138.

16 Men. *Pk.* 151–153.

17 Men. *Pk.* 162–167. Körte 1938 (in the Teubner edition of this play) suggests instead ending

The fact that Polemon gets excessively angry and cuts Glykera's hair is said to be the origin of all the following events. Agnoia, as prologue-speaker, says that she is the cause of Polemon's reaction.[18] However, we should reflect on how much the quality of Polemon's reaction is dependent on a totally external force. The fact of not knowing the truth about Glykera and Moschion is not something that Polemon can control; it is a circumstance that Agnoia, the Old Corinthian and Glykera contribute in creating. In this sense Agnoia does have an effect on Polemon.[19] However, we know that Agnoia acts on a subject who is already violent (σφοδρός)[20] in his responses. Finally, Polemon's decision to cut Glykera's hair is an extreme act that he decides to perform himself and cannot be considered as the necessary outcome of the anger that Agnoia produced. Menander makes the goddess create the accident but the characters on stage respond to this in their own specific way once the circumstances have been created outside their own control.

What Agnoia goes on to say, in the remaining lines of her speech, is that what has taken place will eventually bring about a happy ending; thus the goddess reassures the audience without giving further details about how this is going to happen. Agnoia says that there are going to be discoveries which all these events, leading Polemon to anger (εἰς ὀργήν θ' ἵνα οὗτος ἀφίκητο), will set in motion (ἀρχὴν δ' ἵνα λάβηι).[21] The influence of the goddess on Polemon is made clear by the prologue speaker; however, the discovery of the truth depends on Agnoia only in a specific way. The happy discoveries are brought about by human reactions produced by a state of ignorance. It is thanks to the figures' responses to Agnoia that the goddess is able to achieve her desired end. The

---

the parenthetical expression of Agnoia at "I brought him to this as he is not like this by nature" (ἐγὼ γὰρ ἦγον οὐ φύσει τοιοῦτον ὄντα τοῦτον), so to oppose her negative influence on Polemon to the rest of the sentence, "so as to set the beginning of all the remaining things to be revealed and so that they finally discover their families" (ἀρχὴν δ' ἵνα λάβηι μηνύσεως τὰ λοιπά τούς θ' αὑτῶν ποτε εὕροιεν), describing the good effect of the discovery produced by Polemon's anger.

18 See also Men. *Pk.* 169.

19 See Barigazzi 1965, p. 155 and Cinaglia 2014. For a broader discussion of the modes of the influence of Agnoia on Polemon see Fortenbaugh 1974, pp. 430–443 and Zagagi 1990, pp. 63–91.

20 Men. *Pk.* 128.

21 "L'inciso è inoltre importante per la caratterizzazione di Polemone, che per la prima volta viene presentato come privo delle abituali proprietà di *miles* comico: anche se egli è σφοδρός (v. 8), l'eccessiva violenza della sua ira è causata dalle circostanze eccezionali, non è un aspetto costante del suo carattere" (Lamagna 1994, p. 178). However, Lamagna describes Polemon's anger as misfortune (ἀτύχημα). See also Capps 1910; Gomme and Sandbach 1973, ad loc.

unfolding of the plot, including Polemon's violent reaction, depends on how people handle their state of ignorance and knowledge or, as we might say, the presence of Agnoia in their lives.

In conclusion, I suggest, the presence of Agnoia in the prologue is meant to highlight the fact that states of unintended ignorance are possible and that unforeseen circumstances can occur: it is the human response to them that gives them ethical meaning. Her presence highlights from the beginning that human beings can face situations in which it is not possible to have full knowledge of the circumstances of the action. Nevertheless, characters are still responsible for their behaviour and the play underlines this responsibility. In any case, this being a comedy, Agnoia also assures the audience that everything will end up well, exactly as she planned. However, the happy ending is not exclusively the result of her deliberation; in this sense she does not completely control the actions of the characters.[22]

1.1.2 Polemon and Moschion

The last point leads to the interpretation of the two male characters, Polemon and Moschion. If we suppose that, instead of Moschion and Polemon, a perfectly virtuous and balanced person had found himself in the same situation, we would expect such a person to react differently. Several scholars have defined Polemon's reaction as misfortune (ἀτύχημα)[23] caused by ignorance. This is true up to a point. Polemon, like the other characters, was deliberately kept in the dark about Glychera's kinship with Moschion. Accordingly, the soldier would have been right to be angry with Glykera for kissing Moschion: his indignation would have been justified; his misunderstanding and his hurt feelings could have been characterised as a misfortune. However, Polemon's reaction does not stop at simple indignation and a prompt (but non-violent) interruption of his relationship with Glykera. Polemon bursts out with excessive anger and this emotion completely clouds his judgment about Glykera and the facts of the situation.

First of all, Glykera is offended because Polemon has completely misjudged her character. For instance, Polemon is convinced that the fact that Glykera has left his house and sought protection from Myrrhines confirms that she has betrayed him for Moschion. But, in a dialogue with Pataikos, the joung girl gives him a list of reasons why she would not have done something like that, considering the kind of person she is and the kind of relationship she had with

22 See Zagagi 1990.

23 See Tierney 1935, p. 249; Webster 1950, pp. 204–205 and Lamagna 1994 p. 56.

the soldier.[24] She feels she has been mistreated and misunderstood and she does not want to go back to Polemon, since he has reacted in this violent and ill-judged way.[25] Secondly, we know that when Polemon realises that Glykera has left him, he decides to plan an assault to take her back with force. This rushed decison is prevented by the more reflective Pataikos. As Pataikos points out to him, Polemon did not take into account some relevant facts: Glykera was not Polemon's legitimate wife, and, from a strictly legal point of view, she had no obligations in his respect. Now that Polemon has dismissed and mistreated her, he does not have the right to take her back by force.[26] Also, Polemon should control his temper with respect to Moschion. The soldier can indeed make a complaint against Moschion for seducing Glykera; but he is not justified in seeking revenge and harming him physically as if Moschion had seduced a legitimate wife and Polemon had actually caught them making love.[27] So, as Pataikos helps us to recognise, driven by anger, Polemon does not only misjudge Glykera's character but his response is crude and ill-considered.

> **Πα:** εἰ μέν τι τοιοῦτ' ἦν, Πολέμων, οἷόν φατε
> ὑμεῖς τὸ γεγονός, καὶ γαμετὴν γυναῖκά σου—
> [...]
> **Πο:** ἐγὼ γαμετὴν νενόμικα ταύτην.
> **Πα:** μὴ βόα.
> τίς δ' ἔσθ' ὁ δούς;
> **Πο:** ἐμοὶ τίς; αὐτή.
> **Πα:** πάνυ καλῶς.
> ἤρεσκες αὐτῆι τυχὸν ἴσως, νῦν δ' οὐκέτι·

24 Men. *Pk.* 708–719. 'Glykera uses arguments that appeal to the intellect, not to the emotions. The behavior he [Polemon] "suspects" would be implausible, rash, and politically stupid; the idea that she acted recklessly and senselessly is absurd and insulting' (Traill 2008, pp. 144–145).

25 Men. *Pk.* 722–723.

26 Men. *Pk.* 489–490. Polemon's treated Glykera as a wife but, technically, she was not. Glykera was Polemon's *pallake* and Polemon has no rights on her, on paper. For further details on this topic see Konstan 1987, p. 127; Omitowoju 2002, pp. 216–217; Traill 2008, pp. 40–44; Sommerstein 2014, pp. 17–20.

27 See Lys. *Or.* 1 where the speaker, Euphileto, claims that, by law, a legitimate husband who caught his own wife in the middle of the adulterous act, was indeed entitled to kill the man who seduced her. For discussion and bibliography on this aspect of Lys. *Or.* 1 ('Concerning the Killing of Eratosthenes') see in particular Carey 1989 and 2012 and Todd 2007.

ἀπελήλυθεν δ' οὐ κατὰ τρόπον σου χρωμένου
αὐτῆι.
Πο: τί φῄς; οὐ κατὰ τρόπον; τουτί με τῶν
πάντων λελύπηκας μάλιστ' εἰπών.
Πα: ἐρᾷις·
τοῦτ' οἶδ' ἀκριβῶς· ὥσθ' ὃ μὲν νυνὶ ποεῖς
ἀπόπληκτόν ἐστιν. ποῖ φέρει γάρ; ἢ τίνα
ἄξων; ἑαυτῆς ἐστ' ἐκείνη κυρία.
λοιπὸν τὸ πείθειν τῶι κακῶς διακειμένωι
ἐρῶντί τ' ἐστίν.
Πο: ὁ δὲ διεφθαρκὼς ἐμοῦ
ἀπόντος αὐτὴν οὐκ ἀδικεῖ με;
Πα: ὥστ' ἐγκαλεῖν
ἀδικεῖ σ' ἐκεῖνος, ἄν ποτ' ἔλθῃις εἰς λόγους.
εἰ δ' ἐκβιάσει, δίκην ὀφλήσεις· οὐκ ἔχει
τιμωρίαν γὰρ τἀδίκημ', ἔγκλημα δέ.

PATAIKOS: Even if the fact is really as such as you say, and she was your wedded wife—[…]
POLEMON: I have considered her my wife!
PATAIKOS: Don't scream. Who was the one that gave her to you?
POLEMON: Who gave her to me? She did.
PATAIKOS: All right. Perhaps you were agreeable to her, but not anymore! She has gone away because you have not treated her appropriately.
POLEMON: What are you saying? Not appropriately? By saying this you have hurt me greatly.
PATAIKOS: You do love her. I know this for sure and, as a result, what you are doing now is senseless. Where are you going? Taking away whom? That girl is mistress of herself. Persuasion is what is left for a lover who is in [such a] bad state.
POLEMON: But he who has seduced her while I was away has he actually not committed an injustice toward me?
PATAIKOS: He wronged you, so you can bring a charge against him if you ever get into dispute with him; but if you get violent, you will be charged. This offence does not involve vengeance but a complaint.[28]

28 Men. *Pk.* 485–503. On Pataikos' legal position see the Gomme and Sandbach commentary on the play: "The points on which Pataikos is clear are (1) that Polemon has a cause for

As Fortenbaugh points out,[29] Polemon's attitude can be linked with Aristotle's description of the *akrasia* regarding anger as described in Chapter 3.[30] Polemon can appropriately be characterised as someone who, being impulsive by nature, would flare up in anger as soon as he thinks he has received an insult[31] and, in this respect, he is similar to Demeas, as I have interpreted his responses in Chapter 3.[32] Polemon transforms what would have been a misfortune (ἀτύχημα) into an act of injustice (ἀδίκημα): he does not control his temper and he misjudges the degree of indignation he should feel in the relevant situation and what action he should take in response. Similarly, in *Samia*, Demeas fails to control his temper and becomes excessively angry and this prevents him from acknowledging the truth. Polemon here does not have enough evidence to discover the truth, but, even so, because of his excessive anger, he does not understand the right way to act in this situation.[33] This kind of ignorance depends entirely on him and shows Polemon's lack of ability to make the right, well-judged choice.[34]

When Polemon has the chance to look back at his action, he understands his mistakes and regrets the fact that he reacted so violently with Glykera before discovering she is Moschion's sister. Thus, he recognises that, independently of his state of knowledge, he has not behaved properly and that he was inappropriately driven by his temper (θυμός).[35] Ignorance of the facts affected a character who was already predisposed to impetuous reactions: although his angry reaction could be partly justified, Polemon's emotional response was excessive and

private complaint at least, 'if he can discuss the matter with Moschion', (2) that Moschion's offence is not one that can be redressed by forcible means but that if Polemon uses force to recover Glykera he will be acting illegally and be condemned when brought to trial" (Gomme and Sandbach 1973, ad loc.).

29 In Fortenbaugh 1974.

30 See Chapter 3, pp. 95–100.

31 As in Arist. *EN* VII 7, 1149a33–34.

32 See Sander 2014, pp. 158–160 for a parallel discussion of Demea's and Polemon's cases and the kind of emotions felt by these two characters.

33 See Arist. *EN* IV 12, 1126b14–16.

34 On this point see Fortenbaugh 1974, pp. 435–436 and compare Arist. *EN* III 2, 1110b31–1111a2 and V 10, 1135b18–20.

35 Men. *Pk.* 985–988. "The variation in Menander's portrayal of his soldier's despair is thus the direct result of the poses he has had each one adopt. Polemon is essentially a distraught husband, as his dialogue with Pataikos makes clear. [...] Thrasonides is the excluded lover of epigram, and his threat of suicide accidentally brings him help unmasked" (Goldberg 1980, pp. 52–53). See also, for a contrasting account of Polemon's character, Friedrik 1953, pp. 164–165.

caused a state of confusion that prevented him from reasoning appropriately. Agnoia is well aware that she is acting on a person whose individual personality is particularly suitable for fulfilling the plan she has in mind:[36] she puts pressure on character traits and weaknesses already present in Polemon[37] and, in turn, Polemon reacts as expected. Polemon's error does not depend on Agnoia completely; it also depends on a different kind of ignorance, namely ethical ignorance. The goddess, as a supernatural agency, is only partly the cause of his mistake: she provides him, through the decisions of Glykera and the Old Corinthian, with a state of knowledge that, because it is associated with Polemon's already impetuous character, leads him to anger and to making wrong decisions.[38]

If we now consider Moschion, we can recognise that his attempt to seduce Glykera is made, to some extent, out of ignorance and, for this reason, we may be inclined to excuse him for this. However, we do not fully discharge him; instead, we are more inclined to agree with Pataikos that what Moschion has done is an act of injustice towards Glykera and Polemon. Pataikos, by contrast with the audience, does not know the real identity of Glykera and Moschion at the relevant moment; but his characterisation of Moschion's act as injustice still seems appropriate.[39] The fact that Moschion falls in love with his sister unknowingly is a misfortune. By contrast, the fact that he forms a plan to kiss her, though knowing that Glykera was given to Polemon and that she lived with him almost as his wife and Polemon loved her, cannot be described in this way.

36 Analogouly, in the *Iliad*, "*Ate*, sent by Zeus, takes away the *phrenes* of the person concerned; as a result, his *thymos* is rendered uncontrollable, his heart swells with *cholos* and the knowledge how to make the right decision which he possesses is rendered ineffective. The gods put a fierce *thymos* in his [Achilles'] chest but at the same time he himself puts it there" (Lloyd-Jones 1971, p. 23).

37 Analogously, with regards to Homeric heroes see Schmitt 1990, pp. 87–129.

38 Also in Homer, heroes seem to act apparently according to gods' plans. However, gods often just intervene in the case of a hero who already has a certain disposition. The action that it is presented as the gods' plan is often rooted in the nature of the hero himself: "The wrath of Achilles is seen together with its fearful consequences, which are described as the working out of the god's plan (Hom. *Il.* I, 5). [...] In the dreadful slaughter lies the fulfilment of Zeus plan, which, in turn was caused by Achilles' wrath. Thus the divine intervention followed on the action of the human individual, which was rooted in his own nature. [...] What matters for us, however, is that the final *aition* is not an overreaching plan of Zeus but the unconsidered act of a human being who performs it not under the influence of a god but rather in resistance to one" (Lesky 2001, p. 175). See also Lesky 1961.

39 See Men. *Pk.* 502–503.

Moschion knows that he is doing something wrong in kissing Glykera, but he persists in his intent. Without asking the girl and feeling ever more strongly the desire to possess her, he plans a way to kiss her. When she appears at the door, he runs to her, suddenly and embraces her.[40] He does commit an injustice because he does not control his desire for the girl and decides to obtain a kiss that he knows it is wrong to have: not because Glykera is his sister—that he is not supposed to know—but because she is Polemon's girl and he is well aware of this fact.[41]

Moreover, in the unfolding of the plot, Moschion is shown as persisting with the insolent behaviour that Agnoia has attributed to him in the prologue. In fact, after kissing Glykera, he goes on wanting to see her and he does not consider that she might not want to. Daos needs to tell him to stop his stubborn attempts to enter Myrrhine's house and make contact with the girl immediately after these events.

> **Δα:** μὰ τὸν Ἀσκληπιόν,
> οὐκ ἔγωγ', ἐὰν ἀκούσῃς. τυχὸν ἴσως οὐ βούλεται,
> μανθάνεις, ἐξ ἐπιδρομῆς ταῦθ', ὡς ἔτυχεν, ἀλλ' ἀξιοῖ
> π[ρὶν τάδ'] εἰδέναι σ', ἀκοῦσαι τὰ παρὰ σοῦ γε, νὴ Δία.
> οὐ γὰρ ὡς αὐ]λ̣[ητρ]ὶς οὐδ' ὡς πορνίδιον τρισάθλιον
> ἦλθε.]

> DAOS: By Asclepius, no I am not! If you would just listen! Maybe, you understand, she does not want either these things [to take place] summarily, anyhow. But she expects that, [before] you know [this], [(that she is here for you)], she hears what you have to say. Of course! she has not come here as a [flute girl] or as a wretched prostitute.[42]

Moschion's actions are analogous to those of his namesake, Moschion, in the *Samia*: both characters display what might be called, in Aristotelian terms, *akrasia* or lack of self-controll because of appetite (ἀκρασία τῶν ἐπιθυμιῶν).

---

40 Men. *Pk.* 152–156.

41 It is true that the status of Glykera in Polemon house was not clear: she had been not given to the soldier by her (citizen) father but by the old Corinthian woman who claimed to be her mother. For this reason Glykera is not marriageable and Polemon has no rights on her. However, those who knew the situation, including Moschion, knew the kind of affectionate relationship between Glykera and Polemon. On this point see Rosivach 1998, p. 54; Omitowoju 2002, p. 216; Traill 2008, p. 41.

42 Men. *Pk.* 336–341.

However, by contrast with Moschion in the *Samia*, in the *Perikeiromene*, this Moschion plans his action[43] and he does not feel shame after having done it. His action is wrong: driven by desire he plans a way to assault a girl who is held in someone else's house, when she does not expect it. His response to his own action is also different from that of Polemon: the soldier, like Moschion in *Samia*, feels regret after having assaulted Glykera but this Moschion does not.[44] The difference in their response is sensed by the audience, which sympathises with Polemon but not with Moschion. In this context, Moschion "remains an essentially shallow figure whose disparate acts serve only to initiate the main action and then move it onto its close. His presumed success with Glykera is an illusion based on his own ignorance. His comic bravado is used in counterpoint with Polemon's despair to highlight interest in the soldier".[45] We might say that Moschion's injury has been done with premeditation and deliberate choice and, therefore, that Moschion has behaved unjustly; and this is independent of his state of knowledge about his kinship with Glykera.

The accidents that happen in the *Perikeiromene* seem, therefore, to have their origin in the characters' agency and in the way they handle their states of knowledge or ignorance. In this respect, what we might otherwise call an 'accident' is not caused entirely by external factors. It is revealing that, at the end of the play, Polemon's injury to Glykera will be excused not as an accident provoked by the fact that he did not know the kinship between her and Moschion, but because all the troubles he created were resolved in a happy revelation.[46] I hope to have shown that, even though the prologue presents the plot as divinely directed, Menander is careful to show how the characters' choices influence their good or bad actions, given the accidental circumstance in which they find themselves acting. This means that the perspective introduced by the goddess does not necessarily affect the whole plot, and that when Menander introduces his figures on stage we need to pay attention to what their perspective is and consider their actions for what they are and not merely as products of Agnoia as a goddess.[47] The *Aspis* presents cases which are in many ways analogous.

43 In the prologue we are told that Moschion is always hanging around Glykera's and Polemon's house with a bad intent (Men. *Pk.* 31–33).

44 See Arist. *EN* VII 7, 1149b14–21.

45 Goldberg 1980, p. 57.

46 See Fortenbaugh 1974.

47 See also Cairns 2001, pp. 16–20 on the narrator's reasons for introducing different, shifting perspectives on a figure's actions with referece to Homer.

1.2 *Aspis*

I have already mentioned the *Aspis* in Chapter 2, when discussing cases of mistaken recognition.[48] At the beginning of this comedy, the slave Daos, after an assault on their camp, wrongly identifies his master Kleostratos with a corpse lying close to Kleostratos' shield, and reports this news to Smikrines, Kleostratos' greedy uncle. During the dialogue that opens the comedy, Smikrines immediately shows an interest in Kleostrato's quite rich war chest that Daos has managed to recover and that will be given to Kleostratos' sister. This situation will trigger a series of events.

1.2.1 The Prologue of Tychē

After the first scene, the goddess Tychē enters the stage and explains that Kleostratos is not dead; Daos and the others do not know what really happened and they are going astray (ἀγνοοῦσι καὶ πλανῶνται).[49] She explains the situation and, at the end, she says who she is and claims that she is in control of the entire plot, "The steward and judge controlling all this. I am called Tychē".[50] I will argue that a closer analysis of the play will reveal that, after various chance accidents orchestrated by Tychē, the plot starts from a human error in recognition: Daos misidentification, as described in Chapter 2. Furthermore,

48 Chapter 2, pp. 29–30.

49 Men. *Aspis* 99.

50 Men. *Aspis* 146–148. The fact that the name of the goddess is postponed after the beginning of the prologue is a shared feature with *Dyscolos* (12) and—most probably—*Perikeiromene* (21). In the case of *Dyscolos*, Dworacki infers that the audience already knew Pan thanks to his characteristic mask and clothing (Dworacki 1973, p. 34). This might also be the case here. In the fourth century BC, *tychē* became quite an important concept: its cult seems to start in this very period in Athens, Thebes, Megara and Corinth (*DNP*, s.v.). If this is true, it is possible that she was characterised like Pan with a particular kind of mask. "Tychē se présente sous la forme d' une figure féminine drapée, généralement debout, plus rarement assise. Elle se définit en général par le port d' une corne d' abondance sour le bras gauche; et c' est, semble-t-il, le premier attribut qui lui soit sûrement reconnu, à partir du IVe s. av. J.-C.; s'y ajoute assez tôt un gouvernail tenu de la moin droite, parfois remplacé par une phiale ou par un sceptre. La tête de Tychē enfin est fréquemment surmontée d' un polos ou d' une couronne tourelée" *LIMC*, *s. v.* Accordingly, it is possible that, in the prologue of *Aspis*, "the dramatist may wish to keep his audience wondering, perhaps looking at the mask and costume for some clue", and, consequently, the revelation of her identity comes only later in the prologue (Gomme and Sandbach 1973, p. 73). This being said, it is interesting to note that also in Euripides' prologues, the prologue speakers, especially if they are human beings, pronounce their name some lines after the beginning of their speech: *Andr.* 5; *Supp.* 6; *HF.* 1–3; *IT.* 5; *Hel.* 22; *Ph.* 12; *Or.* 23 and *Heracl.* 30.

this error unleashes a wide variety of human reactions that constitute the main focus of the plot. These reactions, in turn, create a situation that will need human intervention in order to bring about the plot's happy ending. Consequently, the prologue speaker has a plan and she expects it to be fulfilled; however, like Agnoia, she needs characters to react in a certain way to obtain this final result. The prologue itself, in fact, seems to direct the attention of the audience to Daos' error in the identification of his master and to Smikrines' evil plan. Daos' error and Smikrines' plan are the result of the characters' own weaknesses; they are caused by Daos' inability to carry out correct reasoning based on evidence[51] and by Smikrines' wicked intentions.[52]

Tychē explains what really happened to Kleostratos and, in explaining this, she attributes to Daos the error of identifying his master with someone else who had accidentally taken Kleostratos' shield.

> **Τύχη**: οὕτως ὁ μὲν παρὰ τῶι τροφίμωι τούτου τότε
> ὢν ἐξεβοήθει τήνδ' ἔχων τὴν ἀσπίδα
> εὐθύς τε πίπτει· κειμένης δ' ἐν τοῖς νεκροῖς
> τῆς ἀσπίδος τοῦ μειρακίου τ' ὠιδηκότος
> οὗτος διημάρτηκεν.
>
> TYCHE: In this way then, the one who was with this one's [Daos] young master went out to help holding this shield and fell immediately. Since the shield lay there among the dead and since the [corpse of the] young man swelled up, he made a mistake.[53]

It is possible to attribute to Tychē various events that, taken together, lead to Daos' final mistake: for instance, Kleostratos' friend taking the shield and Kleostratos taking someone else's armour and being captured. However, in the end, it was Daos who made a mistake, that is, he failed to put together properly the evidence he had and announced Kleostratos' certain death to everyone.[54] However, what Smikrines has called 'an unexpected misfortune' (ἀνέλπιστος τύχη),[55] Kleostratos' death, has not happened at all; it is Daos' wrong interpretation that has caused it. Certainly Menander wanted to emphasise the role of chance in human affairs and he does so by creating a prologue-speaker that

51 See Chapter 2, pp. 29–30 for fuller discussion of this topic.
52 Goldberg 1980, pp. 34–35.
53 Men. *Aspis* 106–110.
54 See on this point Vogt-Spira 1992, pp. 78–81.
55 Men. *Aspis* 18; see also Konet 1976, pp. 90–91.

emphasises this theme. The goddess, like Agnoia, represents what happens when accidents and chance events occur in someone's life; but she also gives the characters the scope for independent action.[56] Some of the events that initiate the action are not in the characters' control; what is in their control is how they decide to interpret these events and take them as a basis for action: their actions are what Tychē needs in order to lead the play to the end she wants.

1.2.2 Smikrines and Daos

In the rest of her prologue, the goddess directs attention to Smikrines. The wicked old man is not shown feeling any sorrow at Kleostratos' death and, consequently, his greedy nature is immediately revealed to the audience.[57] Smikrines' intention is to obtain Kleostratos' war chest and, to do so, he plans to marry Kleostratos' sister, though she was promised originally to Kleostratos' cousin.[58] From a legal point of view Smikrines, in principle, can ask the girl in marriage.[59] Now that Kleostratos is dead, he will not have a reliable administrator for his property when he dies.[60] In fact, Smikrines does not trust his younger brother Chairestratos: Smikrines believes that the latter is behaving irresponsibly in giving the girl in marriage to Chaireas. Therefore, for the sake of his own property, Smikrines considers the best option that of marrying the girl himself. Smikrines' plan is to mask his wicked intrigue as a wise solution to a misfortune, namely, Kleostratos' death.

> Σμ: πάντα ταῦτ' ὀργίζομαι
> ὁρῶν. ἐπειδὴ δ' ἐστὶν ἀλλοτρίως ἔχων
> πρὸς ἐμέ, ποήσω ταῦτ' ἐγώ· τὴν οὐσίαν
> οὐχὶ καταλείψω τὴν ἐμὴν διαρπάσαι
> τούτοις, ὅπερ δὲ καὶ παραινοῦσίν τινες

56 Lloyd-Jones 1971, p. 162 and, on these two specific plays, Zagagi 1990. "Such characters [Menander's prologue speaker: Ignorance, Fortune and Proof] may be purely inventions of the playwright to suit the dramatic circumstances of the moment, but the fact that personifications were presented in physical form must have helped, alongside representation in the visual arts, to give them substance in the popular imagination" (Stafford 2002, p. 13).

57 Men. *Aspis*, 143–145.

58 Men. *Aspis*, 114–120; see Goldberg 1980, p. 34.

59 Being Kleostratos and Kleostratos' father dead, the girl has in fact become an *epiklēros* (heiress) and Smikrines, as her paternar uncle, is entitled to ask her hand. For further discussion on this point see Harrison 1968, pp. 10–11 and, with specific reference to this play, Gomme and Sandbach 1973, p. 29 n. 1 and pp. 76–77; MacDowell 1982 and Brown 1983.

60 Men. *Aspis*, 167–171.

> τῶν γνωρίμων μοι λήψομαι τὴν παρθένον
> γυναῖκα ταύτην· καὶ γὰρ ὁ νόμος μοι δοκεῖ
> οὕτω λέγειν πως, Δᾶε. ταῦτ' οὖν ὃν τρόπον
> πράττοιτ' ἂν ὀρθῶς καὶ σὲ φροντίζειν ἔδει·
> οὐκ ἀλλότριος ⟨εἶ⟩.
>
> SMIKRINES: I get angry looking at all this. Since he deals with me as a stranger, this is what I will do. I will not leave this property of mine for them to tear in pieces, I will take this girl as my wife as some of the people I know suggest to me. It seems to me that the law says this, Daos. In fact, you should have looked into this, how these things should be done properly. You ⟨are⟩ not unfamiliar with this matter.[61]

This decision is perceived, by the other characters, as a demonstration of a lack of decency and human feeling.[62] The audience knows that Smikrines is not suffering a misfortune, as he pretends to be, but, instead, is committing an injustice. The old man does not consider the relevance of his age; his desire of acquiring wealth is so strong that he is not able to appreciate how improper is his pretence of marring his much jounger niece.

From the perspective of the other characters, Smikrines, in his turn, is himself causing a misfortune. He is making himself the author of an unfortunate circumstance that is imposed on the others and which they do not know how to control. This passage has a similar structure to the *Perikeiromene*: I will now explain how. In the *Perikeiromene*, Glykera and the Old Corinthian decide to dispose of their knowledge in the way they think is most suitable for everyone. Thus, their role is associated with that of the prologue speaker because they create states of ignorance in the other characters. In an analogous way, in the *Aspis*, Smikrines' decision to marry the girl surprises everyone and leaves everyone in great distress as if another misfortune has fallen on the characters after what has been announced about Kleostratos' death.

Confronted with Smikrine's resolution to fulfil his plans, the slave Daos makes an attempt to resolve the situation planning to stage Chairestratos' death. We might say that, to some extent, also Daos' role here can be associated with that of Tychē and Agnoia because, like the goddesses, he decides to surprise the other characters with an accident which is intended to bring about certain discoveries. Indeed, it is in order to reveal Smikrines' true intention that

61 Men. *Aspis*, 180–189.

62 Men. *Aspis*, 257; 260 and 309.

Daos makes up a plan: Chairestratos' family will pretend that Chairestratos has suddenly died. Smikrines will then be interested in Chairestratos' daughter as she will inherit his father's much more substantial property and he will show everyone which kind of person he is.

> **Δα:** [ ]. φερόμενον εὐθὺς ἐπ̣[
> προπετῆ, διημαρτηκότ', ἐπτ[οημένον
> ὄψει μεταχειριεῖ τε τοῦτον εὐπόρως.
> ὃ βούλεται γὰρ μόνον ὁρῶν καὶ προσδοκῶν
> ἀλόγιστος ἔσται τῆς ἀληθείας κριτής.

> **Daos:** You will see him falling, making mistakes, [carried away by excitement] so you will have him in your hands easily. He is only looking and thinking about this thing he wants and he will be an unreasoning judge of the truth.[63]

That said, they plan a way to make Chairestratos' accidental death credible. The alleged tragedy is announced by Daos who quotes tragic verses pretending that all these unforeseen misfortunes have been sent by the gods. But this last misfortune is skilfully planned by Daos and is meant to lead Smikrines to engineer another act of injustice with the intention of making his wicked nature evident to everyone: in this way, all the other characters would have enough evidence to condemn Smikrines' wicked intentions. An interesting aspect of this scene is that, when Daos announces that Chairestratos has just died, he says, with a tragic quote, that it is *tychē* and not sound judgement (εὐβουλία) that controls human beings.[64] However, Daos' clever orchestration of the whole situation proves the contrary: it is true that chance affects people's life in various ways, however, people's responses to it are also important and do have an impact in the way events develop. Daos thinks that Smikrines is not acting in a humane way (ἀνθρωπίνως) and that something needs to be done to resolve the situation: his association with Tychē becomes more evident here. In the prologue we are told by Tychē that Smikrines is someone who does not behave correctly with respect to the members of his own family and the community in general.[65] The plot will reveal to everyone what a bad person he is.[66] Daos' plan helps Tychē in making the revelation possible. We will see

63 Men. *Aspis*, 323–327.
64 Men. *Aspis* 411.
65 Men. *Aspis* 114–120.
66 Men. *Aspis* 138–146.

that, in the prologue of *Dyscolos*, Pan makes an analogous point: Knemon does not behave well with respect to his family and the community in general: this situation needs to change.[67] Pan himself, therefore, provokes an accident to which characters will respond in various ways and, with their responses, they will produce certain results.[68]

Looking back at the *Aspis*, the fact that Daos creates a situation, as Tychē would have done it, means that sound judgement and human intellectual ability have a significant role in the accidental circumstances in which people often find themselves in life. Human rationality is able to take accidental events as a basis for further actions: this is what finally determines the ethical quality of the agents and their acts. Daos (similarly to what Glykera and the Old Corinthian do in the *Perikeiromene*) takes up here the role of the prologue speaker, the goddess Tychē. He stages an accidental event and he lets it affect Smikrines and, from the outside, he watches the reactions of his character and waits to see where they lead, imagining in advance how the situation will unfold. The rest of the play is largely lost; however, we possess a part of the intrigue made up by Daos: the plan consists in pretending that a false doctor diagnoses Chairestratos' death by a sudden attack of "choking spasm". The play probably concludes with the arrival of Kleostratos on stage which resolves the situation and decisively subverts Smikrines' plans.

What is clear is that, from the beginning, the events that happen on stage are for the most part created by the characters themselves. Daos makes a mistake in identifying Kleostratos' corpse (ἁμάρτημα); Smikrines takes advantage of Kleostratos' death (ἀδίκημα) and the other characters are affected by his decision. However, a pretended, and skilfully crafted, misfortue engineered by Daos will resolve the problem. Tychē produces the initial accident and she expects that figures will react in a certain way so she will fulfil her plan; however, the plot unfolds according to the characters' intentions and their wise or wicked ethical choices.

1.3 *Divine Prologue Speakers and Related Matters*

So far, I have argued that Menander seems to be interested in the range of ways in which people react to unexpected situations. Independently of what might happen or what one might happen to know, people should be able to handle properly at least the portion of reality of which they are aware. When they do

67 This theme seems to be set out explicitly by Plautus' *Rudens*. In the prologue Arcturos states that Jupiter sends gods into the world to ascertain those who act correctly and those who do not so that he can then punish or reward them accordingly (Pl. *Rud.* 9–30).

68 For further discussion about *Dyscolos* see Chapter 5, section 1.

not, they show their flaws; the spectators are amused because they recognise the characters' mistakes but they know that, on stage, everything will end up in a happy way as the goddesses announce at the beginning. The audience is informed of everything by an external entity that declares she produced certain circumstances in order to achieve a specific result. In fact, the actions of the central characters of these comedies originate as reactions to something that the characters did not originally determine, but which was offered, thus giving scope for action. In this way, the audience understands how characters will react to a situation of which all or most of them are not fully aware, by contrast to the audience and the goddesses who see the situation from outside these events. Consequently, the relationship between divine prologue speakers and characters is one of (external) cause and response:[69] the prologue speakers organise things in a certain way so to provoke certain reactions and the characters respond to these events accordingly. Nevertheless, eventually, it is the characters' response that qualifies them as a certain kind of person and that makes them the targets of the audience's laughter. The audience is able to recognise the characters' flaws with laughter because the actions and events that develop from the figures' accidents are finally intelligible at a psychological, human level. After the divine speaker leaves the stage, Menander draws the audience's attention to the characters, how they reason, why they act and which actions they decide to perform.

These general points also apply to previous tragic texts. Here, I discuss some examples from Euripides' *Ion* and *Hippolytus* that exhibit a comparable relationship between divine prologue speakers and human characters.[70] In Euripides, in fact, we often find that gods and goddesses appear at the beginning and at the end of the dramatic action, delivering a prologue or an epilogue often as *dei ex machina*.[71] At the end of the *Ion*, for instance, the goddess Athena appears to explain to Ion and Kreusa the series of events in which they found themselves involved. She explicitly states that the god Apollo was the one who planned the

---

69 See analogously Williams 1993, pp. 51–66 with reference to Homer and Greek tragedy.

70 Segal argues that New Comedy shares with Euripides a similar treatment of divine intervention: they simply suggest that the gods have planned everything as a mere dramatic pretext (Segal, E. 2001, p. 19). After the prologue they promptly vanish from the play, since their sole function is to explain the situation (*ibidem*, pp. 12–13).

71 "When it seems that events have reached an *impasse*, the gods suddenly appear from nowhere and shout 'Stop!' [...]. What strikes one is its artificiality: the endings have been imposed in what seems a perfunctory manner. Has the action really been rounded off in a satisfactory sense? Has resolution really been achieved? Perhaps not—but a god willed it" (Wright 2005, p. 361).

whole plot and that everything that has happened to them was caused by him in order that they could recognise each other.[72] However, Athena also says that Apollo had to modify his original plan about Ion,[73] which Hermes presented in the prologue. Apollo planned that Kreusa and Ion should recognise each other once they arrive in Athens; however, this plan was spoilt by Kreusa's intention of killing Ion. Apollo, fearing that Ion would actually be killed by his mother's firm resolution (μητρὸς ἐκ βουλευμάτων), had to anticipate their recognition using devices (μηχαναί) on which Athena does not linger further. Analogously to what happens in Menander, it seems that Euripides introduces in the plot two shifting perspectives (human and divine) that seem to interact and motivate each other.[74] The circumstances of the plot are created by an external force, Apollo, so that he could produce certain results; however, in turn, Kreusa's human resolution influences Apollo's plan and the god needs to devise new routes to obtain his desired end. Apollo will finally achieve the result he wishes; however, he needs Kreusa to comply with him in some way. He needs Kreusa to choose to react in one way rather than another for his plan to be fulfilled. Gods' decisions are final, and Athena's epilogue seems to remind characters of this, but characters are given scope for independent action: more precisely, it seems that the gods themselves need figures to react in a certain way in order to have their desires fulfilled.

The prologue of Euripides' *Hippolytus* offers another example which might constitute a useful point of comparison with the prologues of *Aspis* and *Perikeiromene*. In the drama, the prologue-speaker, Aphrodite, summarises the previous events and introduces the actual circumstances of the play:[75] Phaedra, Theseus' wife, is in love with her step-son Hippolytus and the goddess declares that she wants to bring this affair to Theseus' notice.[76] In fact, she says, it is part of her plan to punish Hippolytus[77] for his disrespectful behaviour towards

72 E. *Ion* 1565–1568.

73 E. *Ion* 1563–1564.

74 Giannopoulou 2000, p. 262. See also Lloyd 1986.

75 E. *Hipp.* 1–40.

76 δείξω δὲ Θησεῖ πρᾶγμα κἀκφανήσεται (E. *Hipp.* 42). "The straightforward meaning of this is that she will reveal to Theseus that Phaedra is in love with Hippolytus. But she does not: she causes Theseus to learn not the truth but Phaedra's false accusation that Hippolytus has raped her; only in the end, when everything is over, is Theseus told the truth by Artemis. This contradiction is not to be resolved by assuming a corruption [...]; the truth is simply that Euripides is not being straightforward. He is not concerned here to give an exact synopsis of his plot, but rather [...] to mislead and mystify without outright misstatement" (Barrett 1964, ad loc.).

77 E. *Hipp.* 28–46.

her and his excessive reverence for Artemis. As in the *Ion*, the goddess has a clear plan but she needs Phaedra to take the *right* decision in order for her plan to be fulfilled. We know that Phaedra is contemplating various possible ways of escaping from her miserable conditions. She says that she is victim of a love passion that is ambiguously characterised as *Kypris*, a term that signifies both the goddess Aphrodite and the human affection of 'love' or 'passion' that is growing in her soul.[78] She lists to the audience the three solutions that she has been thinking about in her mind in order to free herself from this painful state: as a final solution she plans to die so as to put a definite end to her struggles.

> **Φα:** λέξω δὲ καί σοι τῆς ἐμῆς γνώμης ὁδόν.
> ἐπεί μ' ἔρως ἔτρωσεν, ἐσκόπουν ὅπως
> κάλλιστ' ἐνέγκαιμ' αὐτόν. ἠρξάμην μὲν οὖν
> ἐκ τοῦδε, σιγᾶν τήνδε καὶ κρύπτειν νόσον.
> γλώσσηι γὰρ οὐδὲν πιστόν, ἣ θυραῖα μὲν
> φρονήματ' ἀνδρῶν νουθετεῖν ἐπίσταται,
> αὐτὴ δ' ὑφ' αὑτῆς πλεῖστα κέκτηται κακά.
> τὸ δεύτερον δὲ τὴν ἄνοιαν εὖ φέρειν
> τῶι σωφρονεῖν νικῶσα προυνοησάμην.
> τρίτον δ', ἐπειδὴ τοισίδ' οὐκ ἐξήνυτον
> Κύπριν κρατῆσαι, κατθανεῖν ἔδοξέ μοι,
> κράτιστον—οὐδεὶς ἀντερεῖ- βουλευμάτων.

> PHAEDRA: I will tell you the course my judgement took. When love wounded me, I searched for the best way to endure it. I made myself start with this: to keep silent and to conceal my illness. For there is no trusting the tongue, which knows how to correct the thoughts of others but invites untold troubles when it speaks on its own behalf. After that, I determined to endure the passion bravely, overcoming it with self-control. Thirdly, because I could not suceed to win love with these [means], I resolved to die, the best resolution (as no one will deny).[79]

Phaedra is not the passive victim of Aphrodite's plan: her human perspective is relevant for the unfolding of the plot and for characterising her as an agent of a certain kind. First of all, if Phaedra had actually committed suicide before confessing her secret to her nurse, we must imagine that Aphrodite would have

78 LSJ, s.v.

79 E. *Hipp*. 391–402. Translation by Shaw 2007 (modified).

thought of some other way to bring about her desired end. In addition to that, as an audience we know how the plot will end and we know that Aphrodite will succeed but, looking at Phaedra's struggle and the solutions she thinks about to escape the goddess' plan, we are invited to see the whole story in different terms. The perspectives offered by the goddess and by the characters are different, and they shift during the play. In fact, when we compare Aphrodite's prologue "with the concrete details of the play, the explanations which the goddess gives are thin and over-simple. They suit the complex of power politics upon Olympus better than they suit the complexities of human life".[80] Phaedra is a woman who happens to be caught by passion for the wrong person: but the ways in which she tries and fails to hide and fight against the feelings that the goddess aroused in her and the consequences that this produces, are humanly and rationally understood and explained. Accidents, events and emotions come into being for no reason—or, at least, for reasons that the figures, as human beings, cannot fully explain: they are produced by external forces, gods, chance and, more generally, accidents proper to the human condition;[81] the figures on stage do not understand the cause of certain events, but their response is crucial to bringing about a certain ending and to showing themselves as people of a certain kind.

Analogously, in Menander, characters' decisions are presented as clear examples of good or bad choices independently of what the divine figure involved in the plot says. The audience is able to witness and to appreciate from an outside perspective and along with the goddesses what is wrong with their actions.[82] It is interesting to see that, in the prologues of the *Aspis* and *Perikeiromene*, the divine figures are personifications of abstract concepts rather than Olympian goddesses, and the broad ideas that they embody (i.e. ignorance and chance) are often recalled in the plots to explain what has hap-

80 Winnington-Ingram 2003, p. 215.

81 "Chance and the gods might be alternative and equivalent ways accounting for the operation within human life of factors which cannot be explained in entirely human terms" (Halliwell 1986, p. 230).

82 See Gutzwiller 2000 who argues that it is exactly this kind of complicity between the goddesses and the audience that makes Menander's prologues different from the Euripidean models: "The gods of Euripidean prologues generally explain past happenings and reveal their control over coming events, without direct address to the audience. In Menander, however, the deity of the prologue reveals past and future while making a kind of compact with the audience to accept and enjoy the illusion of the play" (Gutzwiller 2000, p. 115). For a discussion of divine characters in Menander in the context of the previous tragic and comic tradition see also Miles 2014.

pened to the characters involved. In the *Dyscolos*, we will find a more conventional deity, Pan, as prologue speaker. However, his function here seems to be not very different from that of Tychē and Agnoia: the god seems to be equally interested in creating for his characters accidents that are meant to produce certain human reactions on stage.[83]

As a matter of fact, in the *Dyscolos*, Pan does not do anything really characteristic of his status as rural divinity: he makes his appearance, he explains the situation and he declares that he has been the one who produced the incident that will provoke the following events.[84] After that, Pan disappears and, as in the other plays, the characters are left in charge of their action and their mistakes. In this particular case, it is also difficult to suppose that Pan represents a particular force, such as the compelling motive of passionate love, which is in some way at work in the play and that Pan states he has produced in Sostratos;[85] nor does Pan represent Knemon's cantankerous character. Therefore, it is tempting to say that the function of his prologue seems to be rather that of presenting the characters on stage and preparing a clear setting for the following actions.[86]

On the other hand, Pan does appear and he does express his disappointment at Knemon's bad behaviour: the way in which Knemon is behaving is against human nature[87] and something has to be done to resolve the troubles that this is creating for his family, particularly, his devoted daughter.[88] Pan's plan is to arouse in Sostratos love for the girl and to see what happens after he has done it. This circumstance created by Pan will produce two main outcomes: the first one is the effect that Pan arguably wanted to bring about, that is, to restore Knemon's daughter to society with her marriage to Sostratos. The second one

83 See Vogt-Spira 1992 who similarly associate Pan (pp. 138–145) with Agnoia (pp. 116–120) and Tychē.

84 See Kantzios 2010 for a discussion on the figure of Pan in the *Dyscolos*. Kantzios argues that the Pan we have here is quite different from its classical image of crusty and reclusive deity: this "new" Pan is more urban and interested in promoting the civil costums like marriage and the bearing of legitimate children. Knemon, on the other hand, represent a sort of alter ego of the classical Pan: quite wild, reclused and not interested in the civil costums to which he is forced to participate at the end of the commedy.

85 Men. *Dysc.* 39–44.

86 "In the *Dyscolos*, [...] the one feature that the audience does not take seriously is the agency of Pan. He is a dramatic convenience, imparting an aesthetically pleasing shape to the scheme of coincidences upon which the plot depends, and by his unseen presence adding piquancy to the country-setting of the comedy" (Anderson 1970, p. 217).

87 Men. *Dysc.* 6.

88 Men. *Dysc.* 34–39.

is more unexpected, and this is the partial conversion of the old misanthrope, which finally takes up a great part of the play that is named after Knemon's bad disposition.

The external force, with the mask of Pan, does intervene in the play creating the first accident, after which characters advance the plot by responding to it in various ways. Pan, Tychē and Agnoia end up having the same functions: they bring to the stage the accidents that start the action off and they watch with the audience the characters' reactions knowing that they will have a specific ending. This function is closely mirrored at a human level by what Daos does in Act Three of the *Aspis*: he stages for Smikrines an accident and he expects to obtain a certain response from him. He does not determine Smikrines' reaction but offers him the chance to reveal his nature in a way that Smikrines himself will decide.

2 Aristotle on Chance, Ignorance and Rational Agents

Before going on to explain Aristotle's treatment of chance and accidental ignorance, I would like to explore his aesthetic theory about the function of the divine prologues in the context of the dramatic plot.

2.1 *Prologues and Likelihood*

In Aristotle's *Poetics*, divine explanations or the gods' presence in drama are categorised as illogical (ἄλογος) and external to the plot. Aristotle suggests that the playwright should deploy them just to fulfil certain functions.

> μηχανῇ χρηστέον ἐπὶ τὰ ἔξω τοῦ δράματος, ἢ ὅσα πρὸ τοῦ γέγονεν ἃ οὐχ οἷόν τε ἄνθρωπον εἰδέναι, ἢ ὅσα ὕστερον, ἃ δεῖται προαγορεύσεως καὶ ἀγγελίας· ἅπαντα γὰρ ἀποδίδομεν τοῖς θεοῖς ὁρᾶν. ἄλογον δὲ μηδὲν εἶναι ἐν τοῖς πράγμασιν, εἰ δὲ μή, ἔξω τῆς τραγῳδίας.
>
> The *machina* should be used for things that are outside the dramatic action, either events that have happened before and which it is not possible for a man to know or events that happen in the future and need a prediction and an announcement, as we attribute to the gods the fact that they see everything. Nothing illogical has to take place in the dramatic action or otherwise [it has to take place] outside of the tragic action.[89]

89 Arist. *Poet.* 15, 1454b2–7.

The plot, according to Aristotle, has to possess an internal coherent logic so that the action is rationally intelligible by the audience in its picture of human actions and interactions. If the playwright conforms to this principle, his audience will be led step by step to the final understanding of the human motivations and mistakes that took place on the stage.[90]

This comes as a consequence of the fact that drama should represent people that act and think as we would probably (τὸ εἰκός) act and think in their position, and being the kind of people they are. Drama should also represent an intelligible motivational chain that links events to actions and to other events that develop necessarily (τὸ ἀναγκαῖον). That is to say, once the events have been created, someone with a specific type of character will probably respond in a certain way because his character will necessarily lead that person to take one decision rather than another.[91] To explain these thoughts, motivations, actions and events from a divine perspective does not help the understanding of this chain. The understanding of what has happened on the stage has to be produced from inside the stage, that is, from inside the plot, within human agency and not outside it.

> χρὴ δὲ καὶ ἐν τοῖς ἤθεσιν ὁμοίως ὥσπερ καὶ ἐν τῇ τῶν πραγμάτων συστάσει ἀεὶ ζητεῖν ἢ τὸ ἀναγκαῖον ἢ τὸ εἰκός, ὥστε τὸν τοιοῦτον τὰ τοιαῦτα λέγειν ἢ πράττειν ἢ ἀναγκαῖον ἢ εἰκὸς καὶ τοῦτο μετὰ τοῦτο γίνεσθαι ἢ ἀναγκαῖον ἢ εἰκός. φανερὸν οὖν ὅτι καὶ τὰς λύσεις τῶν μύθων ἐξ αὐτοῦ δεῖ τοῦ μύθου συμβαίνειν, καὶ μὴ ὥσπερ ἐν τῇ Μηδείᾳ ἀπὸ μηχανῆς.
>
> It is indeed necessary to aim always at the necessary and the plausible in the characters just as in the structure of the facts. So that [it is] either necessary or plausible that a person of such and such a sort says and does things of the same sort and that [it is] either necessary or plausible that

90 The aim of drama, however, is not educative but cognitive, as Halliwell notes, "The emphasis on the comprehension of tragedy does contain an element of reassurance and rational confidence: understanding where the failures of action are concerned might imply that in principle things might be effected otherwise, that they might be controlled so as to avoid suffering and misfortune" (Halliwell 1986, p. 236).

91 For further discussion of this topic see Frede 1992 who interprets the kind of necessity of which Aristotle is talking about here as "necessity in the sense that the character's action springs necessarily from the kind of person (character) he is. For the critical spectator it is a pleasure to recognise how and why the decision the agents are making, or the sufferings they have to undergo, are *necessary* or *plausible* ones, so that in the end the tragedy appears as an organic whole" (Frede 1992, p. 214). I shall come back to this point in Chapter 5.

> this thing happens after that one. It is evident, indeed, that the unravelling of the plot must arise out of the plot itself, and not, as in the *Medea*, *ex-machina*.[92]

It seems, therefore, that Aristotle suggests that the divine prologue should be used in the way that Menander does, according to my analysis of *Perikeiromene* and *Aspis*. The divine voice should be essentially external and separate from the rest of the plot. It supports the playwright in that it should help him in making clear what the circumstances of the action are and what the story is that the playwright himself has invented: it also clarifies what the accidents are which the playwright has created to surprise his characters. If the illogical and unforeseeable has to be included in the plot and the audience needs to be informed about this in order to understand the circumstances of the action, this explanation has to take place outside the dramatic action where the characters cannot hear it and where the audience may share the playwright's knowledge. In this way the audience and the playwright comply in creating and observing the accidents to which human condition is liable and occupy a privileged position.

More specifically, watching Menandrian comedy, people in the audience see on stage characters that are similar to them: they see human beings affected by accidents and feelings as they are and they see human nature represented as the playwright understands this. Accordingly, they are aware that the events on stage are likely to take place in everyone's life, but they enjoy the opportunity of experiencing those events from a distance, being conscious that, at the moment of the performance, they will not be affected by what is happening or what the playwright, within the prologue, announces for them. Once events and accidents have been explained in the prologue, nothing that goes beyond human intelligibility should enter in the plot. This is why, human rational choice cannot be explained by a *super*-human perspective: characters will explain themselves and their actions throughout the plot, while the figures in prologues create circumstances that the characters do not yet know about and explain these to the audience, drawing the attention to the external force that they represent and that is about to challenge the characters' lives.

2.2 *Aristotle, Tychē and Agnoia*

These ideas can plausibly be linked to Aristotle's treatment of chance and accidental ignorance in his works on ethics and physics. Before exploring this point

92 Arist. *Poet.* 15, 1454a33–b2.

further, I need to clarify that I am using here the expression 'accidental ignorance' in order to distinguish ignorance of particulars which we cannot control, namely, a kind of 'non-culpable ignorance',[93] from the ethical ignorance to which we are led by incontinence and intemperance. Having said that, the common ground that, in Aristotle, chance and accidental ignorance share is that of events that are external to human agency and which just happen to fall in a human being's life.[94] Moreover, it seems to me that we find in Aristotle the same attention as in Menander to the response that the agent gives to accidental events. We find the idea that once chance or accidental ignorance affects someone, this event necessarily requires a response from the agent and, that once the agent responds, the person becomes involved in the action. It is this involvement that identifies someone as the performer of an action which he may or may not have expected to be in the position to perform. What seems to be crucial is that, given an unexpected circumstance, the agent and the action itself are labelled with a name, which indicates the ethical quality of the action, *after* the agent has given his response to the accidental circumstance in which he found himself acting. Thus, the agent, being involved in an event, inevitably becomes significantly active because, depending on the response he gives, he decides what significance the accident has for him and his ethical life. In fact, when someone chooses what to do in a given situation, he also determines the quality of the resulting action and justifies its being characterised as good or bad.

In support of this point, I consider Aristotle's *Physics* II, 4–6: here rational beings are differentiated from animals, inanimate beings and children by reference to Aristotle's explanation of how events affect the natural and the human world. In the *Physics*, Aristotle argues that accidental events are designated differently according to the agents they affect: when something unexpected or with no apparent purpose happens to a rational being, this can be transformed into an accidental cause that contributes to the performing of an action that the rational being chooses to do; in this case, the event takes the name of *tychē*. Moreover, as Aristotle makes clear in the *Ethics*, the quality of the agent's response to *tychē*—the accidental event that involves him as rational agent—is fundamental for carrying out an ethically relevant action and also for characterising the action as good or bad. This process does not apply to irrational beings.

93 Sorabji 1980, p. 235.

94 This is also analogous to what I have pointed out in Menander at pp. 128–129—above: on this analogy see Tierney 1935, especially p. 224 and Gutzwiller 2000, pp. 116–124.

This last point opens scope for debate about the responsibility that one holds when chance or accidental ignorance intervenes in someone's life: more specifically, it opens up debate about the distinction between voluntary and involuntary action as presented in the *Nicomachean Ethics* and the *Eudemian Ethics*. Here, the attitude of the agent, *before* the deed done in the context of chance or accidental ignorance, and *after* it, becomes crucial for the definition of the *ēthos* of the agent and also for defining the act itself as voluntary or not, unfortunate or unjust. At the end of this analysis, it will be clear that, for Aristotle, very few acts can be identified as completely involuntary and all of them require a human response in order to be characterised in a certain way.

2.2.1 Chance and Mere Chance

In the central chapters of *Physics* II, Aristotle offers an extensive treatment of the topic of chance. The context in which he is treating this topic is a general inquiry on nature (*physis*), which is defined as a source and "cause of change and remaining unchanged in that to which it belongs primarily and of itself and not by virtue of concurrence".[95] That is to say, Nature is not the cause of everything but only of those things that have an internal principle that develops in accordance with nature;[96] thus, nature is not the cause of what happens by virtue of concurrence.[97]

> Some things, says Aristotle, are by nature, others as a result of other causes (i.e. of τέχνη, τύχη and προαίρεσις, [...]).[98] [...] Aristotle does establish a distinction between two classes of things, one consisting of things which as such have an internal principle of movement (i.e. animals and their parts, plants, and the four simple bodies earth, water, air, fire), the other of things such as beds and clothes which as such have no internal principle of movement, though in virtue of the simple bodies of which they are made they have such a principle.[99]

Thus, it is possible that certain things have other causes and they owe their movement and rest not to nature but to causes that are external to the *physis*, the nature, of the moving or resting beings: these causes contribute from the

95 Arist. *Ph.* II 1, 192b20–23, Charlton 1970, ad loc.

96 Arist. *Ph.* II 1, 192b35–193a2.

97 Arist. *Ph.* II 1, 192b23.

98 See Arist. *Metaph.* Z 7, 1032a11–15.

99 Ross 1936, pp. 499–500.

exterior to their rest or movement.[100] Initially, Aristotle just provides us with examples of stones and coats as instances of things that owe their change to something other than nature. In the case of the coat, for instance, Aristotle says that it comes into being by *technē* (art).

At first, human beings are included in the category of things that are made and develop according to nature's plan and possess an internal origin of change, namely, their own nature.[101] However, in *Physics* II, chapters 4 to 6, we find cases in which rational beings are shown to be able not only to develop and bring to an end their inner *physis* but also to adapt to things or events that are external to it, for instance, accidental events. At this point, Aristotle discusses whether events of this kind can be considered as natural causes of a human being's change: in fact, even if accidental events are external to the nature of animal and human organisms, they may still somehow produce change and rest in both the natural and the human realms.

One element that Aristotle considers in discussing whether accidental events can be characterised as natural causes, derives from the fact that, when an accidental event happens in the human realm, it seems to change its nature: it does not seem any longer to have been produced by chance but appears *as if* planned by nature. That is, the outcome produced is one that nature or thought would have produced. Aristotle explains that all events that happen accidentally can be ascribed to *to automaton*—that is, mere chance or spontaneity; but if an accidental event affects a human being, this is no longer so described but is characterised as *tychē*, that is 'chance'. Hence, *tychē* constitutes a subset of *to automaton*: its being a subset depends on the fact that the subjects to which *tychē* relates are rational animals, namely human beings.

Regarding *tychē*, one has the impression of seeing something happening as nature would have produced it.

> ἔστι δ' ἕνεκά του ὅσα τε ἀπὸ διανοίας ἂν πραχθείη καὶ ὅσα ἀπὸ φύσεως. τὰ δὴ τοιαῦτα ὅταν κατὰ συμβεβηκὸς γένηται, ἀπὸ τύχης φαμὲν εἶναι.
>
> Events that serve a purpose might be brought about by thought or by nature. When such things happen *per accidens*, we say that they do so by chance.[102]

100 Arist. *Ph.* II 1, 192b18.

101 Arist. *Ph.* II 1, 193a35–b25.

102 Arist. *Ph.* II 5, 196b21–24. For extended commentary on the meaning of these lines, see Lennox 1984, especially, pp. 58–60.

To expound, when a rational being is affected by an event *per accidens*, he transforms it into chance using the event itself as a means through which, with thought and choice, he can create his own good or bad luck; thus, the accident turns out not to be in vain but to take place for some sort of purpose (ἕνεκά του). This is why, when an automatic event strikes a human being, it is categorised as *tychē*.

> δῆλον ἄρα ὅτι ἡ τύχη αἰτία κατὰ συμβεβηκὸς ἐν τοῖς κατὰ προαίρεσιν τῶν ἕνεκά του. διὸ περὶ τὸ αὐτὸ διάνοια καὶ τύχη· ἡ γὰρ προαίρεσις οὐκ ἄνευ διανοίας.
>
> It is evident then that chance is a cause *per accidens* of things done according to choice that serve a purpose. Hence, chance [is concerned] with the same [class of events] as thought is for there is no choice without thought.[103]

On the other hand, accidental events that occur in the natural word, and affect inanimate beings or animal, do not bring about outcomes of the same kind; more precisely, they do not imply choice or thought. Therefore, such events do not appear to have been produced with the precision of rational choice that belongs only to human beings who can transform them in order to obtain certain ends; for this reason the results are simply called automatic outcomes and not *tychē*.[104]

Concluding, accidental events are defined as concurrent external causes that, together with human choice, produce change and rest in human beings and, thanks to human rational choice, they appear to happen for some purpose and not in vain, that is to say, they produce the opportunity for further rational action. Moreover, to be called *tychē*, these accidental events must happen for the sake of something and, in order to produce some results, they need a rational being who takes advantage of them. To develop this point, I will refer to the example that Aristotle himself offers. He describes as a case of *tychē* the circumstance in which a man, walking in the market place, finds by chance the man who owes him money and, taking advantage of the fact that he has met him, asks him to have his loan back.[105] If we now suppose that, in the

---

103 Arist. *Ph.* II 5, 197a5–8.

104 Arist. *Ph.* II 6, 197b14–20. On this passage Judson comments "Thus *E* is the outcome of chance (τὸ αὐτόματον) iff (1) *E* is among the things which come to be for the sake of something 'without qualification', (2) *E* does not come to be for the sake of what results, and (3) the cause of *E* is external" (Judson 1991, p. 93).

105 Arist. *Ph.* II 4, 196a3–5.

same situation, the same man, meeting his debtor, does not ask him for his loan back, then we conclude that the man has not taken advantage of the fortunate situation, that is, he has missed the chance to recover his money on that day and on that occasion. Accordingly, in this case, the fact that the man was at the market, and the fact that he happened to see his debtor, did not produce any effect. That is, this event was not chance or fortune but something that happened in vain.[106]

Nevertheless, Aristotle concludes that chance events cannot be classified in any case as determinate causes of change and movement of living beings because chance events do not produce this change necessarily or for the most part and they are posterior to reason and nature because they need reason and nature in order to happen for some purpose and not in vain.[107] Hence, the changes that chance events combine to produce are not already determined by a natural plan, for instance, it is not necessary that the man will ask for his loan back when he sees his debtor even if it is a fact that the two men actually meet at the market. Certain things happen because they are necessitated by causes that do not depend on the agent (for instance, the meeting of debtor and creditor at the market) but the moment in which the agent chooses (that is, the man decides to ask for his loan back) makes him the author of a conscious plan that he himself directs towards an end that *he* thinks to be the best.[108] By contrast, things that do not have the capacity of choosing and directing their movement according to a plan are not agents of *tychē* but only of *to automaton*.

I believe that, turning back to my analysis of Menander's *Perikeiromene* and *Aspis*, we can find the kind of human material suitable for illustrating what I have just said about Aristotle's thinking on this topics. Accoring to my reading of the *Aspis*, Menander presents us with a plot in which accidental events of different type are produced by the rational thought and choices of his characters: I have already explained how, in this play, it appears that a misfortune has

106 Arist. *Ph.* II 6, 197b23–28.

107 Arist. *Ph.* II 6, 198a9–13. "Because the beneficial results of natural processes occur regularly 'always or for the most part' they cannot be the outcome of chance which would yield beneficial results only irregularly" (Granger 1993, p. 168). See also Hankinson 1998, pp. 133–140.

108 Certain things are necessitated by prior causes. "But if one traces the chain back, one must eventually reach a self-mover which responds to a final cause. So although such phenomena are not themselves in accordance with a conscious plan that aims for the best, they are at least the eventual results of such a plan. It is because they are not directly dependent on the volition of a conscious agent that Aristotle sometimes attributes them to necessity" (M.L. Gill 1982, p. 132). See also Sorabji 1980, pp. 227–245, on which M.L. Gill comments in the article just quoted.

happened to Kleostratos, and that Smikrines has taken advantage of it. When Daos conceives his plan to unmask Smikrines, he stages Chairestratos' death, that is, he pretends that another misfortune has happened to Smikrines' family. The interesting thing here is that Daos provides an accidental event because he wants to achieve an explicit aim, that is, to unmask Smikrines. Menander shows us here the way in which he thinks about chance events: Daos knows that, by providing the accidental event, Smikrines will take advantage of it in some way and it will be clear to everyone that he and his actions are wicked. The unfortunate event, that is, Chairestratos' death, will create the desired results: as predicted by Daos, Smikrines uses it as an opportunity to take Chairestratos' daughter as his wife with the intention of getting a richer dowry. The alleged misfortune (Chairestratos' death) did not happen accidentally but was invented by Daos who, like a director or a playwright, wished to produce certain reactions in the characters involved, and actually succeeded in doing so. Chairestratos' death was determined by Daos but Smikrines' response was not a necessary outcome of this event: Smikrines was not forced to choose Chairestratos' daughter as his wife, but he chose her when he was given the chance by Daos.

A further example from the *Epitrepontes* shows the expression of a similar point of view. A first glance at the plot of this play, analysed in Chapter 2, might lead us to think that the story that Menander is creating is based on fortunate events which lead, *per accidens*, to the solution of the plot. Accordingly, it is in these terms that the slave Onesimos, at the end of the play, gives his interpretation of what has just happened. Onesimos' lines, reported below, offer a warning to Smikrines who wants to take his daughter back into his house, since Pamphile was wrongly accused and disregarded by her husband, Charisios. At this stage of the action, everyone knows that Charisios is the legitimate father of the child that Pamphile has exposed; Smikrines is the only one who is not aware of this and he still intends to take revenge on Charisios.

> **Ον**: τοῦτόν τις ἄλλος, οὐχ ὁ τρόπος, ἀπολλύει;
> καὶ νῦν μὲν ὁρμῶντ' ἐπὶ πονηρὸν πρᾶγμά σε
> ταὐτόματον ἀποσέσωκε, καὶ καταλαμβάνεις
> διαλλαγὰς λύσεις τ' ἐκείνων τῶν κακῶν

> ONESIMOS: No one else, if not his character, is destroying him. But now, while you were starting to do a bad action, chance saved you and you arrived to find a complete mutation and release from your sorrows.[109]

109 Men. *Epitr.* 1106–1109. For further discussion of this passage see Barigazzi 1965, pp. 192–217.

Onesimos says that *to automaton* is the cause of the sudden reversal and solution (λύσις) of the plot. Gomme and Sandbach explain that Onesimos here is not satisfied with the use of the familiar word '*tychē*', but he uses a grander word.[110] In my opinion, his statement is just a confirmation of his partial view of the whole situation.[111] Onesimos has observed the unfolding of the process of recognition initiated by Habrotonon: from his narrow point of view mere accidents have reconciled Pamphile and Charisios, as he did not play a significant role in the process of recognition as Habrotonon did.[112] Indeed, when he first discovers the ring, he is afraid to communicate the discovery to his master.[113] Onesimos does not take advantage of the fortunate circumstances that have happened as he is afraid to use them as evidence to reveal the truth to Charisios. Had the action depended on him, the truth would not have been discovered: Pamphile's rape by Charisios and the discovery of the exposed child would not have been chance events but they would have happened in vain. The intervention of Habrotonon changes the course of the action as she wants to understand clearly what happened: from her particular perspective, she sees the whole story as a good opportunity to obtain her freedom.[114] Conversely, once Onesimos sees his master's ring in the cradle of the exposed child, he does not want to speak and he is afraid to take part in the plan. Consequently, at the end of the play it seems to him that only mere chance has led to the happy ending of the story. On the other hand, Habrotonon helps the action by taking

110 Gomme and Sandbach 1973, p. 379.

111 This hypothesis is perhaps reinforced when Onesismos quotes two lines of Euripides' *Auge* few lines later to explain to Smikrines what has happened. He says "ἡ φύσις ἐβούλεθ', ἧι νόμων οὐδὲν μέλει·/ γυνὴ δ' ἐπ' αὐτῶι τῶιδ' ἔφυ" (Men. *Epitr.* 1122–1124). That is to say, "it is as nature intended": Pamphile, like Auge, was raped, she bore a child for nine months, she gave birth to it and now the child has been recognised by its legitimate father; however, the story, and the role of Pamphile in it, is more complex: "It is not enough to dismiss the act of rape, with the subsequent pregnancy, as a deed of overriding nature. We then recognise the irony in the citation from the *Auge*, its inappropriateness for the emotional and ethical circumstances that we have witnessed in the comedy" (Anderson 1982, p. 174). For a detailed discussion of this passage see Furley 2009, ad loc.

112 Vogt-spira also suggests that it is not because of an automatic outcome that the truth has been discovered, the revelation of identities has been taken further by the characters. "Gleichwohl spielt auch in diesem Stück der Zufall eine Rolle", because it gave the "causa efficiens"—that is to say, the various coincidences that brought to the discovery of the ring—which the characters will take as a chance to bring to an end the multiple recognitions (Vogt-Spira 1992, p. 169). See also Stockert 1997, pp. 7–9.

113 Men. *Epitr.* 419–429.

114 Men. *Epit.* 546–549.

advantage of the accidental pieces of information they progressively discover. In the *Epitrepontes*, *tychē* "brings separate strands of action all together"[115] and Habrotonon's lively mind is needed: the plot needs her quick-wittedness[116] to help mere chance—*to automaton*—to become a fortunate event—*tychē*.

This brief survey of Aristotle's treatment of chance, including the discussion of the *Aspis* and the *Epitrepontes*, is intended to underline the importance that Menander and Aristotle give to the role of human rationality regarding accidental events. Menander and Aristotle agree in saying that, in the natural world of coming to be and changing, human rationality is decisive in classifying the accidental events that affect it as *to automaton* or *tychē*. Nature has a plan and its own teleological aims; but, if human rationality gets involved and chooses, it is able to create something that seems to be nature's design, though it is not. Aristotle calls this *tychē* and the attribution of this name depends on how human rationality uses it: accidental events might or might not contribute to the performing of an action and it is up to the agent to decide when this is the case or not.

2.2.2 Voluntary, Non-Voluntary, Involuntary Actions

The last point in the previous paragraph is crucial for the ethical implications of this topic. The quality of the action that, following the accidental event, one decides to perform can be, of course, good or bad. Consequently, I will now examine how accidental events contribute to the process of ethical deliberation and how the agents' response to these events is again crucial for classifying the event itself in ethical terms. I will show that—as in the realm of natural causes, accidental events need human rationality to be classified as 'chance' or external non-determinate causes of change—analogously, in the field of ethics, accidental events take on a different meaning according to how the rational agent responds to these events.

In the *Eudemian Ethics*, we are told that good chance and knowledge are indispensable ingredients that help practical wisdom (φρόνησις) to achieve welfare and virtue.[117] Aristotle points out that when the wise person is involved in accidental events that he cannot control, or when he happens to be ignorant about particulars of an action in which he is involved, his path towards virtue can be obstructed.[118] When the agent is caught by unexpected and confusing situations he may become the agent of an action that he did not originally

115 Arnott 1975, p. 21.
116 Henry 1985, p. 50.
117 Arist. *EE* VIII 2, 1247a1–5.
118 Arist. *EE* VIII 1, 1246b25.

want to perform; that is to say, he may perform an involuntary action. However, the line that divides voluntary from involuntary action in Aristotle's account is blurred, and this distinction depends largely on Aristotle's treatment of chance and rational choice.

The previous section has shown that when accidental events happen to someone, if he is a rational agent, he comes to terms with what has happened and chooses to do something about it. When he exercises choice (προαίρεσις), the agent inevitably becomes the cause (αἰτία) of his action: he cannot choose what happens but he can choose what to do about things that have happened to him.[119] The situation, as in Menander, may be said to be created by divine intervention or by unpredictable chance; however, the choice itself is made by people who have the opportunity to exercise agency. However, it is clear that it is difficult to specify properly the nature of an action that is the result of chance. For instance, in these cases, it is difficult to determine wheather the action is completely involuntary or not.

According to Aristotle, it appears that an agent acts involuntarily only in situations in which he contributes nothing by his choices. In the *Nicomachean Ethics*, Aristotle explains that only in cases in which the agent is completely controlled by an external force can we say that he did something involuntary; for all other cases involving a choice, a sharp distinction is difficult. The case studies offered below may clarify this point. CS 1 presents an action done throughout the agency of an external force; CS 2 refers to an action done under external compulsion but one that requires, to some extent, human choice in order to be performed:

> CS 1: βίαιον δὲ οὗ ἡ ἀρχὴ ἔξωθεν, τοιαύτη οὖσα ἐν ᾗ μηδὲν συμβάλλεται ὁ πράττων ἢ ὁ πάσχων, οἷον εἰ πνεῦμα κομίσαι ποι ἢ ἄνθρωποι κύριοι ὄντες.
>
> CS 2: ὅσα δὲ διὰ φόβον μειζόνων κακῶν πράττεται ἢ διὰ καλόν τι, οἷον εἰ τύραννος προστάττοι αἰσχρόν τι πρᾶξαι κύριος ὢν γονέων καὶ τέκνων, καὶ πράξαντος μὲν σῴζοιντο μὴ πράξαντος δ' ἀποθνήσκοιεν, ἀμφισβήτησιν ἔχει πότερον ἀκούσιά ἐστιν ἢ ἑκούσια.
>
> CS 1: Forced is the action whose origin is outside of the subject, this being [the action] in which the one who acts or is acted upon contributes nothing, for example if the wind carried him away somewhere or men held him under their power.[120]

119 Arist. *EN* III 5, 1112a18–35.

120 Arist. *EN* III 1, 1110a1–4.

> CS 2: But those things that are done by fear of greater evils or for some sort of good—for example if a tyrant, who has in his power [someone's] parents and children, orders [him] to do something shameful and, if [he] does it, they would be saved and, if [he] does not, they would die—give room for a debate on whether they are non-voluntary or voluntary.[121]

The difficulty that Aristotle has in defining as voluntary or not cases that are different from CS 1 is that, in cases such as CS 2, the agent chooses something. And once the agent chooses, even if does so under constraint, he becomes the origin of this action.

> καὶ γὰρ ἡ ἀρχὴ τοῦ κινεῖν τὰ ὀργανικὰ μέρη ἐν ταῖς τοιαύταις πράξεσιν ἐν αὐτῷ ἐστίν· ὧν δ' ἐν αὐτῷ ἡ ἀρχή, ἐπ' αὐτῷ καὶ τὸ πράττειν καὶ μή.

> Thus, they [the actions explained by CS 2] have in the agent the origin of the movement of the parts of the body instrumental to the act. And because the origin is in the agent it is up to the agent to do it or not to do it.[122]

Consequently, a circumstance such as that presented in CS 2, is defined as a mixed case, and it is closer to a voluntary than to an involuntary action. According to this line of thought then, the evaluation and the characterisation of an action that takes its origin from an external event are finally based on the person that responds to it: we can say that the external event is a concurrent cause but it does not determine the agent's choice.[123] To give a list of cases is difficult as each event is defined by the choice of each person concerned. However, Aristotle subdivides involuntary action into two groups, namely as i) acts done under compulsion and ii) acts done through ignorance.[124] Also, Aristotle subdivides these cases further, depending on the agent's attitude before and after the deed; and it is at this point that the parallel with Menander becomes more striking. In treating acts done under compulsion, Aristotle states that what we sometimes claim to have done under compulsion and involuntarily is indeed

---

121 Arist. *EN* III 1, 1110a4–8.

122 Arist. *EN* III 1, 1110a15–18.

123 "Admittedly, he [Aristotle] thinks that there is an internal origin of voluntary conduct, but an internal origin may be a member of a chain which stretches back ultimately to external factors [...] the notion of an internal origin needs not to exclude external co-operating influences" (Sorabji 1980, p. 321). See also Meyer 1994, p. 71 and Cinaglia 2014.

124 Arist. *EN* III 1, 1109b35–1110a1.

not well described in those terms. One cannot claim, for example, that one has acted under the compulsion of passions.[125] In this case, the person is just lacking in self-control and the cause of the action is internal and not external to the agent:[126] so his action is voluntary. The truly involuntary action made under compulsion is what we find in CS 1 and only to some extent CS 2.

If we consider actions done through ignorance, we cannot indiscriminately list all of them as involuntary: we need to know the agent's attitude *before* and *after* he performed the action. Actions that are done in ignorance of the right choice to be taken are definitely voluntary: this ignorance is again internal to the agent as he, first of all, does not know the best thing to do before performing the action. Accordingly, this case cannot be identified as accidental ignorance concerning particulars, that is to say 'non-culpable ignorance'.[127] On the other hand, if the agent acts in ignorance of the particular circumstances of his action, we characterise his deeds in different ways once we consider the reaction of the agent *after* he performed the action and recognised how things really were. In this context, if the agent regrets what he has done in ignorance, the action is genuinely unintended, that is to say involuntary. On the other hand, if the agent does not regret what he has done, then the action is described as not genuinely involuntary. In fact, his lack of regret shows that he is happy about what he has done in ignorance and he does not feel pain about it. This means that the agent acted with a genuine intent to produce certain results and he would do that again even in circumstances when he exactly knows how things stand.

> Τὸ δὲ δι' ἄγνοιαν οὐχ ἑκούσιον μὲν ἅπαν ἐστίν, ἀκούσιον δὲ τὸ ἐπίλυπον καὶ ἐν μεταμελείᾳ· ὁ γὰρ δι' ἄγνοιαν πράξας ὁτιοῦν, μηδέν τι δυσχεραίνων ἐπὶ τῇ πράξει, ἑκὼν μὲν οὐ πέπραχεν, ὅ γε μὴ ᾔδει, οὐδ' αὖ ἄκων, μὴ λυπούμενός γε.
>
> Every action done through ignorance is non-voluntary, but involuntary is the one which [produces] pain and regret; for the person who has done something through ignorance [and] is not displeased by that action, though he did not act voluntarily, as he did not know [what he was doing], nor did he act non-voluntarily, since he feels no pain.[128]

---

125 Arist. *EN* III 1, 1110b9–17.

126 Arist. *EN* III 3, 1111a22–b3.

127 See also Arist. *MM* I 33, 1195a26–34.

128 Arist. *EN* III 2, 1110b18–22. See Williams for a contemporary account of the concept of 'agent regret' and its relevance in the field of unintentional acts: "the regret takes the form of self-reproach and the idea is that we protect ourselves against reproaches from

The characters of Polemon and Moschion in the *Perikeiromene* provide interesting examples to illustrate Aristotle's point. Both are driven by a kind of passion and, in this respect, they act voluntarily, performing actions that are classifiable as unjust and are criticised as such by the other characters. At the same time, both Polemon and Moschion are also ignorant about the real identity of people affected by their actions, therefore, we can say that, to some extent, they act in ignorance. The crucial element that distinguishes the characterization of the two figures is, however, the description of their reaction when they discover the truth. When the real identity of Glykera is revealed, Polemon is even more ashamed of his actions but Moschion is not: their different responses affect the way in which their charachters and their acts are viewed by the audience. Polemon's assault on Glykera is an impetuous act performed in ignorance of the actual circumstances: it is still an unjustice but it is clearly an act that Polemon himself admits, in retrospect, that he should not have performed. Moschion's kiss is a plain act of bravado typical of a profligate young lover who does not show regret—neither after having done it or hafter having acknowledged the truth.

In addition to that, Aristotle also specifies that, in order to classify an injury as an act done through ignorance, from a juridical point of view, it is also necessary to evaluate the attitude of the agent *before* the deed. He argues, in fact, that there are three kinds of injuries that might be done with respect to other people:[129] misfortune, error and injustice (ἀτύχημα, ἁμάρτημα and ἀδίκημα). In the case of misfortune, the agent is completely ignorant of the person, the instrument and the aim of the action. That being said, to distinguish between the two other cases of injury, the critical element that we need to specify is the attitude of the agent *before* the deed. The fact that the person acted with or without vicious disposition defines the deed as an error or an act of injustice.

> 1] ὅταν μὲν οὖν παραλόγως ἡ βλάβη γένηται, ἀτύχημα· 2] ὅταν δὲ μὴ παραλόγως, ἄνευ δὲ κακίας, ἁμάρτημα (ἁμαρτάνει μὲν γὰρ ὅταν ἡ ἀρχὴ ἐν αὐτῷ ᾖ τῆς αἰτίας, ἀτυχεῖ δ' ὅταν ἔξωθεν)· 3] ὅταν δὲ εἰδὼς μὲν a] μὴ προβουλεύσας δέ, ἀδίκημα, οἷον ὅσα τε διὰ θυμὸν καὶ ἄλλα πάθη, ὅσα ἀναγκαῖα ἢ φυσικὰ

our future self if we act with deliberative rationality: 'nothing can protect us from the ambiguity and limitation of knowledge, or guarantee that we find the best alternative open to us. Acting with deliberative rationality can only ensure that our conduct is above reproach, and that we are responsible to ourselves as one person over time'" (Williams 1976, p. 130).

129 Arist. *EN* V 10, 1135b16–22 and [Arist.] *Rh. Al.* 4, 1427a25–40.

> συμβαίνει τοῖς ἀνθρώποις· ταῦτα γὰρ βλάπτοντες καὶ ἁμαρτάνοντες ἀδικοῦσι μέν, καὶ ἀδικήματά ἐστιν, οὐ μέντοι πω ἄδικοι διὰ ταῦτα οὐδὲ πονηροί· οὐ γὰρ διὰ μοχθηρίαν ἡ βλάβη· b] ὅταν δ' ἐκ προαιρέσεως, ἄδικος καὶ μοχθηρός.
>
> 1] When the harm done is contrary to calculation, it is a misfortune; 2] when it is not contrary to calculation yet without vice, it is an error, (for one is mistaken when the source which causes the harm is in him, [and] one is unfortunate when it is outside [him]); 3] when a man acts knowingly but a] without previous deliberation, the harm is an injustice (e.g. like those through anger or passion which are compelling or natural to men), for although men act unjustly when they cause harm and are mistaken, and the effect is unjust, still they are not yet unjust and wicked because of these actions, since the harm done results not through an evil habit; but b] when a man acts with deliberation, he is unjust and evil.[130]

If someone acts without a vicious disposition, this affects the ethical quality of the action and the way in which this is seen by external observer. This is why, in the *Rhetoric to Alexander*, it is argued that, if one wants to defend someone from the accusation of having acted unjustly, he would need to present the deed as a mistake (ἁμάρτημα) rather than an act of injustice (ἀδίκημα). He would have to demonstrate that the agent did the act but that the damage done to the other person was not done voluntarily; that is, it was done through genuine ignorance and without a vicious disposition.[131] Polemon again offers an example suitable to clarify this distinction: the soldier is furious with Glykera because he does not know of her kinship with Moschion and, because of this kind of ignorance, Polemon decides to assault her and cut her hair to punish her. This decision is taken through anger or temper (διὰ θυμόν) and it is an act of injustice of the first kind (that is, of the kind 3(a) according to the passage quoted above). Polemon's reaction can be definied as an act of ingustice because it is excessive independently of his ignorance of the facts. As a matter of fact, he feels regret immediately for what he has done in a moment of anger even before discovering the whole truth about Glykera's origins. Had Polemon's indignation being managed more appropriately and had he chosen simply to dismiss Glykera without resorting to violence, his harm could have been classified as error because it would have been done in ignorance, responding to a supposed slight: therefore it would have been

130 Arist. *EN* V 10, 1135b16–25.

131 [Arist.] *Rhet. Al.* 4, 1427b5–8.

done with calculation but without a vicious disposition (that is, case 2 in the above passage). During the comedy, in fact, Polemon regrets his actions for two reasons: he recognises that he has misbehaved because he acted out of i) excessive anger and ii) in ignorance.[132]

Moschion, on the other hand, performs an action that is characteristic of someone that is unjust. He kisses a girl who lives in someone else's house as his 'unwedded wife', a girl who was given to a specific man and who is now involved with him in a trusting and loving relashionship—which is acknowledged as such by everyone in their community. Moschion has planned for a long time to assault her and he finally does this while she is not expecting the kiss. Moschion had all the pieces of information he needed to refrain from kissing Glykera but he did it nonetheless; he took his decision according to the prompting of his erotic desire and he carefully planned his actions. His deed then is more clearly classifiable as an act of injustice of the kind 3(b): that is, he acts knowing and with previous deliberation. Smikrines, in the *Aspis*, represents another example of 3(b): we know that he has a vicious disposition because, stimulated by his greed, he tries to marry Kleostratos' sister as a consequence of Kleostratos' unfortunate death and he shows himself capable of the same action when he is given the chance by Daos' clever plan. Independently of the legal position, Smikrines' motivations are, in both cases, ethically wrong. In conclusion, it appears that the way in which Menander presents these three characters to his audience corresponds to the analysis that Aristotle would give of their actions; that is to say, the ethical parameters within which Menander constructs his characters are analogous to the ones suggested by Aristotle.

3 Conclusions

What has turned out to be relevant, for both Aristotle and Menander, in matters of accidental event and accidental ignorance, is the response that the agent gives in these cases. Ultimately, the specification of the agent's character and the ethical quality of his choices depends on what the agent decides to do according to his good or bad motivation. Even in circumstances when an external element interferes with one's life, the agent should be able to make appropriate use of this event to produce an ethically correct action. Accordingly, my aim has been to show that, in both Aristotle and Menander, this external element is not the significant source or basis of the action. Tychē and Agnoia,

132 Men. *Pk.* 982–989. See also Cinaglia 2014.

chance and non-culpable ignorance, are just seen as opportunities offered to the agent that do not compel the agent to do what he decides to do. If people act according to what an external force tells them to do, there is no space for human choice; there is no reason to talk about voluntary and involuntary actions; and there is also little reason to become engaged in what happens on the stage as the audience would not be sympathetically involved in the sequence of reasonings, emotional responses, and actions that constitutes the plot.

In this chapter my aim has been to demonstrate that Aristotle and Menander have a special interest in this aspect of human life and that they give an analogous account of the role that human rationality plays in situations involving chance or accidental ignorance. In summary, I have explained that, in Aristotle's *Physics*, chance events are given different names according to the way that human beings respond to them and how they decide to deal with them and, for this reason they are described as concurrent non-natural causes. In the *Nicomachean Ethics*, Aristotle states that the response that the agent gives, in cases of accidental events, and his attitude before and after the deed, are crucial factors in defining the quality of the action: that is, they are relevant for characterising actions as good or bad, voluntary or non-voluntary. On this basis, Aristotle concludes that few of the so-called 'involuntary actions' can be said to have been compelled by accidental external events. For the most part, in cases of accidental events or accidental ignorance, human choice and motivation and right or wrong ethical habituation are the variables to take into account in order to classify the specific action as a voluntary action, an error or an act of injustice. Also, considering evidence from the *Perikeiromene* and *Aspis*, I have concluded that Menander underlines an analogous point: he seems to exhibit, in fact, a positive interest in writing plots in which characters are challenged by various sorts of accidents, and in this context, they are induced to make choices that will reveal their true nature. In particular, Menander appears to be interested in drawing distinctions between the ethical quality of the different kinds of choices made by characters who act in comparable situations of misfortune or ignorance. These distinctions have been shown to be higly comparable with Aristotle's ethical thought.

CHAPTER 5

Character, Ethics and Human Relationships: Aristotle and Menander on How We Learn to Be Good and How We Become Bad

The *Dyscolos* is one of the plays that has perhaps given most scope for debate about the possible influence of Aristotle on Menander.[1] As pointed out in the Introduction, scholars have often noted that there are similarities between some statements found in Menander's comedies, fragments and *gnomai*, and the general framework of Peripatetic ethical thought. In this play, in particular, it is often possible to find sentences and statements that recall the ideas of Aristotle in his works on ethics and psychology. Therefore, scholars have often agreed on the fact that, although it is not possible to establish a clear Peripatetic influence on Menander, it is, however, possible to argue that there is an *allgemeine Lebensweisheit*[2] that Menander shares with Peripatetic ethics and this comes out particularly clearly in this play. I believe that this argument could be taken further. The analogies between Menander and Aristotle go beyond the similarity suggested by a limited number of fragments, statements or single *gnomai* appearing in the plays. I hope to show in this chapter that it is possible to find various themes involved in the *Dyscolos* that, together with the topics analysed in the previous chapters, make up a consistent system of ideas that constitutes Menander's thought about ethics, human nature, psychology and also politics. It is this comprehensive whole, rather than specific points of similarity, that makes Menander's thought analogous to Aristotle's philosophy.

In Chapter 4, I analysed the role of chance and accidental ignorance in people's life, taking into account how, in Menander and Aristotle, these factors are relevant to matters of ethics. I concluded that it is the agent's approach to the accidental event that determines its significance within the agent's ethical life. What leads one to describe an accident or a state of accidental ignorance as 'misfortune', 'error' or 'injustice' is the way the agent chooses to react to the immediate circumstance and how he feels after the accident has taken

1 See Post 1960; Barigazzi 1965; Ramage 1966; Gaiser 1967, pp. 34–35; Anderson 1970; Patterson 1998, pp. 177–211 and Lape 2004, pp. 125–126.

2 Gaiser 1967, p. 14. For possible Peripatetic influence on the *Dyscolos* see Barigazzi 1965, especially pp. 70–115 and Wehrli 1970; for possible analogies between the *Dyscolos* and Theophrastus' thought about character and education, see Steinmetz 1960 and Gaiser 1967.

 | DOI: 10.1163/9789004282827_007

place. Nature or chance determines the occurrence of a certain event; however, these factors do not determine the specific approach that the individual chooses to take in dealing with it. The quality of the agent's deliberation, responding to a given accidental circumstance, defines him as an ethical agent of a certain kind. The agent's emotional state subsequent to the accidental event reveals his true (good or bad) disposition and intention in performing the action; in this sense, it reveals who he really is. Smikrines, in *Aspis*, is a good example of this: he expresses his wicked nature fully when he finds himself responding to a series of accidents. I concluded, therefore, that, for both Aristotle and Menander, life's circumstances and accidents constitute the mirror in which we learn how to know ourselves and others. Hence, I have explored how Aristotle and Menander treat cases in which people react in different ways to similar circumstances and are judged according to their response to them.

Also, in Chapter 4, I pointed out the way in which accidental events represent a chance to correct our inclinations and, as a result, our character, after having had such experiences or having seen other people going through them. In particular, the discussion of the examples of Polemon, in *Perikeiromene*, and Demeas, in *Samia*, in the light of Aristotelian philosophical thought has supported this point more clearly. Both Polemon and Demeas are figures who, more explicitly than others, show, at the end of the play, that they have understood what they did wrong and what they should avoid doing in future. For instance, they learn that their inclination to get angry has caused them troubles and this needs to be somehow controlled in the future.[3] This theme of learning through experience goes back to Chapter 2. There, I observed that, both in Menander and in Aristotle, the role of experience, through perception, in theoretical and practical understanding, is essential in order to form a better and more comprehensive view of how things stand and how one should act in facing certain, more or less expected, circumstances. To engage with life's experiences and accidents and to examine our actions, trying to understand retrospectively what we did right or wrong, is indispensable for the correct development of one's character and this builds up a fund of experience and knowledge that helps one's future understanding.

The aim of this chapter is to take this inquiry further and to explore how understanding, experiences and accidents relate to character formation in Menander and Aristotle. To my mind, Aristotle and Meander share a common view of how people develop their ethical character. With respect to character

3 Men. *Pk.* 439–442 and *Sam.* 703–705.

formation, I believe that the analogy between their points of view lies ultimately in the fact that both seem to believe that ethical character depends on the individual because it is up to him to develop certain dispositions (ἕξεις) in the course of his life. It is up to him to develop his natural emotional inclinations and habits with the aim of forming a good character according to correct ethical knowledge. This implies, in turn, a reasoned understanding of what it means to be human and what the aims of a human life are. Both Aristotle and Menander share the idea that these natural inclinations and habits cannot be correctly educated to form a consistent character, *ēthos*, outside the context of human relationships and the shared discourse about relevant values that these relationships involve. Interpersonal relationships, providing examples and discussion of relevant ethical issues, are fundamental for the achievement of each person's successful ethical understanding and, in turn, this understanding contributes to the happiness of all. In an ideal society, where everyone cares about the other for the sake of everyone's mutual benefits, every member should contribute to discussion about these topics. Accordingly, the experiences and examples of the good or bad dispositions of other people that form part of the shared life of citizens of the same *polis*, members of the same family or community of friends, inevitably influence the development of one's own character and one's own practical understanding.[4]

To explore these themes in Menander's comic production, I have chosen to focus my attention on the *Dyscolos*. I believe that this is the play that most clearly explores the issues involved in matters of character development. More specifically, the play illustrates how interpersonal relationships help to educate a person's dispositions and, eventually, contribute to forming practical understanding. Moreover, the *Dyscolos* sets out clearly that the achievement of this understanding and the successful development of a good character is not only beneficial for the individual involved, but also for the people around him. Some of these topics have been mentioned in previous chapters and the themes that I am going to treat in the *Dyscolos* have been discussed also with reference to the other plays. However, I have chosen to focus on this comedy because I believe that it offers a set of themes that are particularly relevant for establishing a comparison with Aristotle's thought in matter of character.

It is possible to identify in this play Menander's ideas about the way in which ethical habituation operates, the causes of the formation of a specific character, and also the possible problems involved in this process and what

4 For the idea that fifth-century BC Greek thought and literature reflect what he calls an 'objective-participant' conception of the person of the kind discussed here, see Gill 1996.

can be done to avoid them. The theme of character development, and the role that interpersonal relationships play in this process, will provide further explanation of some of the issues raised at the beginning of my discussion. This is why I have decided to explore these themes in this final chapter, examining the play that more clearly than others illustrates and brings together the set of ideas explored in this book.

Accordingly, following the procedure used elsewhere, in the first part, I will analyse Menander's *Dyscolos*, focusing, in particular, on two characters: Knemon, an old misanthrope, and Sostratos, a young man who falls in love with Knemon's daughter. The play is particularly relevant for my argument as it presents us with two opposite examples of behaviour that offer parallels with Aristotle's ethical thought. On the one hand, we have Knemon: the old man has spent his whole life outside the community and he has lost sight of how a human being should behave and what the human community is there for. He has grown old in this misanthropic disposition and the play shows how difficult it is for him now to change despite the fact that, at the end, he recognises his mistakes. Sostratos, on the other hand, is a young man: he does not have enough experience of life to face with a firm disposition the difficult situation that he finds himself in. Consequently, he relies on the other characters who advise him on the right way to gain Knemon's daughter and to deal with the old misanthrope. At the end of the play, Sostratos partly changes as he seems to have gained some understanding from his experiences. However, his youth does not enable him to reach complete self-awareness as, for instance, seems to happen to Moschion at the end of the *Samia*.[5]

In any case, the play leaves us with the impression that the young Sostratos will develop a good character, over the years if not at present, and that, on the other hand, Knemon has been responsible for the bad shaping of his own dispositions. Moreover, the reason why we think that Sostratos will grow up as a good person is that we realise that he has proved himself able to engage successfully with diverse experiences and that he has somehow taken advantage appropriately of what circumstances offered and people suggested. Knemon, instead, has become a grouch hated by everyone because he did not take these opportunities and engage with life's experiences and, more generally,

---

5 David Konstan argues that the anger that Moschion shows in Act V of the *Samia* is a kind of emotion that is usually attributed to mature Athenian men: the fact that Menander attributes it to Moschion at the end of this comedy means that Moschion now considers himself mature and has the right to be angry. (D. Konstan, unpublished lecture notes "Ancient comedy and its influence", Brown University, Providence, RI-USA, Fall 2008). See also Dutch and Konstan 2011 and Konstan discussion of the *Samia* in Konstan 2013.

did not engage with the other members of the community in the ethical values promoted by a shared life.

In the second part of this chapter, I will explore how a reading of Aristotle's ethical and political philosophy clarifies, and gives further significance to, what we have analysed so far in regard to Menander. It is an important feature of Aristotle's ethical thought that one's own natural, inborn inclinations are only a part of ethical character. What is also needed in order to build up a consistent character is to achieve a sound ethical understanding and to educate one's emotional inclinations in the form of consistent ethical dispositions. In order to cultivate these dispositions, it is fundamental that we share and exercise them in the context of human relationships: it is by engaging with other people and situations that one sharpens one's own practical understanding and trains one's inclinations. To have various experiences, and to discuss them with others, helps us to form a comprehensive view that is fundamental for achieving any kind of understanding, as discussed in Chapter 2, and that also forms the basis of the process of deliberation, as discussed in Chapter 3.[6] This is also why, in Aristotle's opinion, a young man cannot be properly virtuous: the reason for this is that he needs to develop, through learning and experience, a consistent practical understanding and an adequate education of his emotional inclinations. In this way, by maturing through age, being educated by others in a certain manner and listening to what they have to say about him, he will learn how to be good.

In addition, what I will stress, in the second part of the chapter, is that the correct shaping of one's own character, in Aristotle too, necessarily takes place within a context of interpersonal relationships. A community of fellow-citizens, family or friends, more generally, a community of *philoi*, helps each of its members to understand what is good and what is not. Discussion, feedback and suggestions within these various communities constitute an indispensable ingredient to promote each person's virtuous life in a mutual way. On the other hand, a life lived in isolation keeps the individual away from the possibility of having this sort of dialogue: a man who wants to live alone misses the chance of being observed and corrected by his neighbours and friends and progressively loses sight of what is good and what is not.

In conclusion, it seems that, in both Menander and Aristotle, to discuss and reflect publicly with other members of a community about relevant ethical

6 See Arist. *EN* III 5, 1112b10–24, where Aristotle compares deliberation to a search (ζήτησις) where, as when we are constructing a figure, we need to find the principle that makes the figure (or the ethically good deliberation) possible.

values is important, and this offers the chance of an improved ethical understanding and also the actual practice of the ethical virtues promoted by a shared life. In the light of these observations about drama and ethical philosophical discourse, I will attempt a final parallel analysis of Aristotle and Menander concerning the relationship between character, ethics and human relationships. This discussion is also intended to conclude and bring together in a comprehensive argument the topics analysed in the previous chapters.

1 Dyscolos: The Young Man and the Old Man

In the *Dyscolos* there is a clear distinction between Knemon and all the other characters: Knemon positions himself apart from them—probably also visually on the stage. Menander accentuates his isolation by surrounding him with people that, at a distance and outside his presence, reflect and comment on his solitary nature.[7] The role of these other characters, however, is not solely reduced to the function of commenting on Knemon's bad behaviour. Their presence is crucial for identifying certain topics implicit in the apparently extreme presentation of Knemon. For instance, the character of the young man, Sostratos, underlines the characterisation of the meaning of the old grouch by forming a contrast.

This kind of interaction between the figures of Sostratos and Knemon is reflected in the organisation of their movements on the stage. The way in which Menander organises the structure of entrances and exits of these two characters, and the way in which he seems to have positioned them on stage, underlies their being opposite and complementary at the same time. The two figures, in fact, embody two different kinds of movement. Knemon represents a movement directed toward the interior, towards increasing seclusion; Sostratos, on the other hand, introduces a movement directed toward the exterior and towards inclusion. He arrives on the stage coming from abroad (probably from Athens); he immediately starts sending people on and off the stage, and thus, he sets in motion a series of events that alter the normal order of exits. His movement affects everyone concerned with a force that seeks to include also the space occupied by Knemon. Both these two movements, that of Sostratos and that of Knemon, are, nonetheless, extreme and need to be modified

7 "Menander rations out the effects that the *dyscolos* can produce as the play develops a set of situations to which he must respond. Sostratos' romance, the sacrifice to Pan, and the lost pot are separate events welded into the plot by the cumulative challenge that they make to Knemon and each situation is enacted by a different set of characters" (Goldberg 1980, p. 74).

to bring them to a more moderate form of action. Thus, Knemon and Sostratos represent two different, but equally extreme, versions of the same defect: they embody the kind of character that results from lack of ethical development and significant human relationships. I will now give an outline of their characters trying to explain how I see their complementary traits operating in the drama.

Pan[8] himself, in his prologue, describes Knemon as an inhuman figure (ἀπάνθρωπος),[9] one that is completely opposite to the idea of humanity that the members of the audience share:[10] he has a wife but she left him because of his bad character and he now refuses to talk to her in the same way that he refuses to talk to his neighbours. He does not address a word or a greeting to anyone and he insists on living alone inside his house and fields.[11] In this way, Knemon positions himself apart from social conventions represented here by marriage or the simple act of greeting people. The audience immediately has the impression that there is nothing natural in how he is behaving and in where he is living:

> The play begins with Pan's description of the barren landscape of Phyle, where men are forced to work rocks rather than soil, and of Knemon's fragmented household [...]. The sterility of Knemon's land and house is depicted as the outgrowth of his character: Knemon's misanthropic dream of seceding from social relations leads to an obsessive concern with physical boundaries.[12]

His behaviour is painful for his daughter, who is kept away from normal social interactions, and also for the other characters whose projects are blocked by Knemon's misanthropic disposition.[13] Knemon wishes to spare his daughter from any sort of human interaction and he does not want her to be married to anyone except someone equal to him in character;[14] he also wishes that everyone would share his isolated way of living. This attitude is visually stressed

---

8 See Chapter 4, pp. 128–129 for a more detailed discussion of Pan's prologue.

9 It is important to stress that Knemon is respectful towards Pan and the Nymphs (Men. *Dysc.* 2–4; 10–12): his being inhuman, therefore, applies mainly to his relationship with other human beings.

10 Men. *Dysc.* 5–8.

11 Men. *Dysc.* 8–12.

12 Lape 2004, p. 134. See also Kantzios 2010 that interpret Knemon's character as an alter ego of the classical representation of Pan himself (see p. 128 n. 84).

13 Men. *Dysc.* 103–116.

14 Men. *Dysc.* 321–336.

by his stubborn attempt to stay inside his property and to protect it and his daughter from any external intrusion.[15] Knemon's behaviour is anti-social not only in the sense that he hates the very sight of other people but also that, by his attitude, he blocks the growth and proliferation of society itself. His daughter will never be married; she will never give birth to legitimate citizens and, when Knemon dies, she will be left without a proper guardian: Knemon's land will gradually be less productive as his old age will prevent the effective farming of his property and no one will inherit it to make it flourishing again.[16]

Knemon also refuses to establish any sort of business contract (συμβόλαιον) with other people or any form of informal friendly agreement: when the slave Getas knocks at his door to ask for a small brazier for the sacrifice that Sostratos' mother wants to celebrate close to Knemon's house, Knemon is surprised that someone would ask him for something by calling at his house. He asks Getas if there is any contract that binds them (ἐμοὶ γάρ ἐστι συμβόλαιον, ἀνόσιε, καὶ σοί τι;)[17] and that would explain Getas' presence at his front-door. Getas, in his turn, thinks that Knemon is asking for a formal contract that can officially testify the lending of the brazier and he is surprised by Knemon's question.[18] In any case, Knemon refuses to be involved in the exchange. This is particularly significant as we know that loans of this kind were considered common practice among fellow citizens or neighbours.[19] Moreover, in this specific case, Getas asks

---

15 Men. *Dysc.* 160–172.

16 See Paoli 1961; Harrison 1968 and Martina 1979 on the legal aspects of the play. "The question is not only that the girl cannot leave the house and no one else can come in; she is also not allowed to grow up—there is a kind of timelessness in Knemon's house. [...] Knemon is in effect seeking stasis, not just solitude, and like a folk-tale villain, he deprives his daughter of her rightful transition towards adulthood" (Traill 2008, p. 51).

17 Men. *Dysc.* 469–470.

18 Men. *Dysc.* 466–480. "The question [about the existence of a contract] represents in Knemon's mind the only reason why anyone should wish to approach him. The old man probably intends it in a wide non-specific sense, though Getas' reply, with its mention of witnesses, shows he interprets the question more narrowly and overlaid with financial implications" (Ireland 1995, ad loc.).

19 "Knemon thinks that a *sumbolaion* (contract) exists for this loan, which was the case only in a very specific kind of debt. *Sumbolaia* were drawn up only in instances of professional money-lending [...] in a civic context, loans were much more frequently given on a voluntary basis or reciprocally between neighbours. In these cases no contract was written and their return was based on trust" (von Reden 1998, p. 264; see also Millett 1991 for a broader discussion of this topic). According to von Reden it is this kind of reciprocity that Menander is promoting in this play. On the development of the concept of 'reciprocity' from archaic Greece to the formation of the *polis* see Seaford 1994.

Knemon for the loan of a small brazier in order to celebrate a sacrifice to Pan, a god.[20] But Knemon refuses to become involved with what is going on just outside his door and he does not understand the reason why he has been asked to be involved, or, probably, the reason why people would need a brazier for a sacrifice.[21] Getas, on the other hand, does not understand why Knemon gets so upset at his request. The two characters clearly lack a common ground of understanding; they almost speak different languages, and the scene sets this out very clearly, playing on their mutual misunderstanding. Finally, Knemon manages to send Getas away empty handed and, in doing so, he adds that he does not want anyone else to think that he is a friend, a *philos*: he makes clear that he is different from other people and that he does not want to be involved in any kind of intercourse that is normal for human beings.

> Κν: ἀνδροφόνα θηρί'· εὐθὺς ὥσπερ πρὸς φίλον
> κόπτουσιν.

> KNEMON: Murderous beasts! They knock at the door straightway as at a friend['s door].[22]

Knemon's seclusion from others is presented on the stage by a movement pointed towards the interior of his house and his property where his life is centred. This kind of movement is in sharp contrast with the sudden entrance of Sostratos, Pyrrhias and Chaireas, the young man and his attendants, that appear on stage immediately after Pan's prologue. These three characters introduce a movement that points outward from Knemon's house: in fact, they wish to take the girl out of Knemon's custody and, by joining her in marriage with Sostratos, to restore her to the context of human relationships from which she has been abstracted by her father.[23] It is clear, in fact, that the isolation into

---

20 This is not because Knemon does not respect Pan: his refusal to lend the brazier necessary for the sacrifice is based on "his minimalist approach to life" (Wilkins 2000, p. 414). See n. 21 here below.

21 Handley notes that Knemon seems to have a shocked reaction to the word 'λεβήτιον' (brazier) that Getas just pronounced to formulate his request (Men. *Dysc.* 473–474): "There is nothing extraordinary with the word λεβήτιον or in the request: what shocks Knemon is the thought of having enough meat to need a stew-pot" (Handley 1965, ad loc.).

22 Men. *Dysc.* 481–482.

23 "Marriage in classical Athens was not a wholly personal matter; it was also part of the nexus of social relations that bound into a community the discrete citizens' household of which the city state was constituted" (Konstan 1995, p. 95).

which Knemon has forced himself did not benefit him, his daughter or his property. His progressive isolation from the outside world has been responsible for what he is now and how he lives. He himself confesses all this after Gorgias, his step-son, has saved him from the dangerous accident in which he falls into a well.

> **Κν:** οὐδ' ἂν εἷς δύναιτό με
> τοῦτο μεταπεῖσαί τις ὑμῶν, ἀλλὰ συγχωρήσετε.
> ἓν δ' ἴσως ἥμαρτον ὅστις τῶν ἁπάντων ᾠόμην
> αὐτὸς αὐτάρκης τις εἶναι καὶ δεήσεσθ' οὐδενός.
> νῦν δ' ἰδὼν ὀξεῖαν οὖσαν ἄσκοπόν τε τοῦ βίου
> τὴν τελευτήν, εὗρον οὐκ εὖ τοῦτο γινώσκων τότε.
> δεῖ γὰρ εἶναι—καὶ παρεῖναι—τὸν ἐπικουρήσοντ' ἀεί.
> ἀλλὰ μὰ τὸν Ἥφαιστον—οὕτω σφόδρα ⟨δι⟩εφθάρμην ἐγὼ
> τοὺς βίους ὁρῶν ἑκάστους τοὺς λογισμούς ⟨θ'⟩ ὃν τρόπον
> πρὸς τὸ κερδαίνειν ἔχουσιν—οὐδέν' εὔνουν ᾠόμην
> ἕτερον ἑτέρωι τῶν ἁπάντων ἂν γενέσθαι. τοῦτο δὴ
> ἐμποδὼν ἦν μοι. μόλις δὲ πεῖραν εἷς δέδωκε νῦν
> Γοργίας, ἔργον ποήσας ἀνδρὸς εὐγενεστάτου·

> KNEMON: No one could change my mind on this, but you will agree. Perhaps I was wrong about one thing, the fact that I thought myself to be, alone among all, self-sufficient and that I did not need anyone. Now, having seen the end of life, being so quick and unexpected, I found that I was not getting it right then. There is always a need for someone to be—and to be there—who will take care [of you]. But, by Hephaestus! I had been really misled by looking at everyone's life and their calculations, how they are disposed towards making profit, I have never thought that there was someone, among all, that was well-disposed towards another. That was the obstacle for me. Gorgias, alone, has given me the proof, performing an act [worth] of a noble man.[24]

Knemon wanted to be self-sustaining but he did not realise that the way in which he was actually leading his self-sufficient life was harmful to himself, his possessions and others.[25] The value that the old man has attributed to his

---

24 Men. *Dysc.* 711–723.

25 See Gomme and Sandbach 1973, p. 245 who note that, according to Arist. *EN* I 5, 1097b8–11, the one who is self-sufficient (αὐτάρκης) is not the one who can provide just for himself,

self-sufficiency has been absolute: Knemon wished to be self-sufficient from an economical, reproductive and ethical standpoint.[26] He was determined to live and work his field alone, reducing his household, his *oikos*, to a minimum and to avoid establishing any sort of contract with other people outside it, what we can call 'economical self-sufficiency'. With respect to his own family, he did not want his daughter to marry and produce heirs: he did not care about expanding his *oikos* and, therefore, contributing to the proliferation of the community. He was content with being on his own, what we can call 'reproductive self-sufficiency'. Finally, Knemon thought that he was the only one who was right: he considered that, by himself, he could provide what was needed for his ethical development. He thought that other people just offered a bad example or, even worse, they spoiled his virtuous, solitary way of life, what we can call 'ethical self-sufficiency'. The play shows that this way of thinking is not the right one. As Knemon himself says, he understands now that he did not get things right.[27]

From this specific point of view, we might say that Knemon shares some traits with another Menandrian character, Smikrines, in the *Aspis*. As discussed in Chapter 4, Smikrines is described as a greedy old man and, like Knemon, his attitude is self-centred and this poses a danger for his community of *philoi*. In fact, he tries to take his relatives' possessions and Kleostratos' war chest for himself. He also tries to disrupt, rather inappropriately, his family's reproductive life, as he, an old man, wants to marry his young niece who is already promised to a more suitable young man. He does this because he reasons from his own particular perspective and he does not consider that of his *philoi*. Moreover, no one has yet demonstrated to him that his nature is defective. The slave Daos will be the one who will show the real character of the old man, and what is wrong with it, to everyone, perhaps, also to Smikrines himself. Daos will demonstrate this by engineering a plan with the intention of bringing out a specific aspect of Smikrines's character: his greed and wickedness.[28] Unfortunately, we do not possess the end of the comedy and we do not know whether Smikrines, seeing clearly his mistakes and his actions from the others' perspective, actually acknowledges his wrondoing and makes progress in his ethical understanding

---

living alone, but also for his family and friends. It is clear that the meaning that Knemon gives here to this word is different.

26 I thank Richard Seaford for sharing with me his thoughts on this subject and pointing out to me these distinctions.

27 See Anderson 1970, p. 215 who makes of the *Dyscolos* a "complex ethical comedy" exactly because, after having made a mistake, Knemon recognises what he did wrong.

28 Refer to Chapter 4, section 1.2.2 for a more detailed discussion of these points.

as Knemon does here. However, we can trace in his character a particular trait that we also find in Knemon and that is shown, in both cases, to be a problem: namely, the fact that he thinks and acts considering only his own point of view and he excludes an interest in the other people around him.

Returning to Knemon, after the accident, the old man admits he was reluctant to open himself up to the external world because he believed that all human beings were corrupt by nature. The experience of the accident has shown him that at least one human being, Gorgias, was not like this, and that people might actually care for him sincerely. The accident is a further element that forms a contrast to Knemon's stubborn resolution to stay inside his boundaries: falling into the well has forced him to ask for external help and this accident has taught him something.[29] When Knemon, under compulsion, steps outside his seclusion, he seems to change his mind about the external world and the rightness of his isolation, but this change of mind is only apparent because he does not wish to change his way of life. Pan's prologue suggests to the audience the reason for this: Knemon is an old man and he has lived in isolation for a long time. He has refused to be acquainted with anyone but himself, which means that he did not share with anyone the knowledge he had of himself, his choices and his dispositions. He wished to remain as he was and refused to listen to what others had to say about this; consequently, he got used to this condition and what had begun just as an inclination became transformed into a permanent disposition. This is why, despite his bad accident and the lesson he learned from it, he declares that he wants to go back again inside his house and he still refuses to be involved in any kind of social intercourse. Accordingly, he entrusts his daughter to his step-son Gorgias in order to avoid dealing with others in the attempt to find her a husband.[30] Marriage represents a further movement outwards that he does not wish to undertake at present for his daughter in the same way as he did not in the past for himself.

29 "His [Knemon's] dislike for people is the product of the way the world is, a noisy and thoughtless world from which he prefers to try to live in exile. But even Knemon is not an island, as the play proceeds to demonstrate; nor is it fair to require the others to share an obsession" (Arnott and Walton 1996, p. 101).

30 "In explaining and amending his character, his speech integrates the variant perspectives presented by the others [...]. He therefore proposes the changes that make possible the play's happy resolution, but they have a curious limitation of their own. Knemon's acknowledgement of social responsibility is immediately followed by his delegation of it. He explicitly wishes to continue living his own way, and his reason for adopting Gorgias is to avoid the social intercourse otherwise necessary to secure his daughter's fortune" (Goldberg 1980, p. 86).

> Κν: ποοῦμαί σ' ὑόν, ἅ τ' ἔχων τυγχάνω
> πάντα σαυτοῦ νόμισον εἶναι. τήνδε σοι παρεγγυῶ·
> ἄνδρα δ' αὐτῆι πόρισον. εἰ γὰρ καὶ σφόδρ' ὑγιαίνοιμ' ἐγώ,
> αὐτὸς οὐ δυνήσομ' εὑρεῖν· οὐ γὰρ ἀρέσει μοί ποτε
> οὐδὲ εἷς.
>
> KNEMON: I make you my son, consider all the things I happen to have as yours. I entrust her [my daughter] to you. Provide her with a husband. Even if I made a complete recovery, I will not be capable of finding [him] by myself. No one will ever please me.[31]

This is also why, at the end of the comedy, Knemon is determined not to join the others in the celebration of the double wedding. To expose himself to other people, to engage with the outside world, is not something in which he is interested because it is something he is not used to. On the other hand, the fact that he decides to adopt Gorgias is a considerable step in the direction of human conventions and a step away from his isolation.

> His action in adopting Gorgias as his son and thereby providing for the future of his own family, shows simply and directly that the misanthrope has made a major concession to humanity: his doing what an equitable man would have been expected to do in similar circumstances. He has no son of his own, indeed no close or trusted relations [...] if he dies without meeting satisfactory arrangements for their future, his death will leave his daughter without a guardian and the estate without a master.[32]

At the moment of the final wedding celebration, however, Knemon wants to remain inside the house: Getas and Sikon, two slaves, need to force him outside his house while he is alone peacefully resting.[33] Knemon is now part of an extended family, and his bad misanthropic attitude needs to be corrected or he will continue to be harmful to everyone.[34] He has to recognise his obligation towards his new family as he recognised his obligation towards his daughter and the legal system of the *polis* as a whole when he adopted Gorgias.[35]

---

31 Men. *Dysc.* 731–733.

32 Handley 1965, p. 257.

33 On the different roles of slaves in Menander's *Dyscolos* see Konstan 2013.

34 "Knemon's resistance to commensality is the ultimate step too far in ancient Greece. He must be forced back into 'civilized' life by Sikon the cook" (Wilkins 2000, p. 412).

35 See Patterson 1998, esp. pp. 177–211 for more extended discussion about the type of society

> **Γε**: θόρυβός ἐστιν ἔνδον,
> πίνουσιν. οὐκ αἰσθήσετ' οὐδείς. τὸ δ' ὅλον ἐστὶν ἡμῖν
> ἄνθρωπος ἡμερωτέος· κηδεύομεν γὰρ αὐτῶι,
> οἰκεῖος ἡμῖν γίνετ'· εἰ δ' ἔσται τοιοῦτος αἰεί,
> ἔργον ὑπενεγκεῖν.
>
> GETAS: There is a lot of chaos inside, they are drinking, no one will realise. It is completely up to us to civilise this man. Now that we make of him a kinsman by marriage, he has become part of the family. If he will be forever as he is, [it would be] an effort to endure him.[36]

The two slaves take Knemon violently outside and literally push him into joining the others. This final scene brings to an end the forced inclusion of Knemon in the community[37] and completes the many attempts to move Knemon from inside his house to the outside world. It is clear that, at Knemon's age, some sort of change in his way of life can only be produced by a violent and compelling event, and not by a patient and constant education of his inclinations. Having developed a bad disposition for a long time, Knemon has acquired a consistently misanthropic character. Now that he has experienced the world outside his isolation, having being forced into it by the accident, his daughter's marriage and the two slaves, he has also understood that his behaviour with respect to the others was wrong, but his disposition has now grown too fixed to change suddenly at the end of the comedy. We might conclude that, to some extent, he has changed his mind and his beliefs about other people; however, his emotional disposition of distrust with regards to the outer world is harder to change. For this reason, he needs to be forced by the two slaves in order to offer the audience a happy ending in which his change of mind is also reflected in a (forced) change of attitude towards the others.

Sostratos' character is sharply contrasted to that of Knemon. As Knemon is closed to every sort of experience, Sostratos is indiscriminately open to all of them. He falls in love with Knemon's daughter as soon as he sees her and he immediately resolves to ask her in marriage.[38] Chaireas, a parasite, suggests

---

promoted by the *Dyscolos*. Patterson also links this kind of ideology to the one promoted by Aristotle in the *Politics*. See also Préaux 1957 and Ramage 1966.

36 Men. *Dysc.* 901–904. See Lape 2004, p. 136.

37 For further discussion on the theme of inclusion in *Dyscolos* see von Reden 1998 and Lape 2004, pp. 124–136.

38 It is true that Pan claims that he aroused in Sostratos love for the girl; however, as the plot will reveal, Pan's intervention seems to be directed towards someone who is already

seeking information about the girl and waiting until they know her identity and status for certain. Sostratos declares that he has no intention of doing this, and, he adds, he has already sent a slave to ask the father of the girl for a meeting.[39] Sostratos agrees that sending Pyrrhias, a slave, to talk with the girl's father, was a mistake, but he realises this only after having rushed to send him to knock at Knemon's door. In fact, he admits, the strong love he felt for the girl made impossible any reasonable attempt to reflect on the situation.

> Σω: ἥμαρτον·[40] οὐ γὰρ οἰκέτηι
> ἥρμοττ' ἴσως τὸ τοιοῦτ⟨ό γ'⟩. ἀλλ' οὐ ῥάιδιον
> ἐρῶντα συνιδεῖν ἐστι τί ποτε συμφέρει.
>
> SOSTRATOS: I made a mistake, maybe an act like this was not suitable for a servant. But it is not easy to consider how to behave appropriately when one is in love.[41]

Sostratos' behaviour here mirrors that of Moschion in the *Samia*: the two of them represent two young men whose fresh and lively desires have not yet been trained to take on a consistent, more measured, emotional disposition. Their emotions and desires tend to get exclusive control of their reasoning and lead their actions towards the achievement of the desired target.[42] However, when the *Samia* begins, Moschion has already reflected on his actions; he has understood what he did wrong, he is ashamed and he is determined to make amends for his mistake.[43] In the *Dyscolos*, instead, we follow the various stages of Sostratos' increasing self-awareness and we are able to see how his character and his understanding develop.

When we first see Sostratos on stage we acknowledge that emotions unleashed at the sight of Knemon's daughter have hindered correct reasoning in the mind of the inexperienced, young townsman, whose only objective in visiting Phyle was to enjoy the delight of free time as his age and status enabled

---

predisposed to be driven by sudden overwhelming desires. Compare Chapter 4, section 1.3.

39 Men. *Dysc.* 50–71.

40 "Sostratos realises that he might have been tactless [...]; here, as later [cf. 522–545], he is conscious of his own situation, and capable of seeing himself as other might see him" (Handley 1965, ad loc).

41 Men. *Dysc.* 75–77. See Chapter 4, pp. 128–129 about the role of Pan in this process.

42 See Chapter 3, section 2.2 for further discussion on this topic.

43 Men. *Sam.* 1–56.

him to. After these events, in Act Two, we witness Sostratos' meeting with Gorgias, Knemon's step-son. After having been reassured about Sostratos' good intention towards the girl, Gorgias explains clearly to him the challenge of the situation. Sostratos cannot hope to win Knemon's trust and the girl with his current attitude: his aspect and behaviour need somehow to change.

> Γο: οὐ πρόφασιν εἰπὼν βούλομ' ἀποπέμψαι κενήν,
> τὰ δ' ὄντα πράγματ' ἐμφανίσαι. ταύτηι πατήρ
> ἐσθ' οἷος οὐδεὶς γέγονεν οὔτε τῶν πάλαι
> ἄνθρωπος οὔτε τῶν καθ' ἡμᾶς.
> [...]
> Γο: λόγον τιν' ἐμβαλῶ
> περὶ τοῦ] γάμου ⟨τοῦ⟩ τῆς κόρης· τὸ τοιοῦτο γὰρ
> ἴδοιμι κἂ]ν αὐτὸς γενόμενον ἄσμενος.
> εὐθὺς μαχεῖται πᾶσι, λοιδορούμενος
> εἰς τοὺς βίους οὓς ζῶσι· σὲ δ' [ἄγοντ' ἂν] ἴδηι
> σχολὴν τρυφῶντά τ', οὐδ' ὁρῶν γ' ἀνέξεται.

> GORGIAS: I don't want to send you away with empty excuses, but to show you how things are. The father of that girl is like no other man that has existed in the past or at present.[44]
> [...]
> I will bring up the topic ⟨of⟩ the girl's marriage. I would be glad myself to see that happening. He will fight right away with everyone, reproaching them for the life they live: [if] he sees you [leading] your life in leisure and luxury, he will not stand the very sight of you.[45]

Gorgias invites Sostratos to find with him a more appropriate way to ask for his step-sister in marriage. In order to achieve his aim, Sostratos has to prove his own strength: he has to mask his status as an aristocratic citizen and work with Gorgias on the fields so that, having the appearance of a farmer, he might have some hope of being accepted by Knemon. Sostratos taking up the challenge, accepts Gorgias' suggestion and starts working. In the event, Knemon's accident will eventually simplify the whole situation as Knemon will entrust his daughter to Gorgias and in this way Sostratos will obtain the object of his desires without difficulties.

---

44 Men. *Dysc.* 322–325.

45 Men. *Dysc.* 352–357.

This achievement makes him immediately confident enough to handle the whole situation: in fact, he suggests that Gorgias should marry his sister and he starts organising the double wedding.[46] To persuade his father, Kallippides, of the suitability of this marriage, Sostratos repeats some of the points that Knemon brought out during the monologue following his accident. He talks to his father about the importance of sharing his wealth with others. In particular, Sostratos says that Kallippides must dispose of his property to benefit other people, not only as an act of disinterested generosity, but in order to create with them a relationship of reciprocal interest. If Kallippides does now, or will do in the future, generous acts such as the one that Sostratos is now asking him to perform, then he will always have around him people who care for him and help him in moment of distress.[47] Sostratos' argument seems to be filled with genuine awareness of the ideas that he is expressing. However, Kallippides' abrupt reply quickly dissolves the appearance that Sostratos is offering serious and considered opinions:[48] Sostratos should know that his father is a generous man and he agrees with everything that his son has just said, there is no need to offer these clichés (τί μοι λέγεις γνώμας;).[49] Thus, at the end of the play, we realise that, despite the fact that Sostratos has proved himself able to perform hard work and, more generally, to confront the challenges of a difficult situation, his inclination to get excited quickly at the prospect of what he desires seems not to have left him.[50] We observe him taking up a new confident self with the same speed with which he took up, at the beginning, the role of the young man in love and sent hastly Pyrrhias to meet Knemon. We have the impression that Sostratos' youth, and also his wealthy upbringing, have not allowed him to engage, until now, in significant relationships that could potentially correct his attitude and change his beliefs about himself and about the world. It is only when Sostratos leaves his usual environment that he discovers something new: he is able to face the situation because Gorgias

46 Men. *Dysc.* 791–818.

47 Men. *Dysc.* 808–810. The points mentioned by Sostratos were rather conventional in the context of Athenian society, see Fantham 1977, pp. 412–413.

48 See also Arnott 1964, p. 113 and, by contrast, Post 1960 who makes of Sostratos the flawless hero of the play.

49 Men. *Dysc.* 813–818.

50 "His [Sostratos'] newly won maturity is soon undercut by an imminent boast [Men. *Dysc.* 862]. The resulting irony of Sostratos' self congratulation preserves his comic image. Unlike Charisios of the *Epitrepontes* and unlike [...] Moschion of the *Samia*, the conclusion does not bring Sostratos the self-knowledge that will foster true sympathy for him. He still understands less about his affairs than we do, and that extra knowledge continues the distance between him and us" (Goldberg 1980, p. 88).

helps him to see clearly what he needs to do, thus inducing him to meet the challenge of a totally new experience, that of working in the fields as a farmer. The way in which Menander characterises Sostratos is that of a young man who, at the end of the play, appears dependent on the suggestions and help of other people. He has, perhaps, understood what he did wrong and how, in future, he should control his impetuous character in dealing with other people. However, at the end of the play, Menander shows us that all he can do is to talk to his father repeating sentences that he does not seem to understand fully and that are not reflected in his actual life experience. As Kallippides points out to him, Sostratos should know that his father already believes in the principles of generosity and benevolence that his son has just listed to him and, allegedly, they are the same principles on the basis of which Sostratos has been raised. However, the young man offers them now to make up a misplaced argument to convince his father of values that he already holds.

In any case, Sostratos has learned something. Like Knemon, Sostratos tackles a new way of understanding as soon as he changes his usual way of life, namely, when he moves out of Athens to go hunting in the countryside. This movement outwards is accentuated further as, pushed by the unexpected compulsion of love, he abandons his usual civic lifestyle and he assumes the appearance of a farmer. Like Knemon, he does not show a complete change of character at the end of the play; he is still an impetuous young man and his inclination needs to be properly educated. However, by contrast with Knemon, we are left with the impression that his youth and his friendship with Gorgias will somehow make possible the emergence of a good character. What is finally suggested by the *Dyscolos* is that to live and share experiences and values with others is good. On the other hand, to live alone and persist in one's own way of life, avoiding significant interpersonal relationships, is bad because one risks lacking understanding of the right way to live. Knemon was not happy while he lived alone but we have the impression that now he has at least learned something from his bad experience. His natural tendency to mistrust the outer world is maybe grown too inveterate to change radically now, but, for the sake of the happy ending, his actions can be (literally) forced to match his renewed beliefs at least about the members of his family.

1.2 *Other Examples of Young Men and Old Men*

The theme suggested by the *Dyscolos*, the old misanthrope, living in isolation and distrustful with respect to the outer world is a topic of particular interest for drama not only in Greece.[51] "The misanthrope is not only merely different

51 See Konstan 1983.

from other men; he judges them [...]. He perceives himself as the representative of a social ideal that others have betrayed, and condemns his fellow for their perversity and hypocrisy" and this makes of him an easy target of comic humour.[52] Examples of misanthropes appear also in Middle Comedy such as the work of Mnesimachos, who wrote a play called *Dyscolos*, and of Ophelion and Anaxilas, who both wrote plays called *Monotropos*, and Antiphanes, author of a play called *Misoponeros*.[53] However, we do not have enough evidence to draw detailed comparisons with these plays or to suggest any possible link to Menander's own work. What we can suggest is that the idea of the mature man, living in isolation (in the real or figurative sense) or deaf to others' suggestions, especially those coming from younger people, can be traced back to fifth-century Attic tragedy and Old comedy. For instance, the dialogue between Gorgias and Knemon, after the Knemon incident, might suggest a parallel with Aristophanes' *Wasps* and Sophocles' *Antigone* in a way that I will explain shortly. This comparison is not meant to identify the difference, in general, between Menander, Sophocles and Aristophanes, but rather to stress what is specific in Menander's treatment of character by comparing a particular episode in the *Dyscolos* with two dramatic examples that, on the face of it, present the same pattern. Despite these apparent analogies, I believe that what makes the case of the *Dyscolos* distinctive is the way in which Menander constructs his characters and explains their motivations for action. Moreover, as I have mentioned before, in the *Dyscolos*, the figure of the old misanthrope, Knemon, is characterised also by contrast to the figure of the young man, Sostratos who, at the same time, undergoes a very similar process of increasing self-awareness and self-understanding. The *Dyscolos* is, therefore, not only the story of an old misanthrope but also analyses the interaction among various characters and their process of character-formation. That is to say, although Menander may be addressing here a literary *topos* that others have explored before him, he does so in an interestingly original way.

After Knemon has been rescued from the well, Gorgias, his step-son, reproaches him for the fact that he has confined himself in isolation (ἐρημία)[54] and that he stood apart from the other people's help and support. Knemon

52 Konstan 1983, p. 97.

53 Ireland 1995, p. 14. The figure of Timon of Athens probably inspired this kind of literature and the general reflection on the topic of misanthropy: for a survey about the historical and literary relevance of Timon of Athens see Armstrong 1987.

54 Men. *Dysc.* 694.

affirms that, having seen the result of his choices, he recognises now that the way in which he was living before was not right.[55] Despite the fact that he now seems to have understood his mistakes, the play shows that he cannot completely change his attitudes towards others all of a sudden. However, he makes a step towards a more humane way of acting and allows a double marriage to take place. In the *Antigone*, we find another confrontation between a father and a son (the dialogue between Creon and Haemon) in which Haemon tries to persuade Creon to change his mind about his decisions. Haemon approaches his father in the hope of persuading him to release Antigone from the charge of having disobeyed the civic laws by her decision to honour the corpse of her brother Polyneices. Haemon fails in his attempt as Creon persists in his decision of punishing Antigone, who is his sister's daughter and his son's intended wife, with death. The stubborn determination of a key figure is a recurrent theme in the construction of Sophoclean characters: in the same play, for instance, we find the same feature in Antigone herself.[56] It seems, in fact, to be a common trait of Sophoclean heroes (or, more generally, tragic characters) to follow exclusively what their own usual way of thinking suggests, and not to adopt someone else's *ēthos*.[57] But the reason why I have chosen to focus on Creon's particular case is that this aspect of his character comes out explicitly in his dialogue with his son, Haemon, who points out with sound arguments what Creon's problem is. The nature of this confrontation invites a comparison with the *Dyscolos*: in both plays, we have two stubborn fathers and two sensible sons who point out to their respective parents a more sound way of doing

55 Men. *Dysc.* 713–716.

56 "In both Creon and Antigone the deepest motive for action is individual, particular, inexplicable in any other terms than personal" (Knox 1964, p. 110), Knox describes their behaviour as typical of Sophoclean characters' *heroic temper*. "The Sophoclean hero acts in a terrifying vacuum, [...] an isolation in time and space which imposes on the hero full responsibility for his own action and its consequences", that kind of hero is "one who makes a decision which springs from the deepest layer of his individual nature, his *physis* and that blindly, ferociously, heroically, maintains that decision even at the point of self-destruction" (*ibidem*, p. 5). On the character of Creon, see also Winnington-Ingram 1980, especially, pp. 126–127. Cf. also Iversen 1998, chapter 6 who argues that the *Dyscolos* is Menander's response to the isolated, self-determined, unyielding type of the "heroic temper" represented in tragedies. As such he is the bloking character who represents the presence of tragedy within the play and, as such, is overthrown, mocked, and forcibly brought back into society against his will for the good of himself and his *oikos*.

57 In tragedies, people "do not sleep" on their decisions (E. Hall, 'Greek tragedy, the Sun and the Unity of Time', Jackson Knight Memorial Lecture, 16 June 2010, University of Exeter, Exeter, UK).

things. For these reasons, I believe that a comparison between the confrontation between Creon and Haemon, in the *Antigone*, and between Knemon and Gorgias, in the *Dyscolos*, will bring out more clearly possible analogies and differences that will help the understanding of Menander's specific point of view on these matters.

At the beginning of their exchange, Haemon tells his father that he has come to speak to him in Creon's best interest. Haemon wishes his father to consider other people's opinion, in particular, his son's opinion and that of the citizens of his own city.[58] Haemon adds that to listen to other people's views will help Creon to achieve a more measured attitude and to make better decisions. Haemon suggests to his father that he should to try 'wear' a way of thinking that is different from the one he is used to.

> Αι: Μή νυν ἓν ἦθος μοῦνον ἐν σαυτῷ φόρει,
> ὡς φῂς σύ, κοὐδὲν ἄλλο, τοῦτ' ὀρθῶς ἔχειν·
> ὅστις γὰρ αὐτὸς ἢ φρονεῖν μόνος δοκεῖ,
> ἢ γλῶσσαν ἣν οὐκ ἄλλος ἢ ψυχὴν ἔχειν,
> οὗτοι διαπτυχθέντες ὤφθησαν κενοί.
> Ἀλλ' ἄνδρα, κεἴ τις ᾖ σοφός, τὸ μανθάνειν
> πόλλ' αἰσχρὸν οὐδὲν καὶ τὸ μὴ τείνειν ἄγαν.

> HAEMON: Do not, then, bear constantly only one way of thinking in your heart, just as what you say, and nothing else, is right. For whoever thinks that he alone is right, or that he has such powers of speech and thoughts as no one else has, such people, when exposed, are always shown empty. But even if a man is wise, it is no shame for him to learn much and not to be over rigid.[59]

Creon refuses to take his son's suggestion, asserting that he is a mature man and is also the king and, therefore, he does not need to be taught by younger people (726–727) or be instructed by his own citizens (734). Creon's response shows that he has a problem that is very similar to that of Knemon: he does not believe that other people can provide him with any sort of suggestion

58 S. *Ant.* 688–711.

59 S. *Ant.* 705–711. Translation by Brown 1987 (modified). Griffith takes these lines as referring to Theognis 215–218 and he reads Haemon's speech as "Greek moralistic debate whether men should maintain a pure and consistent character or [...] should be adaptable, and resourceful in self-preservation" (Griffith 1999 ad loc.).

or help.[60] In his turn, Haemon makes against his father the same reproaches that Gorgias makes against the old grouch; Creon has enclosed himself in a deaf and sterile isolation, as Haemon rightly points out to him when he states: "you would do well as a monarch of a desert (Καλῶς ἐρήμης γ' ἂν σὺ γῆς ἄρχοις μόνος)".[61] Because of this resolution, Creon is going against his better interest and is making mistakes. What Creon and Knemon need to do is to open their mind and experience other ways of thinking and behaving so to allow other people to help them for the sake of mutual care and interest.[62]

This point bears another observation: the other feature that characterises both Knemon and Creon is that they struggle to recognise the obligations that they have with respect to their *philoi*, in particular, relatives, and the mutual obligations that this relationship implies.[63] Creon fails to understand that Haemon, as a *philos*, is speaking in Creon's best interest and that his interest also coincides with his son's.[64] Moreover, Creon fails to recognise that he has an obligation towards Polyneices and Antigone as *philoi*: he does not realise the mutual relationship that ties him to them beyond the bounds of the political institution.[65] He only sees them as enemies of his *polis* and, as a consequence, he needs to punish them for the sake of public order.

Despite Haemon's words, Creon's way of thinking does not change until the end of the tragedy and, because of his stubborn insistence on doing what he believes to be right, he fails to understand that what he is doing may be wrong or to appreciate the possible consequences of his actions. On the other hand, Knemon makes possible the comedy's happy ending because he understands his mistake and so he is enabled to see more clearly his actions through the eyes of other people. Knemon has also understood that these other people sincerely

60 In the case of Creon, this is a recurrent attribute of tyrants in Greek tragedy; see Seaford 2003, pp. 104–105.

61 S. *Ant.* 739. Creon and Haemon lack a common ground of understanding: "Creon calls Haemon's speech whining and slavish entreaty for a woman (756)". Haemon notes that his father's speech is full of youthful violence (735). "Confusion in the hierarchy of language parallels confusion in the hierarchy of generations. Language and family are interwoven with politics in the increasing questionable order of Creon's city" (Segal 1981, pp. 164).

62 "Unlike Creon, he [Haemon] understands that *philia* means caring for another for that person's own sake" (Blundell 1989, p. 121).

63 This is another feature of tragic tyrants (see Seaford 2003, pp. 105–106). See Goldhill 1986(a), p. 82; Blundell 1989, pp. 119–121 and Belfiore 2000, p. 143 on the theme of *philia* and its violation in relation to the *Antigone* and, in particular, to the characterisation of Creon.

64 S. *Ant.* 701–704.

65 Goldhill 1986(a), p. 82.

care about him and that they are asking him to show some reciprocal interest in them for the sake of each one's happiness. Even if Knemon, at the end of the play, does not completely change and his inclinations cannot be totally shaped by his new beliefs about the outer word, he develops to some extent and he achieves an understanding that we do not see equally developed in Creon's case. These differences reflect, to a large extent, the obvious difference in genre between the two dramatic works: it is clear that Knemon should make some adjustments to his character in order to make the characteristic comic happy ending possible. However, I think that the differences between the two plays go beyond the difference between tragedy and comedy and reflect certain distinctive features of Menander's dramaturgy.

In the *Antigone*, we see the tragedy brought about by the stubborn determination of two characters, Antigone and Creon, both advancing their own specific claims and both inflexibly committed to the bodies of laws and values in which they believe. The speech between Creon and Haemon has the function of showing more clearly Creon's unyielding determination and the fact that his ideas on the matter are not open to change. In the *Dyscolos*, in partial contrast, we find the divergent (and yet in some ways parallel) presentation of two developing characters, of the way they make choices and, finally, their growing understanding. The exchange between Gorgias and Knemon is a crucial point in this process: it identifies clearly the problems in Knemon's character and it produces some sort of development in Knemon's ethical understanding. This is one of the main focuses of Menander's play, which, significantly, is named *Dyscolos* after Knemon's character. Thus, the comparison with the *Antigone* helps to stress further that for Menander, character (understood in an Aristotelian sense) stands very much as the centre of interest in his dramas.

The other example I wish to consider in comparison with Menander's *Dyscolos*, is Aristophanes' *Wasps*. In the *Wasps*, we face again a situation in which a son, Anticleon, tries to convince his father, Philocleon, to change his way of life. Philocleon, by contrast with Knemon, has not completely separated himself from any form of social interaction. On the contrary, when we first see him at the beginning of the play, he is trying to escape from his house where his son has imprisoned him to prevent him going to the law-court as he does obsessively every day. Despite this point of contrast from Knemon, Philocleon expresses a similarly single-minded attitude: in fact, we know that Philocleon wishes to lead his life as much as possible in the law-courts and to enjoy the exclusive company of his fellow jurymen.[66] The reason why he enjoys this kind of life

66 Ar. *V.* 340–341.

is that it gives him unconditional power. He does not seem to care about who should be rightly punished or not but takes delight in imposing his will indiscriminately on other people.[67] What Anticleon wants his father to do is to listen to what he has to say about his occupation as a juror: he presents his father and the chorus of wasps (his father's fellow jury men) with a long, well-constructed argument. Anticleon says that the government is taking advantage of them: it does not give them enough reward for what they do; they are slaves of the system and they do not see how much they have been deceived.[68] Anticleon, like Gorgias and Haemon, represents a "model of normality",[69] the voice of sound arguments through which we can measure the absurd and extreme character of Philocleon:[70] however, the young men fulfil their function in a different manner and, eventually, they achieve opposite results.

Anticleon wants to try to find some sort of agreement with his father in the attempt to persuade him not to attend law-court sessions endlessly.[71] What is striking in this process of persuasion is that Anticleon tries to change his father's mind about going to law courts, without actually trying to change his father at the ethical or psychological level. He does not try to change his father's motivation for doing what he is doing. Philocleon is interested in going to law-courts because he enjoys exercising his power over other people and harming them; Anticleon, in his turn, suggests that Philocleon could do exactly what he was doing in the law-court by staying at home.

> **Bδ:** σὺ δ' οὖν, ἐπειδὴ τοῦτο κεχάρηκας ποιῶν,
> ἐκεῖσε μὲν μηκέτι βάδιζ', ἀλλ' ἐνθάδε
> αὐτοῦ μένων δίκαζε τοῖσιν οἰκέταις.
> [...]
> ὅτι τὴν θύραν ἀνέῳξεν ἡ σηκὶς λάθρᾳ,
> ταύτης ἐπιβολὴν ψηφιεῖ μίαν μόνην·
> πάντως δὲ κἀκεῖ ταῦτ' ἔδρας ἑκάστοτε.
> καὶ ταῦτα μὲν νῦν εὐλόγως, ἢν ἐξέχῃ
> ἕλη κατ' ὄρθρον, ἡλιάσει πρὸς ἥλιον·
> ἐὰν δὲ νείφῃ, πρὸς τὸ πῦρ καθήμενος·

67 Ar. *V.* 548–616.

68 Ar. *V.* 663–720.

69 Silk 2000, pp. 248–249.

70 "[Anticleon's] main function in the play is to represent the true or sensible view of every question. He serves as a foil to Philocleon, a standard of normality by which the old man's absurdity can be measured" (MacDowell 1995, p. 178).

71 Ar. *V.* 471–478.

> ὕοντος εἴσει· κἂν ἔγρῃ μεσημβρινός,
> οὐδείς σ' ἀποκλείσει θεσμοθέτης τῇ κιγκλίδι.

> ANTICLEON: All right then, since you have enjoyed doing that, don't go to that place any more, but stay right here and pass judgement on the servants [...]. Because the housemaid opened the door secretly, you will decide by vote [to apply to] her only one penalty; you used to do that down there every time, anyway. Well, that works reasonably; and then, if it comes out a fine hot day towards dawn, you can literally judge the accused, out in the sun, or if it's snowing, sitting by the fire. When it rains you go inside. And if you wake up at midday, no presiding magistrate will close the barrier against you.[72]

Philocleon finally changes his mind and he agrees to change his way of life completely. His conversion is abrupt and, as an audience, we do not understand what kind of psychological process brought him to take this decision (and, probably, Aristophanes is not interested in offering his audience this kind of analysis). After his supposed conversion, Philocleon takes instructions from his son about how to behave during a symposium and how to dress in order to start living the normal social life that his son has promised to him.[73] Philocleon accepts that he should change his way of life and wear new kinds of clothes:[74] his son tries to give him a new social identity. However, despite the apparent change in his life-style, he continues to demonstrate the same wicked inclinations that had motivated his occupation as a jury man before.[75] As a result, at the end of the play, as the chorus rightly remarks, Philocleon does not actually change his ethical character:[76] his tendency to impose his will on other people actually gets worse because, now that he enjoys the delight of a more sociable life, he has started assaulting everyone in the street in a state of drunkenness.[77] Philocleon's inclinations are fully reaffirmed and Philocleon enjoys an even greater freedom: he can now affirm his nature without boundaries,

72 Ar. *V.* 764–775. Translation by Sommerstein 1983 (modified).

73 Ar. *V.*1122–1295.

74 See Pütz 2007, p. 84 who stresses that Philocleon's change is accentuated by the complete change of clothes.

75 Silk 1990, p. 163.

76 Ar. *V.* 1451–1465.

77 "One has the situation—rare in Aristophanean comedy—of reason and common sense defeating the chimeras of the hero, only to find that nothing has been achieved, or more precisely, that things are worse than before" (Whitman 1964, p. 152).

abusing drinking and dancing without the burden of having to attend law-courts every day.[78]

We might say that Anticleon's re-education of his father to a more sociable life produces results that are opposite to what we find in Knemon. At the end of the *Dyscolos*, Knemon changes his attitude towards the external world because he agrees to listen to people who care for him; he appreciates his mistakes and admits his bad inclination: we cannot say the same of Philocleon. Moreover, unlike Philocleon, Knemon wishes to maintain the same way of life because, despite understanding what he did wrong, his misanthropic inclinations and old habits remain hard to change. Philocleon, instead, without really changing his mind, embraces a totally new way of life. His change is abrupt;[79] it is a complete reversal in attitude that is not combined with any change in ethical beliefs.[80]

Before concluding this part, I consider a passage in the *Epitrepontes*. There, we find another angry old man, Smikrines, who, nevertheless, does not share the extreme misanthropic character that characterises Knemon. Smikrines does not want to give back his daughter to Charisios, her husband, who has driven her from his house when he realised that she had exposed her child, who was offspring of a rape. Smikrines is the only one who, at this stage, has not yet managed to understand that Charisios has turned out to be, as a matter of fact, the rapist and, therefore, the father of the child. At the end of the play, the slave Onesimos criticises Smikrines for the fact that, without knowing the circumstances, he still wants to keep his daughter away from Charisios. Smikrines' slow-mindedness, says Onesimos, is a consequence of his stubborn character: it is at this point that the slave offers a curious account of character.

> **Ον**: ἑκάστωι τὸν τρόπον συν[ώικισαν
> φρούραρχον· οὗτος ἔνδο̣[ν] ἐπ̣[

78 See Silk 1990, p. 163 and also Whitman 1964, p. 154 who describes Philocleon as the characteristic Aristophanic comic hero. On the other hand, Dover 1972, p. 126 is more cautious in ascribing him such feature: Philocleon is essentially a coward and cowardice is not typically to be found in the comic hero.

79 That is one of the main feature of the people of Aristophanes (Silk 1990, especially pp. 162–163 for the treatment of this particular play).

80 "The characterisation of Philocleon is excellent but its purpose is amusement, not psychological truth. [...] All this is not consistent or realistic, but it is highly entertaining and that is in part why we like the old scallywag" (MacDowell 1995, p. 178). For a general discussion on Aristophanic characters see Ehrenberg 1951; Whitman 1964; Dover 1972; Silk 1990 and 2000.

> ἐπέτριψεν, ἂν αὐτῶι κακῶς χρη[σώμεθα,
> ἕτερον δ' ἔσωσεν. οὗτός ἐσθ' ἡμῖν θεὸς
> ὅ τ' αἴτιος καὶ τοῦ καλῶς καὶ τοῦ κακῶς
> πράττειν ἑκάστωι· τοῦτον ἱλάσκου ποῶν
> μηδὲν ἄτοπον μηδ' ἀμαθές, ἵνα πράττῃς καλῶς.

> ONESIMOS: They [the gods] gave to each one a guardian, the character. This one destroys us within, if [we use] it in a wrong way, otherwise it preserves us. This is a god for us, it is for each one the cause of doing good or bad. To do well, you must appease this god, doing nothing out of place or stupid.[81]

As Gomme and Sandbach point out, commenting on this passage, Onesimos confuses two concepts: that of a man's character and that of a divine guardian spirit sent by the gods.[82] Onesimos is a slave, rather slow-minded and fearful, and we do not expect from him a speech that shows full awareness of the concepts involved. Onesimos seems rather to put forward arguments that he does not fully understand but that he has, perhaps, heard somewhere. He offers these ideas at this point as this seems to be a good occasion to use them and to make fun of Smikrines. Nevertheless, what Onesimos' brief comment gives us is a definition of character, which was, perhaps, part of the shared discourse at that time and that, more importantly, mirrors what we have seen in the *Dyscolos*. The way in which we educate our natural dispositions defines what we are. Depending on how we habituate ourselves to live, we come to be people of a certain kind, and it is why our character is responsible for our fortune and misfortune. As we see in the following section, Onesimos' amusing speech also reflects, in its peculiar way, Aristotle's thoughts about character.

2 Aristotle on the Individual and His Community

In Book II of the *Nicomachean Ethics*, Aristotle states that ethical virtue springs from habituation: *ēthos* is the way in which one develops one's natural

---

81 Men. *Epitr.* 1093–1099. For a detailed discussion of this particular passage see Barigazzi 1965, pp. 192–217.

82 "Onesimos' philosophy here will not stand up. He has confused two ideas: (1) a man's character brings him good and bad fortune, (2) man has in him a guardian spirit which will reward good deeds, but punish offences" (Gomme and Sandbach 1973, ad loc.).

inclinations into settled dispositions in the course of a lifetime.[83] Ethical character depends, in this sense, on the individual, his inborn nature and on how through habituation and reasoning, he educates his natural inclinations and shapes a consistent character. Ethical understanding is improved through experience but also by shared reflection and debate about ethical values: to reflect collectively about what is to be a human being, what constitutes human life and happiness, is fundamental for improving our ethical understanding and guiding our actions.[84] In Aristotle's thinking on this topic, one point that I am especially interested in exploring is how the correct development of one's character is benefited by the social context in which one grows up and lives. More precisely, this context provides the knowledge and the experience needed to shape and develop our ethical identity. I believe that it is in this respect that the analogy with Menander's idea of 'character' as presented in the *Dyscolos* becomes clearer.

The Greek word from which the English expression 'character' derives is '*charaktēr*' (χαρακτήρ), a noun deriving from the verb 'charassō' (χαράσσω). The original meaning of this verb is 'to write on stone, wood, metal' or 'to print something on a coin' and it is with this meaning that the word is mainly used in classical authors, including Plato and Aristotle.[85] The term might also indicate a "distinctive mark or token impressed (as it were) on a person or thing by which it is known from the others". Only rarely, it might also be used for a "type or character (regarded as shared with others) of a thing or person, rarely of an individual nature".[86] This last meaning, which is the one closest to what we mean with the English term 'character', is found mainly in later authors such as Philodemus and Arrian. It seems, however, that we can already find a similar use of this term in a fragment by Menander.[87] Accordingly, Körte concludes that Menander is the first one to use the term '*charaktēr*' to indicate the features identifying an original unique personality.[88] The evidence for this, however, is slight and the other sources, closer in time to Menander, in which we find the

83 Arist. *EN* II 1, 1103a18–26.

84 Arist. *EN* X 9, 1179b20–31. See Gill 2006, pp. 135–136.

85 LSJ, s.v. For extensive discussion of the history of this term see Körte 1929 and van Groningen 1930; see Diggle 2004, p. 4, for a summary of this discussion with reference to Theophrastus' *Characters*.

86 LSJ, s.v.

87 Men. fr. 72 K.A. (ἀνδρὸς χαρακτὴρ ἐκ λόγου γνωρίζεται); see LSJ, s.v. and Körte 1929.

88 "Ganz auf dieser Entwicklungslinie liegt es nun, dass Menander der erste griechische Schriftsteller zu sein scheint, der das wort χαρακτήρ für die individuelle Eigenart eines einzelen Menschen gebraucht hat" (Körte 1929, p. 79).

term used with this meaning, are no less problematic. The term also appears as the title of Theophrastus' work *Characters*, but there is still discussion about the authenticity of this title and, more generally, about the aims of the treatise.[89]

However, in the *Lexicon Menandreo*,[90] we find that Menander makes much more use of terms such as '*ēthos*' or, more frequently '*tropos*', to define one's specific way of acting and behaving, rather than '*charaktēr*' which is only found, with this meaning, in the fragment quoted earlier. His usage might be explained by the fact that the Greek word '*charaktēr*', perhaps because of the etymology noted earlier, implies that this way of acting and being is a trait engraved on us since our birth, which determines our personality and cannot be changed or developed. This is not the same idea that is conveyed by the words '*ēthos*' or '*tropos*': these two words suggest the idea of 'character' as a set of natural traits developed into stable dispositions as a result of habit and a certain way of life.[91] This idea is analogous to what we find in Aristotle. In Aristotle, we do find reference to the idea that one can be born with a natural inclination to make the right choice.[92] However, it is clear that simply having a good natural disposition is not up to us and, therefore, is not object of praise or blame as it is not something that we achieve by our own means. One cannot be said to have a good character or to have developed a virtuous disposition until one exercises this inclination and educates it to respond in a certain way, either well or badly.

> οὔτ' ἄρα φύσει οὔτε παρὰ φύσιν ἐγγίνονται αἱ ἀρεταί, ἀλλὰ πεφυκόσι μὲν ἡμῖν δέξασθαι αὐτάς, τελειουμένοις δὲ διὰ τοῦ ἔθους.
>
> So virtues arise in us neither by nature nor contrary to nature, but by our nature we can receive them and perfect them through habituation.[93]

Accordingly, natural traits cannot be the elements that alone shape our ethical character: what defines it is what we decide to do with our natural inclinations or the goods given by chance. This is the meaning that the Greek word '*ēthos*', as opposed to '*charaktēr*', conveys for Aristotle: and, in using the English word 'character', I will have in mind these connotations of *ēthos*. Character emerges from the way in which one develops emotional and behavioural habits and deals with them over a lifetime. No matter which kind of inclinations we are

89 See for further details Diggle 2004, pp. 4–6.
90 Pompella 1996.
91 LSJ s.v.; see Men. *Epitr.* 1092–1099.
92 Arist. *EN* III 7, 1114b8–12.
93 Arist. *EN* II 1, 1103a23–26.

born with, we should be able to habituate them in a correct way so as to build up a stable virtuous disposition: in this sense our *ēthos* is up to us.[94] It is now possible to include Aristotle's idea of character in a broader definition of the following kind:

> character is "[...] a matter of the shaping of human life by an ethical motivation and agency ascribed, at its core, to the individual himself, and for which he might be held responsible, albeit in a context of forces (inherited status, natural capacities, nature and education, and not least, the larger order of a world controlled by gods) which help to create, and to limit, the conditions within which such agency and its attendant responsibility can operate".[95]

No one needs to become someone else to be able to have a good life; this is something that each one can achieve starting from what each one already is, educating in the correct way one's own natural inclination in the contexts and with the means at one's disposal.[96] Hence, character is something for which we can be praised or blamed as it is up to us to give shape to a good or bad *ēthos*.

2.1 *Listening and Watching Friends*

It is also worth pointing out that the act of ascribing praise and blame to one's own and other people's actions and choices is in itself an important ethical activity that contributes to one's own character formation. It is also this kind of activity, that of identifying someone else's choices and actions as good or bad, that sharpens one's own ethical understanding, since this offers good or bad examples of this kind.[97] I am now going to explain this statement in more

94 Arist. *EN* I 11, 1100b15–23 and III 7, 1114a19–29. "A person's character consists on those long standing actively dispositional qualities and traits—his natural capacity and habits—that (by setting the general direction of his desires and the range of his passions) directs to choices [...]. It is a stable and enduring configuration of these, structured in order of relative strength and importance" (Rorty 1994, p. 61). See also Broadie 1991, pp. 160–165 and Sherman 1997, pp. 240–257.

95 Halliwell, 1990, p. 33.

96 See Arist. *EN* IX 4, 1166a17–21.

97 "Praise and blame are ethical exercises and forces: they are, in fact, paradigmatic forms of ethical judgement. They entail not only the existence but also the sharing of values, since effective praise and blame must be addressed to audiences which will recognise and endorse their function: their function and effect are constituted precisely by people's response to them" (Halliwell 1990, p. 45). See also Broadie 1991, pp. 165–170.

detail by focusing, first, on how this process works for the individual's character development. Secondly, I will consider the implications of this analysis for the larger community in which the individual is embedded.

It is clear that ascribing praise and blame is an act that involves more than one person: first of all, one needs to be surrounded by people who perform choices and actions so that one can observe and judge them—and, maybe, also try to correct them by engaging in a discussion about what is good and what is not. Besides, it is possible that one might not be able to understand, especially at a young age, to whom praise and blame should be attributed; and someone else with more experience needs to step in to show this clearly through reflection and discussion.[98] It follows that to form relationships with other people is fundamental for correct character development. At the beginning of the educational process, one may not understand the reasons why people identify such and such things as good or bad and why one should act in a way rather than in another and habituate one's desires and emotions to respond in a certain way to certain types of situation. This is because achieving a consistent and complete ethical understanding and reaching the level at which virtuous dispositions naturally inform our decisions and actions requires activity and a long process of habituation.[99] Meanwhile, however, it is necessary to have some knowledge of what is right and wrong, even if, at the beginning we might not fully understand the reason for this: attributing praise and blame and reflecting together with other people on these topics is an important part of this process of ethical development.[100] As brought out shortly, it is important, particularly, for young people, who have not yet developed a consistent ethical understanding, to educate their inclinations by imitating those who are praised as virtuous people.[101] However, this activity also helps those who, having failed to develop a virtuous character adequately, need in any case some guidance to get to know the right thing to do.

> εἰ μὲν οὖν ἦσαν οἱ λόγοι αὐτάρκεις πρὸς τὸ ποιῆσαι ἐπιεικεῖς, πολλοὺς ἂν μισθοὺς καὶ μεγάλους δικαίως ἔφερον [...] νῦν δὲ φαίνονται προτρέψασθαι μὲν καὶ παρορμῆσαι τῶν νέων τοὺς ἐλευθερίους ἰσχύειν, ἦθός τ' εὐγενὲς καὶ ὡς ἀληθῶς φιλόκαλον ποιῆσαι ἂν κατοκώχιμον ἐκ τῆς ἀρετῆς, τοὺς δὲ πολλοὺς ἀδυνατεῖν πρὸς καλοκαγαθίαν προτρέψασθαι· [...] οὐ γὰρ οἷόν τε ἢ οὐ ῥᾴδιον

98 See Burnyeat 1980; also, more generally, see Gill 1996 for treatment of these ideas in both Plato (pp. 266–267) and Aristotle (pp. 346–370).

99 Arist. *EN* VII 5, 1147a21–22 and X 9, 1179b4–35.

100 Arist. *EN* I 2, 1095b1–9.

101 See further Chappell 2005, especially pp. 236–239.

> τὰ ἐκ παλαιοῦ τοῖς ἤθεσι κατειλημμένα λόγῳ μεταστῆσαι· ἀγαπητὸν δ' ἴσως ἐστὶν εἰ πάντων ὑπαρχόντων δι' ὧν ἐπιεικεῖς δοκοῦμεν γίνεσθαι, μεταλάβοιμεν τῆς ἀρετῆς.
>
> If arguments were sufficient by themselves to make people good, then they would have brought many great rewards […] As a matter of fact, [arguments] appear to have an effect in exhorting and stimulating the liberally-minded among young men, and, perhaps, in causing the character of someone of high lineage and truly a lover of what is noble to be possessed by virtue, but they are not capable to exhort the masses in the direction of what is noble and good […] For it is not possible or not easy to remove by argument what has been rooted since long time in [people's] characters. And presumably we should be content if, when all the means are available through which we think we become good, we were to get some share of virtue.[102]

In fact, even if, through reasoning, it is possible to modify certain beliefs and make people understand when they are wrong, character traits and natural inclinations that have been growing for long time do not change easily. This is why it is important to train one's emotional inclinations from the beginning in appropriate ethical activity,[103] following the guidance of people who care about one's ethical development. If wrong attitudes, instead, become steadily incorporated in one's character they will naturally inform one's emotional responses at any time. The fact that, after a long time, one understands that these features are wrong might not be enough to extirpate them completely from one's character; they will, to an important extent, always be part of the person.[104] Therefore, the activity of ascribing praise and blame to others and to oneself and listening to other (wiser) people's teachings is fundamental for correct ethical development in people who do not yet have a stable virtuous character but can be also useful to those who, having already developed a

102 Arist. *EN* X 9, 1179b4–20.

103 For recent discussion on this topic see Annas 2011, in particular, chapter 1.

104 See Gill 1996, chs. 4–6, for Platonic-Aristotelian ideas about the psychology of ethical development. See also Gill 1998(b) for a comparison of Platonic and Stoic models of character-development. See Gill 2006, pp. 5–14 and 129–146 (especially pp. 134–135) for a comparison of the Platonic-Aristotelian model of development with Hellenistic-Roman (especially Stoic) ideas. See also Nussbaum 1994, pp. 78–101 for discussion of the Aristotelian approach to emotional dispositions viewed in comparison with Hellenistic thought.

consistently bad character, need to be redirected toward the right way to live; although their character might not be able to be corrected.

The process of ethical development also goes beyond the individual's personal perspective.

> τούτοις δ' ἔοικε μαρτυρεῖσθαι καὶ ἰδίᾳ ὑφ' ἑκάστων καὶ ὑπ' αὐτῶν τῶν νομοθετῶν· κολάζουσι γὰρ καὶ τιμωροῦνται τοὺς δρῶντας μοχθηρά, ὅσοι μὴ βίᾳ ἢ δι' ἄγνοιαν ἧς μὴ αὐτοὶ αἴτιοι, τοὺς δὲ τὰ καλὰ πράττοντας τιμῶσιν, ὡς τοὺς μὲν προτρέψοντες τοὺς δὲ κωλύσοντες.
>
> These statements seem to be confirmed[105] not only by each of us in private life, but also by legislators themselves. For they punish and penalise those who commit evil acts (unless they act by force or through ignorance for which they are not themselves responsible), but they honour those who do noble actions, with a view to exhorting these and deterring the others.[106]

It seems, in fact, that public discussion about ethical values is not only important for the individual involved in the educational process but also for the happiness of the whole community: this would explain why, for instance, the head of a community, whether a *polis* or a family, offers his members the incentive to follow the example of good people and deters them from following bad people. In fact, other people's comments on someone's actions and choices have at least two functions: i) they are necessary to provide the agent with objective feedback on his actions so that he can appreciate his goodness or badness; ii) thanks to this feedback, they help in shaping not only the agent's character but also that of the people who share the agent's life. The combination of these two points is of great benefit for both the individual and the community.

It seems that, for Aristotle, to develop a good character and to perform virtuous actions makes us happy. We learn, in fact, from the first book of the *Nicomachean Ethics* that the proper function (ἔργον) of human beings is to live a certain kind of life: this kind of life is constituted by the activity (ἐνέργεια) of the soul in accordance with reason and this activity is performed well when it

---

105 The context Aristotle refers to is the discussion about actions performed through voluntary ignorance: namely ignorance about the right thing to do.

106 Arist. *EN* III 7, 1113b21–26, and see also Arist. *EN* II 1, 1103b2–6. "Rules and general procedures can be aids in moral development, since people who do not yet have practical wisdom and insight need to follow results that summarise the wise judgement of the others" (Nussbaum 1986(a), p. 179). See also Broadie 1991, p. 165.

is accomplished with the appropriate virtue; thus, one's happiness consists in exercising one's own function well, namely, living a life as a virtuous person.[107] But it also seems that what makes our happiness complete is to live in a community where everyone lives this sort of life.

> εἰ δὲ τὸ εὐδαιμονεῖν ἐστὶν ἐν τῷ ζῆν καὶ ἐνεργεῖν, τοῦ δ' ἀγαθοῦ ἡ ἐνέργεια σπουδαία καὶ ἡδεῖα καθ' αὑτήν, καθάπερ ἐν ἀρχῇ εἴρηται, ἔστι δὲ καὶ τὸ οἰκεῖον τῶν ἡδέων, θεωρεῖν δὲ μᾶλλον τοὺς πέλας δυνάμεθα ἢ ἑαυτοὺς καὶ τὰς ἐκείνων πράξεις ἢ τὰς οἰκείας, αἱ τῶν σπουδαίων δὲ πράξεις φίλων ὄντων ἡδεῖαι τοῖς ἀγαθοῖς (ἄμφω γὰρ ἔχουσι τὰ τῇ φύσει ἡδέα)· ὁ μακάριος δὴ φίλων τοιούτων δεήσεται, εἴπερ θεωρεῖν προαιρεῖται πράξεις ἐπιεικεῖς καὶ οἰκείας, τοιαῦται δ' αἱ τοῦ ἀγαθοῦ φίλου ὄντος. οἴονταί τε δεῖν ἡδέως ζῆν τὸν εὐδαίμονα. μονώτῃ μὲν οὖν χαλεπὸς ὁ βίος· οὐ γὰρ ῥᾴδιον καθ' αὑτὸν ἐνεργεῖν συνεχῶς, μεθ' ἑτέρων δὲ καὶ πρὸς ἄλλους ῥᾷον.
>
> If being happy consists in living and engaging in an activity, and the activity of the good person is good and pleasant in itself, as we said at the beginning; and if what is our own is among the things [that are] pleasant; and if we can contemplate better our neighbours than ourselves, and their actions [better] then our own; and if the actions of good people who are friends are pleasurable for the good person (since they have both [qualities] that are pleasant by nature); then the blessed person will need friends like this, since he prefers to contemplate actions that are good and his own, and such are the actions of a good person who is his friend. People think that the happy person should live pleasantly. Life would be difficult for the one who lives alone, since it is not easy by oneself to engage in activity continuously; but it is easier with other people and in relation to them.[108]

Contemplating people who are doing fine actions is like contemplating oneself doing such actions: the happiness created by this kind of activity is refracted by the examples of the people around us. Moreover, to live in a community offers each member the possibility of exercising his ethical understanding

---

107 See especially Arist. *EN* I 6, 1098a3–18 and I 9, 1098b20–1199a8. For discussion of this topic and the apparent contrast between the definitions of happiness (εὐδαιμονία) in *EN* I and X, see, among others, the essays of Ackrill, McDowell, Rorty, Wilkes in Rorty 1980; Price 1989, ch. 2–4; Broadie, 1991, pp. 366–438; Annas 1993, pp. 27–46.

108 Arist. *EN* IX 9, 1169b30–1170a6. See also *EN* IX 9, 1170a13–19 and IX 9, 1170b9–12.

and using others who care about him, his *philoi*,[109] as a mirror to read more clearly his own actions and choices. Through one's *philoi*, one acquires a clear and objective perception of what one has done and why one has done it. When a *philos* praises or blames our actions, he or she provides us with a clearer insight about what has been done.[110] This, in its turn, invites us to reflect upon, and analyse, our actions and motivations and, consequently, to acquire better knowledge of ourselves with the aim of improving our ethical understanding.

> δῆλον δὲ λαβοῦσι τί τὸ ζῆν τὸ κατ' ἐνέργειαν, καὶ ὡς τέλος. φανερὸν οὖν ὅτι τὸ αἰσθάνεσθαι καὶ τὸ γνωρίζειν, ὥστε καὶ τὸ συζῆν τὸ συναισθάνεσθαι καὶ τὸ συγγνωρίζειν ἐστίν. ἔστι δὲ τὸ αὑτοῦ αἰσθάνεσθαι καὶ τὸ αὑτὸν γνωρίζειν αἱρετώτατον ἑκάστῳ, καὶ διὰ τοῦτο τοῦ ζῆν πᾶσιν ἔμφυτος ἡ ὄρεξις· τὸ γὰρ ζῆν δεῖ τιθέναι γνῶσιν τινά. εἰ οὖν τις ἀποτέμοι καὶ ποιήσειε τὸ γινώσκειν αὐτὸ καθ' αὑτὸ καὶ μὴ [...] οὐθὲν ἂν διαφέροι ἢ τὸ γινώσκειν ἄλλον ἀνθ' αὑτοῦ· τὸ δ' ὅμοιον τοῦ ζῆν ἀνθ' αὑτοῦ ἄλλον. εὐλόγως δὴ τὸ ἑαυτοῦ αἰσθάνεσθαι καὶ γνωρίζειν αἱρετώτερον.
>
> It will be clear if we ascertain what life is in its active sense and end. Clearly it is perception and getting knowledge, and so to live together is to perceive and to get knowledge together. And to perceive oneself and to get knowledge of oneself is more desirable to everyone and hence the desire of living is inborn in all; for living must be regarded as a kind of knowledge. If then one were to cut off and abstract [what is] knowing in itself and what is not [...] there would be no difference between this and another person knowing instead of oneself and this is like another person living instead of oneself. But naturally the perception and getting to know of oneself is more desirable.[111]

The one who keeps himself away from his *philoi*, is deprived of this fundamental experience. Not having someone to suggest to us that we did something wrong will, most probably, lead us to repeat that mistake again and, more importantly, to fail to achieve the understanding of what is good. It is also possible that, eventually, by living a solitary life, we progressively lose sight of what is wrong with our choices; in refusing to listen to other people's comments, we will start

109 Which in an ideal *polis* should be the whole of the citizen body: see Arist. *EN* IX 6, 1167b1–4; *Pol.* III 9, 1280b36–1281a5.

110 Arist. *MM* II 15, 1213a10–20.

111 Arist. *EE* VII 12, 1244b23–34. The greek text follows Susemihl's 1884 Teubner edition.

thinking that what we do is actually right. Wicked people, in fact, deliberately avoid other people's company so that they do not have to acknowledge the wickedness of their actions.[112] Moreover, the one who already has a wicked inclination and only wishes to spend time with people of his own kind is in an even worse situation as he will intensify his own wicked inclination and that of the people he surrounds himself with.

> γίνεται οὖν ἡ μὲν τῶν φαύλων φιλία μοχθηρά (κοινωνοῦσι γὰρ φαύλων ἀβέβαιοι ὄντες, καὶ μοχθηροὶ δὲ γίνονται ὁμοιούμενοι ἀλλήλοις), ἡ δὲ τῶν ἐπιεικῶν ἐπιεικής, συναυξανομένη ταῖς ὁμιλίαις·
>
> The friendship of bad people therefore turns out to be an evil (for because of their lack of stability, they share in bad pursuits and turn evil by becoming like one another). But the friendship of good people is good and increases through their association.[113]

It turns out, therefore, that living in a community or among friends is not the only ingredient of good character development: we also need to take advantage of the presence of our neighbours and their feedback on our action.[114] For this reason, fellow-citizens, friends and offspring are classified as external goods as they are the primary material needed for ethical dialogue and activity, and their existence is important for our happiness according to the relationship of mutual benefit that is involved among *philoi*.

> φαίνεται δ' ὅμως καὶ τῶν ἐκτὸς ἀγαθῶν προσδεομένη [εὐδαιμονία], καθάπερ εἴπομεν· ἀδύνατον γὰρ ἢ οὐ ῥᾴδιον τὰ καλὰ πράττειν ἀχορήγητον ὄντα. πολλὰ μὲν γὰρ πράττεται, καθάπερ δι' ὀργάνων, διὰ φίλων καὶ πλούτου καὶ πολιτικῆς δυνάμεως· ἐνίων δὲ τητώμενοι ῥυπαίνουσι τὸ μακάριον, οἷον εὐγενείας εὐτεκνίας κάλλους· οὐ πάνυ γὰρ εὐδαιμονικὸς ὁ τὴν ἰδέαν παναίσχης ἢ δυσγενὴς ἢ μονώτης καὶ ἄτεκνος.
>
> But [happiness] appears, as we mentioned, to require also [the presence of] external goods since it is impossible or not easy to perform noble actions being without resources. For one does many actions through friends, wealth and political power, as by means of instruments. To be

112 Arist. *EN* IX 4, 1166b13–17.

113 Arist. *EN* IX 12, 1172a8–11.

114 This is why it is important to live close to one's own friends: see Arist. *EN* VIII 6, 1157b5–11.

> deprived of some things such as high lineage, good children and beauty, spoils our blessedness. For anyone who is of utterly ugly figure or of low lineage or solitary or childless is not completely happy.[115]

According to Aristotle, if one is so fortunate to be given external goods of this kind (i.e. wealth, beauty, children and friends), one should be able to use them. One should be able to listen to friends or raise one's own offspring adequately so that they can develop a proper ethical understanding through education, dialogue and a shared life with parents and the rest of the community.[116] The one who is not able to make good use of what he has received in life or does not want to share the goods of fortune with others for the sake of mutual and shared benefit cannot be completely happy.[117] This does not mean that wealth, children and fortune, in general, are sufficient conditions for happiness: but to be provided with external goods, and not make good use of them, somehow limits one's happiness; "Some external conditions [...], while not used for the virtuous person as means to achieve his purposes (as e.g., his money or his personal influence might be), put him in the position where the options for action that are presented to him by these circumstances allows him to exercise his virtues fully and in ways that one might describe as normal for the virtues".[118] In turn, to keep one's life and one's good fortune away from others is bad for the community itself. As pointed out before, each member of any kind of community is an indispensable element for building the larger framework of the good life of his community. Each one provides others with the example of his life, sharing his point of view about matters of importance and, in his turn, he benefits from the lives and the opinions of the other members. Therefore, *philoi* should engage as much as possible in mutually helpful activity such as contemplation and feasting.[119] To withdraw from this natural system of

---

115 Arist. *EN* I 9, 1099a31–b4.

116 "A virtuous man knows the values to himself of having good children, who grow to maturity and fine lives in close mutual dependence with his own, and will, just because he is virtuous, devote considerable effort to procreating and raising such a family" (Cooper 1985, p. 180); "The failure to have good children affects his [the good man's] happiness insofar as it prevents the subsequent activities that might have engaged together with his children" (*ibidem*, p. 189).

117 See Arist. *EN* IV 1, 1120a5–8; IV 3, 1121b9–16; IX 9, 1169b16–19; Arist. *EE* VII 12, 1245a11–20. See Cooper 1985, p. 127.

118 Cooper 1985, p. 182.

119 Arist. *EE* VII 12, 1245b3–10. See also Arist. *Pol.* III 9, 1280b36–38 on which Cooper comments: "And these [marriage, brothrhood, religious festivals], in turn, he evidently means

mutual benefits is not only missing the point of what it means to be a human being, it is also failing to achieve one's own complete happiness and making that of others less complete.

> [αἰσχρὸν ἐστί] καὶ ἐπὶ τούτοις τὸ τῶν καλῶν ὧν πάντες μετέχουσιν, ἢ οἱ ὅμοιοι πάντες ἢ οἱ πλεῖστοι, μὴ μετέχειν—ὁμοίους δὲ λέγω ὁμοεθνεῖς, πολίτας, ἡλικιώτας, συγγενεῖς, ὅλως τοὺς ἐξ ἴσου—αἰσχρὸν γὰρ ἤδη τὸ μὴ μετέχειν οἷον παιδεύσεως ἐπὶ τοσοῦτον, καὶ τῶν ἄλλων ὁμοίως. πάντα δὲ ταῦτα μᾶλλον, ἂν δι' ἑαυτὸν φαίνηται· οὕτω γὰρ ἤδη ἀπὸ κακίας μᾶλλον, ἂν αὐτὸς ᾖ αἴτιος τῶν ὑπαρξάντων ἢ ὑπαρχόντων ἢ μελλόντων.

> [In addition it is shameful] not to share in fine things of which all have a share, or all those like oneself or most of them. By those like oneself I mean those of the same nation, fellow citizens, those of the same age, relatives, generally, one's equals; for in the first place it is shameful not to share to the same extent in such things as education and other similar things, but all these things are more shameful if they appear to be one's own [fault]; because in this way they actually [seem to come] more from vice, if one is the cause of one's own past present or future [deficiencies].[120]

It follows that each person should be interested in the correct ethical development of the other person—and, therefore, in the other's happiness—as this is also part of his own ethical development and happiness.[121] This is why in a community where people live together and are concerned for each other's happiness, it is important that ethical values and examples are discussed publicly so to provide the best education for each one in the interest of all.[122] These principles are manifest if we look not only at how, in the large-scale system of the *polis*, private citizens and legislators comment on their fellow-citizen's actions, but also if we observe how friends and relatives behave in the smaller scale system of a family or a community of friends. What these communities have in

---

to say, provide the specific sort of connectedness that, in Greek cities, grounds the interest in and concern by each citizen for the quality of mind and character of his fellow citizens" (Cooper 1990, p. 232).

120 Arist. *Rhet.* II 6, 1384a8–16.

121 "Aristotle does not have in view the kind of altruism that consists in wanting to benefit, in principle, any other, regardless of his relationship to oneself [...]. Aristotle locates well-wishing firmly within close interpersonal (and mutual) relationships, and not in one-way actions or attitudes" (Gill 1998(a), p. 319).

122 Arist. *EN* IX 4, 1166a1–b29. See Annas 1993, pp. 249–262; Gill 1998(a).

common is that each member is somehow committed to the other in sharing a certain life (the best possible) and, as such, should sincerely care for the ethical development of his neighbour.[123] I will discuss this point at greater length shortly. First, I would like to point out that, according to this line of thought, the correct development of our character does not depend solely on us and on our individual ability to see and do the right thing; it also depends on the way we value other people and their judgements on our actions.[124] Also, the ethical development resulting from this activity produces benefits that go beyond the individual. Other people's opinions about the agent's actions do not just have an individual-centred educational aim but they play a fundamental role in the collective understanding of what is good and what is bad. Once someone has been led by others to recognise that he made a mistake, it follows that he will be able not only to correct his error, but, also, finally to understand that what he did was wrong and, possibly, if he is mature enough, why. Accordingly, this understanding should prevent the agent, and the people who witnessed his error, from making the same mistake again and, eventually, it should enable the development of a properly virtuous disposition that would constitute the core of happiness (εὐδαιμονια) for the individual and the community.[125] Thus, it turns out that to live in a community of people who care about their mutual ethical character, a community of *philoi*, is key to having a happy life.

2.2 *Talking and Living with Friends*

I will now explore in more detail how a community of *philoi* should function in order to promote this kind of outcome. I will take as a case study for this analysis the functioning of a *polis* as described in Aristotle's *Politics*. According to Aristotle, the first forms of associations, such as families and villages, originated in the aim of the satisfaction of bare needs of life such as food and protection from danger.[126] What distinguishes the origin of the civic society

---

123 Arist. *EN* VIII 10, 1159b25–1160a30. "Philia is other-concern restricted to those people to whom one has a certain sort of commitment. The commitment can be deep, as with friendship based on good character, or shallow, as in utility friendship, it can be continuing or transitory. It can be based on natural choice, as with adults developing an acquaintance, or can arise from unchosen relationships as with family relationships" (Annas 1993, p. 250). See also Konstan 1997, p. 92.

124 "We learn about ourselves by having another self before us whose similar actions and traits we can study from a more detached and more objective point of view" (Sherman 1989, p. 143).

125 Arist. *EN* I 4–6, 1097a15–1098a20. See in particular Cooper 1977, pp. 300–302.

126 Arist. *Pol.* I 2, 1252b7–15.

is the human need not just for living but living well. The *polis*, therefore, represents the most perfect and complete kind of community, the one in which complete self-sufficiency is achieved (αὐτάρκεια).[127] The desire to reproduce and satisfy the need of food and protection from danger led to the establishment of communities that were self-sufficient only from a reproductive and economical point of view. However, according to Aristotle, these kinds of community could not provide for the satisfaction of another desire constitutive of human beings: the desire to live well (εὖ ζῆν). The self-sufficiency achieved with the constitution of political societies, instead, does include this third aspect: this is why the kind of self-sufficiency that we find in the *polis* is of the perfect, fully achieved, kind.

The transition from communities such as families and villages to political states is, therefore, a natural development of human nature: human beings do not only eat, reproduce, fight and build fortifications; they also have the natural desire to speak and to communicate to other people what they think and feel, and to discuss the reasons why they do so in one way rather than another. Consequently, at the basis of the formation of the *polis* is discussion about what constitutes a good life, and this is done through discourse (λόγος) about what is right and wrong.

> διότι δὲ πολιτικὸν ὁ ἄνθρωπος ζῷον πάσης μελίττης καὶ παντὸς ἀγελαίου ζῴου μᾶλλον, δῆλον. οὐθὲν γάρ, ὡς φαμέν, μάτην ἡ φύσις ποιεῖ· λόγον δὲ μόνον ἄνθρωπος ἔχει τῶν ζῴων· ἡ μὲν οὖν φωνὴ τοῦ λυπηροῦ καὶ ἡδέος ἐστὶ σημεῖον, διὸ καὶ τοῖς ἄλλοις ὑπάρχει ζῴοις (μέχρι γὰρ τούτου ἡ φύσις αὐτῶν ἐλήλυθε, τοῦ ἔχειν αἴσθησιν λυπηροῦ καὶ ἡδέος καὶ ταῦτα σημαίνειν ἀλλήλοις), ὁ δὲ λόγος ἐπὶ τῷ δηλοῦν ἐστι τὸ συμφέρον καὶ τὸ βλαβερόν, ὥστε καὶ τὸ δίκαιον καὶ τὸ ἄδικον· τοῦτο γὰρ πρὸς τὰ ἄλλα ζῷα τοῖς ἀνθρώποις ἴδιον, τὸ μόνον ἀγαθοῦ καὶ κακοῦ καὶ δικαίου καὶ ἀδίκου καὶ τῶν ἄλλων αἴσθησιν ἔχειν· ἡ δὲ τούτων κοινωνία ποιεῖ οἰκίαν καὶ πόλιν.
>
> It is also clear why a human being is more of a political animal than a bee or any gregarious animal. Nature makes nothing pointlessly as we say and no animal has speech except the human being. A voice is a signifier of what is pleasant and painful, this is why it also belongs to other animals (for their nature goes this far: to perceive what is pleasant or painful and signify this to each other) but speech is for making clear what is beneficial or harmful and hence also what is just or unjust. For this is peculiar

127 Arist. *Pol.* I 2, 1252b28–32. See Irwin 1988, p. 406 and 1990, p. 85.

> to human beings, in comparison to the other animals, that they alone have perception of what is good or bad, just, unjust and the rest and it is community in these that makes a household and a city-state.[128]

Aristotle also explains that the act of getting together and speaking about these things is built into every human being: the ones that do not feel this need are similar either to beasts or gods.[129]

> For if the conception of a good has to be expanded in terms of such notions as those of practice, of the narrative unity of human life and of a moral tradition, then goods, and with them the only grounds for the authorities of law and virtues, can only be discovered by entering into those relationships which constitute communities whose central bond is a shared vision and understanding of goods. To cut oneself off from shared activities from which one has initially to learn obediently as an apprentice learns, to isolate oneself from the communities which find their aim and purpose in such activities, will be to debar oneself from finding any good outside of oneself.[130]

This is why the *polis* needs to promote those activities that bring citizens together; participating in public gathering such as sacrifices or festivals that facilitate citizens' interaction and the sharing of viewpoints on subjects that are of relevance for collective happiness.[131] If each member brings to the attention of the community his own point of view, and the example of his own conduct, this can be related and compared with that of other people and this will finally produce an improved shared understanding.[132] It is interesting that, in the

128 Arist. *Pol.* I 2, 1253a7–18. See Sorabji 1993, pp. 79–96 on the possession of speech as a criterion to differentiate humans from animals.

129 Arist. *Pol.* I 2, 1253a26–30.

130 MacIntyre 1981, p. 258, here identifies a feature of Aristotelian ethics (the recognition of the communal dimension) that MacIntyre regards as fundamental for any credible ethical theory.

131 "Il gioco regolato delle asserzioni e delle obiezioni, l'andare e venire delle domande e delle argomentazioni formano il metodo adatto per la costituzione di convinzioni condivise intersoggettivamente" (Bubner 1994, p. 235). See also Barnes 1980, p. 130; Nussbaum 1986(a), pp. 160–179; Starr 1986, p. 220 and Cooper 1990, p. 232.

132 For a very similar contemporary account of these topics, see Habermas 1981, especially volume II, pp. 99–118, where Habermas explains that the pooling of different examples of conduct (*Verhaltendisposition*) is important for generating an interpersonal dialogue that,

Politics, Aristotle criticises the Spartans, because they cannot offer every citizen the opportunity of joining the whole community in participating in the kind of gatherings that facilitate this dialogue.[133]

The importance of these meetings lies also in the fact that they provide the actual material for shared discussion; they allow people to speak about their own collective experiences and their points of view on these experiences. In this sense, to discuss does not actually interrupt the ethical activity but it actually provides it with concrete examples and new cases about which people can reason together.[134] The getting together of people naturally gives the opportunity of sharing, for instance, one's life experiences or discussing something that has happened in the community: this is something that people cannot do alone and this is why the "intersubjective communication"[135] of these experiences through dialogue is fundamental.[136] To describe something as good or bad, to give meaning to certain experiences, to establish the values on which the community should build its good life, we necessarily need to get together and to speak about this.

> Experience that is intersubjectively communalized in the strict sense cannot be conceived without the concept of meaning that is communicated and shared by different subjects. Identical meanings are not formed in the intentional structure of a solitary subject that confronts his world in isolation.[137] For meanings to be identical in any intelligible sense, they must have the same validity for different subjects.[138]

---

through discussion, will finally attune (*abstimmen*) these different examples and provide a shared understanding constituted by the harmonious unity of various points of view.

133 Arist. *Pol.* II 9, 1271a29–37.

134 This is a substantial point in common between Aristotle and Habermas (Bubner 1994, p. 236).

135 I am borrowing here the term from Habermas 2001, ch. 2.

136 "We know how to learn what we owe to one another; and each of us, respectively, as members of a community, can self critically appropriate our past histories, in the light of such moral obligations, for the sake of articulating a proper ethical self-understanding [...]. The right ethical self-understanding is neither revealed, nor in any other way 'given' to us, but achieved in a joint effort. From this perspective, the enabling power built into language is of a trans-subjective, rather than an absolute, quality" (Habermas 2006, p. 123).

137 In this part of the chapter Habermas is discussing and responding to Husserl's treatment of subjective intentionality as it appears in the *Cartesian Meditations* and in the fifth *Logical Investigation*.

138 Habermas 2001, p. 43.

Consequently, the *polis*, originating from smaller kinds of communities, provides, through dialogue, the fundamental criteria for distinguishing between what is good and what is not and this helps shared understanding of the fact that "the best life, both for the individual alone and for the city-state collectively, is a life of virtue sufficiently equipped with the resources needed to take part to virtuous actions".[139] To be part of a community means that we have already agreed with other members about certain shared values,[140] it means that our ethical development, and that of our *philoi*, proceeds on the basis of a definition of 'right' and 'wrong' as it has been discussed and agreed upon by the whole—or at least the most part of—the community. Accordingly, to be part of a community means to be actively involved in a dialogue that shapes those universal principles that are fundamental for guiding our practical understanding and our choices. They are, in some cases, the principles that are the premises of the so-called practical syllogism as analysed in Chapter 3.[141] By contrast with the universal principles of science, the principles of practical understanding are what they are because they are formed by "abstracting the core, the essential—and in this sense universal—aspect of the ethical life from the incidental, context-specific ones":[142] this process of abstraction is possible through experiencing a life with others and sharing a discourse about what is good. The one who willingly puts himself outside this dialogue deprives himself of the possibility of recognising these principles and thus deprives the community of his opinions and his example on important ethical matters.[143] That is why Aristotle says that someone who lives outside the community is a beast or a god: someone who does not say a word to his fellow human being about what is good and what is not is not a human being as we understand it. He is, in Pan's words, inhumane (ἀπάνθρωπος): he does not reciprocate the interest that the community has in him and he does not understand the mutual benefits that this relationship would produce for both the individual and the community.[144] In fact, it is natural for human beings—but also for animals—to feel a bond,

139 Arist. *Pol.* VII 1, 1323b40–1324a2.

140 "The justification of state intervention in the lives of individuals is in general provided first by the individuals themselves in so far as they have voluntarily entered into an association which aims at the good life" (Gerson 1987, p. 212).

141 See Chapter 3, section 2.2.

142 Gill 2005, p. 21. See also Nussbaum 1978, essay 4.

143 "A crucial feature of the thinking involved is the idea that *communicating* the ultimate preferability of post-reflective knowledge is the most profound way to benefit others, and that doing so is an integral part of living the best possible human life" (Gill 1996, p. 325).

144 Arist. *EN* X 6, 1167b2–9. Gill 1998(a), especially pp. 318–319.

some kind of *philia* among members of the same species;[145] and, once one has identified fundamental ethical values by sharing one's life with others, it is also necessary that one expresses those values in the everyday life of interpersonal relationships in order to be properly virtuous and, therefore, happy. As pointed out in the previous chapter and at the beginning of this one, experience helps to sharpen not only theoretical but also ethical understanding. This, of course, requires the presence of other people with whom one can develop this understanding until one's own inclination toward doing the right thing becomes fully natural.[146]

If we now look back at the *Dyscolos*, after this analysis of Aristotle's thought on human communities, we can find a number of analogies with Aristotle's account. Knemon made a mistake when he decided to withdraw from every kind of human relationship. Knemon's life provided him with several bad experiences and, in consequence, he became distrustful of other people in general. According to the portrait of the typical old man in the *Rhetoric*, we know that, for Aristotle too, old people usually tend to be overly suspicious precisely because of their experiences.[147] But Knemon, as an old man, offers an extreme version of Aristotle's stereotype: his misanthropic inclinations have become so accentuated that he has started to mistrust every human being completely and to refuse to share his life with others altogether. His bad character over the years could not be amended by anyone, as no one was allowed to speak to him. He kept himself, his property, and his daughter isolated and condemned to a pointless sterility, painful for his household and for the whole community of friends and neighbours.[148] Knemon's bad disposition has become a fixed trait of his character because Knemon abstracted himself from any human relationship and from the praise and blame of other people, gradually convincing himself that he alone offered the right example to follow. In this way, he deprived himself and his fellows of a truly happy life because he blocked any dialogue with them: his own and others' ethical, economical and reproductive development was virtually stopped. His behaviour was harmful not only for himself but for everyone around him and it did not produce any significant dialogue that could

145 Arist. *EN* VIII 1, 1155a15–22.

146 Arist. *EN* VII 5, 1147a22.

147 Arist. *Rhet.* II 13, 1389b21–22.

148 Knemon and his daughter, however, are decent people. Knemon's daughter has been protected from the external world and she is virtuous as she does not know what malice and corruption are (Men. *Dysc.* 34–36). Also Knemon's character promotes an ethic of work and agricultural labour even if he advocates this to an extreme extent (Men. *Dysc.* 718–721).

improve his or any other's understanding of what was right and wrong. When Knemon understands this, it is too late: his emotional disposition to distrust other people and his ingrained instinct to escape their presence can hardly be softened; however, the experiences which he was forced to share have given him some kind of understanding and directed his attention towards values and examples that he now recognises as good and which he should at least try to imitate.

Our understanding of Knemon is deepened by referring to the contrasting character of Sostratos, in the light of what has been said about Aristotle. Sostratos is open to everyone and every experience. What we learn from him is that, while one ought to be open to life's experiences and interpersonal relationships, it is also important to be able to select among them and not pursue one's desires indiscriminately. According to Aristotle, this trait in particular is a common characteristic of young people, who are prone to follow their various, changing desires in an impulsive and quick-tempered way.[149] Because of lack of experience, they are keen to take up all sorts of experiences that life offers them;[150] and this is how Sostratos behaves at the beginning of the play. Young people such as Sostratos, however, have an advantage; by contrast with older people such as Knemon, they enjoy living with others and are more ready to listen to other people's suggestions: young people, says Aristotle "are fond of friends and eager for companions because they enjoy living with others".[151] If they learn how to take advantage of other people's company, they will also learn progressively how to soften their temper and to be good. While they are still young, because they do not yet have a consistently virtuous disposition, young people are more attentive to the opinion of others in their regard;[152] accordingly, they feel shame if they make mistakes as they are afraid of the criticisms of their *philoi*. At a young age, it is this feeling of shame that guides people's actions and choices rather than a clear understanding of what is good and what is bad.[153]

This understanding will come with time, experience and education: we know from the *Nicomachean Ethics* that, if young people are guided by the correct education of their emotional dispositions, accompanied by learning and experience, they have a good chance of achieving finally that level of ethical

149 Arist. *Rhet.* II 12, 1389a2–12.

150 Arist. *Rhet.* II 12, 1389a21–29.

151 Arist. *Rhet.* II 12, 1389a35–b3.

152 Arist. *Rhet.* II 6, 1384a23–25.

153 Arist. *EN* IV 15, 1128b16–23.

understanding. Sostratos represents again a good example of this general picture: at the beginning of the play he is overly confident and he only follows his own judgement about getting whatever he wants. His meeting with Gorgias confronts him with a difficult situation and this enables him to see that his attitude has been impulsive and quick-tempered. He, therefore, decides to follow Gorgias' suggestions. We saw that, at the end of the play, Sostratos is not completely changed but he has had an ethically significant experience that has potentially taught him something. We also have the impression that the presence of a good friend such as Gorgias will probably lead him in the right direction.

3 Conclusions

I hope to have clarified the analogies between Aristotle and Menander on the subject of character. In the first part of the chapter, I discussed how Menander constructs the characters of Knemon and Sostratos and how he presents the kind of problems that they exemplify. Both Knemon and Sostratos, for opposite reasons, lack the basic experience and understanding needed for a stable, virtuous character. Sostratos is a young man and his desires and inclinations need to be educated with the help of a more experienced friend such as, for instance, Gorgias. His ethical understanding will develop progressively if he continues to make good use of his resources and to listen to the feedback of his more expert friends. On the other hand, Knemon is an old misanthrope and, at the end of the play, we realise that Knemon's character will probably never change: Knemon's inclinations have been settled features of his character for a long time. At the end of the play, he progresses in ethical understanding but he cannot bring himself to do naturally what he has now understood to be good. Knemon's problem is the fact that he has lived in isolation for long time: no one had the chance to observe and correct his character discussing with him about the best way to live. This kind of behaviour has been a problem not just for him but for everyone who was around him: Knemon's desire to be isolated spoiled the happiness of his family and his larger community of neighbours.

In Aristotle we have found analogous ideas. Aristotle argues that it is up to us how we make use of our natural inclinations and the goods that we happen to receive in life. Friends, as part of the goods given by fortune, are an indispensable ingredient of our happiness as they provide the possibility of example and dialogue. To talk and reflect together about the best way to act and live constitutes an essential ingredient of our own happiness and that of our friends. The *polis* presents, in a larger scale, an example of how a community of friends or a household (*oikos*) should work: to be part of a *polis* is to get together and communicate in order to contribute to each person's better understanding of what is good or not for the sake of mutual benefit and everyone's happiness. As in the *Dyscolos*, to exist outside this dialogue spoils one's own happiness because, being alone, one loses the opportunity to relate to others and, therefore, the chance to improve one's own ethical understanding. Also it makes less perfect the happiness of the community because other people will be deprived of the example, the point of view and, more generally, the support of that one member who has decided to live alone.

Conclusions

In these final remarks I would like to summarise what has been said so far and reflect, in more general terms, on the nature and objective of my enquiry.

I have started this book by analysing Menander's and Aristotle's treatment of the processes of theoretical and practical understanding. I first focused (Chapter 2) on the process of theoretical understanding and I pointed out that, for both Menander and Aristotle, a complete understanding of how things stand in the world or in the microcosm of the comic plot can only develop out of a combination of empirical evidence based on experience and reasoning that can give meaning to the bare sensory material. The successful conclusion of this thinking process explains everything that has been experienced before giving a unitary and final account of it, as happens in cases of Menandrian dramatic recognitions or in Aristotle's theory of scientific demonstrations. In this respect, I argue, Menandrian comedy also seems to suit Aristotle's aesthetic thought particularly well: watching Menander's comedies, spectators are invited to develop an increasing understanding of the logic of the plot and of the characters' reasoning which eventually leads the audience to a comprehensive understanding of how things stand and who people are.[1]

These reflections induced me to explore further the way in which Menandrian characters progress in their ethical understanding and how the audience is led to follow their ethical reasoning and the acknowledgement of their ethical mistakes that produces eventually the happy ending. Accordingly, in Chapter 3, I focused my attention on Menander's and Aristotle's analogous treatment of ethical understanding. As in the case of theoretical understanding, successful ethical reasoning depends, to an important extent, on how we evaluate the specific particulars with which the action is involved. An adequate perception of what the circumstances of the action are depends on our cognitive faculties and our emotional responses to a given set of circumstances. It seems that, in both Menander's and Aristotle's presentation, we often make wrong ethical choices because emotions aroused in response to the perception of given circumstances hinder our correct ethical reasoning. Perceived particulars often stimulate excessive emotional responses; consequently, our reasoning is distorted because we do not evaluate the particulars of the action correctly.

However, the fact that we act in circumstances that are not clear or are unexpected does not make us any less responsible for our wrong ethical choices,

1 See also Chapter 1, section 2 for further discussion on this topic.

 | DOI: 10.1163/9789004282827_008

as I have explored in Chapter 4. Chance and accidental ignorance, Tychē and Agnoia, provide us with opportunities for action that we should be able to use in the right way. Both Menander and Aristotle seem to agree in saying that a misfortune does not really affect the quality of our choices: what characterises our ethical deliberation as right or wrong is the reasoning that leads to it rather then the more or less fortunate result that we achieve through it. Accordingly, to an important extent, life's fortunate or unfortunate accidents are an indispensable ingredient of human life in that they provide us with occasions to exercise our ability to reason, to make choices and to see how other people go through the same process. Thus, accidental events provide us with the experience that, together with appropriate ethical reasoning, will progressively sharpen our ethical understanding.

In fact, both Menander and Aristotle seem to agree on the fact that we cannot say we are properly virtuous just because once, or occasionally, we have made the right choice. People such as Demeas or Polemon are often prevented from doing the right thing because their excessive temper overwhelms them. Although we understand from the play that they are fine people and they usually do fine actions, the events presented in the plot demonstrate that they do not show a consistently virtuous disposition: they often make wrong choices because they are not habituated to control their temperamental inclinations. Truly virtuous agents exercise the full potential of their ethical understanding if, on every occasion, they respond in the right way and feel the right kind of emotion. Ethical understanding, therefore, like theoretical understanding, requires intellectual and ethical skills that need to be developed into a stable disposition which would enable us to find the right solution to any given issue: Aristotle and Menander, as analysed in Chapter 5, seem to agree on this point. To this degree, the process of character formation is, for both Aristotle and Menander, up to us: we decide how to shape our character on the basis of the choices we make in life. The process is delicate, especially in the early stages, but with the help of more experienced friends, teachers and relatives, we may gradually become more capable of making the right choice according to an ethical understanding that increases with age and experience.[2] If, like old Knemon, we do not carry out this process properly and we indulge in bad habits, not listening to the suggestions of others, we risk preventing forever the possibility of developing a virtuous character: our bad inclinations will become deeply rooted habits and no reasoning would be able to make us change our way of life. Interpersonal debate about what is right and wrong is,

---

2 See Chapter 5, section 3 and Arist. *EN* III 5, 1112b11–24.

therefore, indispensable for adequate character-development. Living a shared life and engaging in dialogue with other people, with members of the same family, friends or fellow citizens, means finding together with them the right way to live, aiming at understanding what it means to live a good and happy life and to base our actions and objectives on this ideal. This sort of dialogue produces mutual benefits for the individual and the other people involved as it contributes to everyone's understanding and, consequently, everyone's happiness.

Concluding, I hope that this book has successfully shown that Menander and Aristotle share a general vision of human nature and happiness. They seem to have a similar understanding of how people reason and make choices and how this affects their life and character. As already indicated, in Menander and in Aristotle, the critical point, in the process that leads people to practical and theoretical understanding, occurs when human emotions and inclinations become involved in this process. Thus, the specific individual perception of a particular that directs our understanding is closely connected to the specific individual desires and emotions that one feels in that context.[3] When the agent's mind is affected by a given perception it can sometimes be imagined as forming a dialogue between reason, emotion and desire[4] on what perception suggests at any given moment. For instance, in the case of *Samia* as analysed in Chapter 3, Demeas' excessive anger and his love for Chrysis underlie his misunderstanding and the formation of defective practical reasoning based on what he has seen and heard. This misunderstanding leads Demeas to make a mistake and to behave badly with respect to others.

In turn, the elements that contribute to the agent's final decision (reason, emotion and desires) are also involved in the explanation that the agent gives of his choices to himself and others; to an important extent, these factors are part of the knowledge that the agent has of himself and his character. For instance, at the end of *Samia*, Demeas, like most Menandrian characters such as Polemon and Knemon, shows that he has understood his errors, he is also able to give an account of what led him into making a mistake and to promise not to do it again. Sharing this kind of understanding with other people helps to improve mutual understanding of the right way to act and to live; the final happy ending, in Menander, produces better understanding for both the

3 Sherman 1997; Cooper 1999; Konstan 2006(b); See also Nussbaum 2001 and Price 2009 for cognate modern theories and Chapter 3, section 2 for further discussion an bibliography on this topic.

4 See Gill 1996, pp. 356–383; 400–443 and 2006, ch. 4. See also Chapter 5 for further discussion and bibliography on this topic.

audience and the characters involved.[5] This shared interest in life's objectives and goals is an indispensable ingredient of human happiness. For instance, the case of Knemon has shown clearly that one's happiness also depends on the ability to share one's understanding with others in order to build a shared vision of life's aims and objectives that can guide our actions and, thus, improve our ethical understanding, giving each person the chance to live the best possible life.

As mentioned in the introduction,[6] the degree of similarity demonstrated here between Aristotle and Menandere gives scope for further lines of inquiry about the significance and implications of these analogies. It is my hope to have provided, with this book, a firm foundation and a clear set of determinate conclusions on ethical understanding for these two key figures of ancient Greek civilization, that will stimulate, in due course, original and exciting research.

5 See Chapter 1, section 2.

6 See p. 3 n. 6 and p. 4 n. 7.

Bibliography

Abel, L. 1963, *Metatheatre: A New View of a Dramatic Form*, New York: Hill and Wang.

Allan, W. 2000, 'Euripides and the Sophist: Society and the Theatre of War', in M. Cropp, K.H. Lee and D. Sansone (eds.), *Euripides and Tragic Theatre in the Late Fifth Century*, (vols. 24–25 *Illinois Classical Studies*), Champain, Illinois: Stipes, pp. 145–156.

——— (ed.) 2008, *Euripides: Helen*, Cambridge: Cambridge University Press.

Anderson, M. 1970, 'Knemon's *Hamartia*', *Greece & Rome*, vol. 17, pp. 199–217.

——— 1982, 'Euripides' *Auge* and Menander's *Epitrepontes*', *Greek, Roman and Byzantine Studies*, vol. 23, pp. 165–177.

Annas, J. 1993, *The Morality of Happiness*, Oxford: Oxford University Press.

——— 2003, 'The Structure of Virtue', in M. DePaul and L. Zagzebski (eds.), *Intellectual Virtue: Perspectives from Ethics and Epistemology*, Oxford: Oxford University Press, pp. 15–33.

——— 2011, *Intelligent Virtue*, Oxfrod: Oxford University Press.

Apostle, H.G. 1969, *Aristotle's Physics*, trans. with introduction and notes, Bloomington: Indiana University Press.

——— 1975, *Aristotle: The Nicomachean Ethics*, trans. with introduction and notes, Dordrecht: Reidel.

Armstrong, A.M. 1987, 'Timon of Athens—A Legendary Figure?', *Greece & Rome*, vol. 34, pp. 7–11.

Arnott, W.G. 1964, 'The Confrontation of Sostratos and Gorgias', *Phoenix*, vol. 18, pp. 110–123.

——— 1968, '*Menander qui vitae ostendit vitam*', *Greece & Rome*, vol. 15, pp. 1–17.

——— 1972, 'From Aristophanes to Menander', *Greece & Rome*, vol. 19, pp. 65–80.

——— 1973, 'Euripides and the Unexpected', *Greece & Rome*, vol. 20, pp. 49–62.

——— 1975, *Menander, Plautus and Terence*, (*Greece and Rome, New Surveys in Classics*, vol. 9), Oxford: Oxford University Press.

——— 1988, 'New Evidence of the Opening of Menander's *Perikeiromene*', *Zeitschrift für Papyrologie und Epigraphik*, vol. 71, pp. 11–15.

——— 1996, *Alexis: The Fragments*, Cambridge: Cambridge University Press.

Arnott, W.G. and Walton, J.M. 1996, *Menander and the Making of Comedy*, Westport: Greenwood Press.

Bain, D. 1979, '*Plautus vortit barbare*. Plautus, *Bacchides* 526–561 and Menander, *Dis Exapaton* 102–112', in D. West and A.J. Woodman (eds.), *Creative Imitation and Latin Literature*, Cambridge: Cambridge University Press, pp. 17–34.

——— (ed.) 1983, *Menander: Samia*, trans. with introduction and notes, Warminster: Aris & Phillip.

——— 1984, 'Female Speech in Menander', *Antichthon*, vol. 8, pp. 24–42.

Bakhurst, D. 2008, 'Laughter and Moral Ambiguity: Particularist Reflections on the Ethical Dimensions of Humour', in M.N. Lance, M. Potrĉ and V. Strahovnik (eds.), *Challenging Moral Particularism*, New York: Routledge, pp. 192–208.

Barigazzi, A. 1965, *La formazione spirituale di Menandro*, Turin: Bottega D'Erasmo.

——— 1970, 'Sulla nuova e vecchia Samia di Menandro', *Rivista di Filologia e di Istruzione Classica*, vol. 98, pp. 148–171.

Barnes, J. 1980, 'Aristotle and the Method of Ethics', *Revue Internationale de Philosophie*, vol. 34, n. 5, pp. 490–511.

——— 1984, *The Complete Works of Aristotle*, trans. with introduction and notes, Oxford: Oxford University Press.

——— 1994, *Aristotle: Posterior Analytics*, trans. with introduction and notes, Oxford: Oxford University Press.

Barrett, W.S. (ed.) 1964, *Euripides: Hippolytos*, Oxford: Oxford University Press.

Barsby, J. (ed.) 1986, *Bacchides*, trans. with introduction and notes, Warminster: Aris & Phillips.

Basset, S. 2008, 'The Late Antique Image of Menander', *Greek, Roman and Byzantine Studies*, vol. 48, pp. 201–225.

Batstone, W. 2005, 'Plautine Farce and Plautine Freedom: an Essay on the Value of Metatheatre', in W.W. Batstone and G. Tissol (eds.), *Defining Genre and Gender in Latin Literature: Essays presented to William S. Anderson on his Seventy-fifth Birthday*, New York: Lang, pp. 13–46.

Baumgart, H. 1887, *Handbuch der Poetik*, Stuttgart: Buchhandlung.

Belardinelli, A.M. 2008, 'Filosofia e scienza nella commedia nuova', *Seminari romani di cultura greca*, vol. 11, pp. 77–106.

Belfiore, E.S. 1992, 'Aristotle and Iphigenia', in A.O. Rorty (ed.), *Essays on Aristotle's Poetics*, Princeton: Princeton University Press, pp. 359–378.

——— 2000, *Murder among Friends: Violation of Philia in Greek Tragedy*, Oxford: Oxford University Press.

Bergson, E. 1911, *Laughter*, trans. C. Brereton and F. Rothwell, London: McMillan.

Bernays, J. 1853, 'Ergänzung zu Aristoteles *Poetik*', *Rheinisches Museum*, vol. 8, pp. 561–596.

——— 1880, *Zwei Abhandlungen über die aristotelische Theorie des Drama*, Berlin: BiblioBazaar.

Bers, V. 1994, 'Tragedy and Rhetoric', in I. Worthington (ed.), *Persuasion: Greek Rhetoric in Action*, London: Routledge, pp. 176–195.

Bloomfield, P. 2000, 'Virtue Epistemology and the Epistemology of Virtue', *Philosophy of Epistemological Research*, vol. 60, pp. 23–43.

Bluck, R.S. (ed.) 1961, *Plato's Meno*, Cambridge: Cambridge University Press.

Blume, H.D. 1974, *Menanders Samia: Eine Interpretation*, Darmstadt: Wissenschaftliche Buchgesellschaft.

Blundell, M.W. 1989, *Helping Friends, Harming Enemies: a Study in Sophocles and Greek Ethics*, Cambridge: Cambridge University Press.

Bolton, R. 1990, 'The Epistemological Basis of Aristotelian Dialectic', in D. Devereux and P. Pellegrin (eds.), *Biologie, logique et métaphysique chez Aristote*, Paris: Editions du centre national de la recherche scientifique, pp. 185–236.

Bonitz, H. 1955, *Index Aristotelicus*, Berlin: Reimer.

Booker, C. 2004, *The Seven Basic Plots*, London: Continuum.

Bowra, M. 1944, *Sophoclean Tragedy*, Oxford: Clarendon Press.

Braam, van P. 1912, 'Aristotle's Use of Ἀμαρτία', *Classical Quarterly*, vol. 6, pp. 266–272.

Braund, S.M. and Gill, C. (eds.) 1997, *The Passions in Roman Thought and Literature*, Cambridge: Cambridge University Press.

Bremer, J.M. 1969, *Hamartia: Tragic Error in the Poetics of Aristotle and in Greek Tragedy*, Amsterdam: Hakkert, 1969.

Broadie, S. 1991, *Ethics with Aristotle*, Oxford: Oxford University Press.

Broadie, S. and Rowe, C. 2002, *Aristotle: Nicomachean Ethics*, trans. with introduction and notes, Oxford: Oxford University Press.

Brown, A. (ed.) 1987, *Sophocles: Antigone*, trans. with introduction and notes, Warminster: Aris & Phillips.

Brown, P.G. 1983, 'Menander's Dramatic Technique and the Law of Athens', *Classical Quarterly*, vol. 33, pp. 412–420.

——— 1993, 'Love and Marriage in Greek New Comedy', *Classical Quarterly*, vol. 43, pp. 184–205.

Brunschwig, J. 2003, 'Epistemology', in J. Brunschwig and G.E.R. Lloyd (eds.), *The Greek Pursuit of Knowledge*, Cambridge, Mass.: The Belknap Press of Harvard University Press, pp. 18–39.

Brunschwig, J. and Lloyd, G.E.R. (eds.) 2003, *The Greek Pursuit of Knowledge*, Cambridge, Mass.: The Belknap Press of Harvard University Press.

Bubner, R. 1994, 'Linguaggio e Politica', trans. L. Cortella, in L. Cortella and C. Vigna (eds.), *L'etica e il suo altro*. Milan: FrancoAngeli, 1994, pp. 228–239.

Burian, P. (ed.) 2007, *Euripides: Helen*, trans. with introduction and notes, Oxford: Oxford University Press.

Burnyeat, M.F. 1976, 'Plato on the Grammar of Perceiving', *Classical Quarterly*, vol. 26, pp. 29–51.

——— 1980, 'Aristotle on Learning to be Good', in A.O. Rorty (ed.), *Essays on Aristotle's Ethics*, Berkeley: University of California Press, pp. 69–92.

——— 1981, 'Aristotle on Understanding Knowledge', in E. Berti (ed.), *Aristotle on Science: The Posterior Analytics*, Padua: Antenore, pp. 97–139.

——— 1990, *The Theaetetus of Plato*, trans. M.J. Levett, introduction by M. Burnyeat, Indianapolis: Hackett Publishing Company.

——— 1994, '*Enthymeme*: Aristotle on the Logic of Persuasion', D.J. Furley and A. Nehamas (eds.), *Aristotle's Rhetoric*, Princeton: Princeton University Press, pp. 3–55.

Butcher, S.H. 1927, *Aristotle's Theory of Poetry and Fine Art*, London: Macmillan.

Cairns, D. (ed.) 2001, *Oxford Readings in Homer's Iliad*, Oxford: Oxford University Press.

Capps, E. (ed.) 1910, *Four Plays of Menander*, with introduction and notes, Boston: Ginn, 1910.

Carey, C. 1989, *Lysias: Selected Speeches*, Cambridge: Cambridge University Press.

——— 2012, *Trials from Classical Athens*, London: Routledge.

Carli, S. 2010, 'Poetry is more Philosophical than History: Aristotle on Mimesis and Form.' *Review of Metaphysics*, vol. 64, n. 2, pp. 303–336.

Carrière, J. 1956, 'Ambiguité et Vraisemblance dans l'*Oedipe Roi*', *Pallas*, vol. 4, n. 3, pp. 5–14.

Cartledge, P. Millett, P. and Todd, S.C. (eds.) 1990, *Nomos: Essays in Athenian Law, Politics, and Society*, Cambridge: Cambridge University Press.

Casanova, A. 2014, 'Menander and the Peripatos: New Insights into an Old Question', in A. Sommerstein (ed.), *Menander in Contexts*, New York: Routledge, pp. 137–151.

Cave, T. 1988, *Recognitions: A Study in Poetics*, Oxford: Clarendon Press.

Chappell, T. 2005, '"The Good Man is the Measure of All Things": Objectivity without World-Centredness in Aristotle's Moral Epistemology', in C. Gill (ed.), *Virtue, Norms and Objectivity: Issues in Ancient and Modern Ethics*, Oxford: Oxford University Press, pp. 233–256.

Charles, D. 1984, *Aristotle's Philosophy of Action*, London: Duckworth.

Charlton, W. 1970, *Aristotle's Physics: Books 1 and 2*, trans. with introduction and notes, Oxford: Oxford University Press.

Cinaglia, V. 2012, 'Aristotle and Menander on How People Go Wrong', *Classical Quarterly*, vol. 62, pp. 553–566.

——— 2014, 'Menander, Aristotle, Chance and Accidental Ignorance', in A. Sommerstein (ed.), *Menander in Contexts*, New York: Routledge, pp. 152–166.

Code, L. 1987, *Epistemic Responsibility*, Hanover: University Press of New England and Brown University Press.

Consigny, S. 2001, *Gorgias, Sophist and Artist*, Columbia (s.c.): University of South Carolina Press.

Cooper, L. 1922, *An Aristotelian Theory of Comedy*, New York: Harcourt, Brace and Company.

——— (ed.) 1960, *The Rhetoric of Aristotle*, trans. with introduction and notes, Englewood Cliffs, New Jersey: Prentice-Hall.

Cooper, J. 1970, 'Plato on Sense-Perception and Knowledge: *Theaetetus* 184–186', *Phronesis*, vol. 15, pp. 123–146.

——— 1975, *Reason and Human Good in Aristotle*, Cambridge Mass.: Harvard University press.

——— 1977, 'Friendship and the Good in Aristotle', *Philosophical Review*, vol. 86, n. 3, pp. 290–315.

——— 1985, 'Aristotle and the Goods of Fortune', *Philosophical Review*, vol. 94, n. 2, pp. 173–196.

——— 1990, 'Political Animals and Civic Friendship' in G. Patzig (ed.), *Aristoteles 'Politik'*, Göttingen: Vandenhoeck & Ruprecht, pp. 221–241

——— 1999, *Reason and Emotion: Essays in Ancient Moral Psychology and Ethical Theory*, Princeton: Princeton University Press.

Cope, E.M. (ed.) 1867, *An Introduction to Aristotle's Rhetoric*, analisys with notes and appendices, London: Macmillan.

——— 1877, *The Rhetoric of Aristotle*, revised by John Edwin Sandys, 3 vols. Cambridge: Cambridge University Press.

Cornford, F.M. 1935, *Plato's Theory of Knowledge*, London: Routledge and Kegan Paul.

Costantinidou, S. 2008, *Logos into Mythos: The Case of Gorgias' Encomium of Helen*, Athens: Kardamitsa.

Cropp, M.J. (ed.) 1988, *Euripides: Electra*, trans. with introduction and notes, Warminster: Aris & Phillips.

Csapo, E. and Slater W.J. 1995, *The Context of Ancient Drama*, Ann Arbor: University of Michigan Press.

Cullity, E. and Gaut, B. (eds.) 1997, *Ethics and Practical Reason*, Oxford: Oxford Univeristy Press.

Curd, P. 2006, 'Gorgia and the Eleatics', in M.M. Sassi (ed.), *La costruzione del discorso filosofico nell'età dei Presocratici*, Pisa: Edizioni della Normale, pp. 183–200.

Cusset, C. 2014, 'Melancholic Lovers in Menander', in A. Sommerstein (ed.), *Menander in Contexts*, New York: Routledge, pp. 167–179.

Dahl, N.O. 1984, *Practical Reason, Aristotle, and Weakness of the Will*, Minneapolis: University of Minnesota Press.

Davidson, D. 1980, 'How is Weakness of Will Possible?', in *Essays on Actions and Events*, Oxford: Oxford University Press, pp. 21–42.

Davies, M. 1998, 'Euripides' *Electra*: The Recognition Scene Again', *Classical Quarterly*, vol. 48, pp. 389–403.

Del Corno D. 1975, 'Da Fedra a Moschione. Immaginazione e fantasticheria', in J. Bingen, G. Cambier and G. Nachtergael (eds.), *Le monde grec: Pensée, littérature, histoire, documents. Hommages à Claire Préaux*, Brussels: Edition de l'Université, pp. 205–213.

Denniston, J.D. (ed.) 1939, *Euripides: Electra*, Oxford: Oxford University Press.

DePaul, M. and Zagzebski, L. 2003, *Intellectual Virtue. Perspectives from Ethics and Epistemology*, Oxford: Oxford University Press.

De Sousa, R. 1987, *The Rationality of Emotion*, Cambridge, Mass.: MIT Press.

Detienne, M. 1979, 'Violentes Eugénies: En pleines Thesmophories, des femmes couvertes de sang', *Acta Antiqua Academiae Scientiarum Hungaricae*, vol. 27, pp. 109–133.

Diano, C. 1968, 'Edipo figlio della Tyche', in *Saggezza e poetiche degli antichi*, Vicenza: Pozza, pp. 119–165.

Di Benedetto, V. 1983, *Sofocle*, Florence: La Nuova Italia.

Diels, H. and Kranz, W. (eds.) 1951, *Die Fragmente der Vorsokratiker*, 3 vols., Berlin-Grunewald: Weidmannsche Verlagsbuchhandlung.

Diggle, J. (ed.) 2004, *Theophrastus: Characters*, trans. with introduction and notes, Cambridge: Cambridge University Press.

Dosi, A. 1960, 'Sulle Tracce della Poetica di Teofrasto', *Rendiconti: Istituto Lombardo di scienze e lettere; classe di lettere, scienze morali e storiche*, vol. 94, pp. 599–672.

Dover, K.J. 1972, *Aristophanic Comedy*, Berkeley: University of California Press.

——— 1974, *Greek Popular Morality in the Time of Plato and Aristotle*, London: Backwell.

Dustin, C.A. 1993, 'Commentary on Sherman', in J.J. Cleary and W. Wians (eds.), *Boston Area Colloquium in Ancient Philosophy*, Boston: Universty Press of America, pp. 34–53.

Dutsch D. and Konstan D. 2011, 'Women's Emotions in New Comedy', in D. Munteanu (ed.), *Emotion, Genre and Gender in Classical Antiquity*, London: Bloomsbury, pp. 57–88.

Dworacki, S. 1969/70, 'The Role of Scenic Accessories in the Comedy of Menander', *Eos*, vol. 58, pp. 299–312.

——— 1973, 'The Prologues in the Comedies of Menander', *Eos*, vol. 61, pp. 33–34.

——— 1977, '*Hamartia* in Menander', *Eos*, vol. 65, pp. 17–24.

——— 1978, '*Anagnorisis* in Greek Drama', *Eos*, vol. 66, pp. 41–54.

Easterling, P. 1990, 'Constructing Character in Greek Tragedy', in C. Pelling (ed.), *Characterisation and Individuality in Greek Literature*, Oxford: Oxford University Press, pp. 83–99.

Ehrenberg, v. 1951, *The People of Aristophanes: A Sociology of Attic Comedy*, London: Blackwell.

El Murr, D. 2006, 'Paradigm and *Diairesis*: a Response to M.-L. Gill', *Journal of the International Plato Society*, vol. 6, www.nd.edu/~plato/plato6issue/contents6.htm.

Else, G.F. 1957, *Aristotle's Poetics: The Argument*, Cambridge, Massachusetts: Harvard University Press.

Entralgo, L. 1970, *The Therapy of the Word in Classical Antiquity*, New Haven: Yale University Press.

Everson, S. (ed.) 1990, *Companions to Ancient Thought: Epistemology*, Cambridge: Cambridge University Press.

Fantham, E. 1977, 'Philemon's *Thesauros* as a Dramatisation of Peripatetic Ethics', *Hermes*, vol. 105, pp. 406–421.

Fendt, G. 2007, *Love Song for the Life of the Mind*, Washington, DC: Catholic University of America Press.

Ferrari, G.R.F. 2000, *Plato: The Republic*, trans. T. Griffith with introduction and notes by G.R.F. Ferrari, Cambridge: Cambridge University Press.

Fine, G. 1990, 'Knowledge and belief in *Republic* V–VII', in S. Everson (ed.), *Companions to Ancient Thought vol. 1: Epistemology*, Cambridge: Cambridge University Press, pp. 85–115.

Finkelberg, M. 2006, 'Aristotle on Episodic Tragedy', *Greece & Rome*, vol. 53, n. 1, pp. 60–72.

Foley, H.P. 1981, 'The Conception of Women in Athenian Drama', in H.P. Foley (ed.), *Reflections of Women in Antiquity*, New York: Gordon and Breach, pp. 127–168.

Fortenbaugh, W.W. 1974, 'Menander's *Perikeiromene*. Misfortune, Vehemence, and Polemon', *Phoenix*, vol. 28, pp. 430–443.

——— 1975, *Aristotle on Emotion*, London: Duckworth.

——— (ed.) 1992, *Theophrastus of Eresus, Sources of his Life, Writings Thought and Influence*, vol. 2: Psychology, Human Physiology, Living creatures, Botany, Ethics, Religion, Politics, Rhetoric and Poetics, Music and miscellanea, Leiden: Brill.

——— (ed.) 2005, *Theophrastus of Eresus, Sources of his Life, Writings Thought and Influence*, vol. 8: Sources on Rhetoric and Poetics, Leiden: Brill.

Fountoulakis, A. 2004, *Αναζητώντας τον Διδαχτικό Μένανδρο*, Athens: Typothito G. Dardanos.

Frede, D. 1992, 'Necessity, Chance and "What Happens for the Most Part"', in A.O. Rorty (ed.), *Essays in Aristotle's Poetics*, Princeton: Princeton University Press.

——— 1995, 'The Cognitive Role of *phantasia* in Aristotle', in M.C. Nussbaum and A.O. Rorty, *Essays on Aristotle's De Anima*, Oxford: Oxford University Press, pp. 279–296.

Friedrich, W. 1953, *Euripides und Diphilos*, München: Beck.

Frow, J. 1986, 'Spectacle Binding: On Character', *Poetics Today*, vol. 7, no. 2, pp. 227–250.

Frye, N. 1957, *Anatomy of Criticism: Four Essays*, Princeton, NJ: Princeton University Press.

——— 1963, *Fables of Identity; Studies in Poetic Mythology*, New York: Harcourt.

Furley, W.D. (ed.) 2009, *Menander: Epitrepontes*, trans. with introduction and notes, London: Institute of Classical Studies.

Gagarin, M. 1997, 'On the Not-Being of Gorgias' *On Not-Being*', *Philosophy & Rhetoric*, vol. 30, n. 1, pp. 38–40.

Gaiser, K. 1967, 'Menander und der Peripatos', *Antike und Abendland*, vol. 13, pp. 8–40.

Gallagher, R.L. 2003, 'Making the Stronger Argument the Weaker: Euripides, *Electra* 518–544', *Classical Quarterly*, vol. 53, n. 2, pp. 401–415.

Garner, R. 1987, *Law and Society in Classical Athens*, London: Routledge.

Gellie, G. 1981, 'Tragedy and Euripides' *Electra*', *Bulletin of the Institute of Classical Studies*, vol. 28, pp. 1–12.

Gerson, L.P. 1987, 'Aristotle's Polis: A Community of the Virtuous', in J.J. Cleary and W. Wians (eds.), *Proceedings of the Boston Area Colloquium in Ancient Philosophy*, Boston: University Press of America, pp. 203–225.

Giangrande, L. 1983, 'Self-knowledge', *Cahiers des Études Anciennes*, vol. 15, pp. 61–67.

Giannopoulou, V. 2000, 'Agency and Τύχη in Euripides' *Ion*: Ambiguity and Shifting Perspectives', in M. Cropp, K.H. Lee and D. Sansone (eds.), *Euripides and Tragic Theatre in the Late Fifth Century*, (vols. 24–25 *Illinois Classical Studies*), Champain, Illinois: Stipes, pp. 257–251.

Gibert, J.C. 2000, 'Falling in love with Euripides (*Andromeda*)', in M. Cropp, K.H. Lee and D. Sansone (eds.), *Euripides and Tragic Theatre in the Late Fifth Century*, (vols. 24–25 *Illinois Classical Studies*), Champain, Illinois: Stipes, pp. 75–91.

Gill, C. 1983, 'The Question of Character-Development: Plutarch and Tacitus', *Classical Quarterly*, vol. 33, pp. 469–487.

——— 1986, 'The Question of Character and Personality in Greek Tragedy', *Poetics Today*, vol. 7, n. 2, pp. 251–273.

——— 1990, 'The Character-Personality Distinction', in C. Pelling (ed.), *Characterisation and Individuality in Greek Literature*, Oxford: Oxford University Press, pp. 1–31.

——— 1996, *Personality in Greek Epic, Tragedy and Philosophy: the Self in Dialogue*, Oxford: Oxford University Press.

——— 1997, 'The Emotions in Greco-Roman Philosophy', in S.M. Braund and C. Gill (eds.), *The Passions in Roman Thought and Literature*, Cambridge: Cambridge University Press, pp. 5–15.

——— 1998(a), 'Altruism or Reciprocity in Greek Ethical Philosophy', in C. Gill, N. Postlethwaite, R. Seaford, (eds.), *Reciprocity in Ancient Greece*, Oxford: Oxford University Press, pp. 303–328.

——— 1998(b), 'Ethical Reflection and the Shaping of Character', J.J. Cleary and W. Wians (eds.), *Proceedings of the Boston Area Colloquium in Ancient Philosophy*, Boston: University Press of America, pp. 193–225.

——— (ed.) 2005, *Virtue, Norms and Objectivity: Issues in Ancient and Modern Ethics*, Oxford: Oxford University Press.

——— 2006, *The Structured Self in Hellenistic and Roman Thought*, Oxford: Oxford University Press.

Gill, M.L. 1982, 'Sorabji and Aristotle against Determinism', *Ancient Philosophy*, vol. 2, pp. 122–133.

——— 2006, 'Models in Plato's Sophist and Statesman', *Journal of the International Plato Society*, vol. 6, www.nd.edu/~plato/plato6issue/contents6.htm.

Goldberg, S.M. 1980, *The Making of Menander's Comedy*, London: Athlone Press.

Golden, L. 1978, '*Hamartia*, Ate, and Oedipus', *Classical World*, vol. 72, pp. 3–12.

——— 1992, *Aristotle on Tragic and Comic Mimesis*, Atlanta, Georgia: The Scholars Press.

Goldhill, S. 1986(a), *Reading Greek Tragedy*, Cambridge: Cambridge University Press.
——— 1986(b), 'Rhetoric and Relevance. Interpolation at Euripides, *Electra* 367–400', *Geek, Roman and Byzantine Studies*, vol. 27, pp. 157–171.
——— 1991, *The Poet's Voice*, Cambridge: Cambridge University Press.
——— 1999, 'Programme Notes', in S. Goldhill and R. Osborne (eds.), *Performance Culture and the Athenian Democracy*, Cambridge: Cambridge University Press, pp. 1–29.
Gomme, A.W. and Sandbach, F.H. 1973, *Menander: A Commentary*, Oxford: Oxford University Press.
Gould, J. 2001, 'Dramatic Character and "Human Intelligibility"', in *Myth, Ritual, Memory and Exchange*, Oxford: Oxford University Press, pp. 78–111.
Gould, T. 2009, 'Comedy', in R. Eldridge (ed.), *The Oxford Handbook of Literature and Philosophy, Oxford*, Oxford University Press, pp. 95–116.
Granger, H. 1993, 'Aristotle on the Analogy between Action and Nature', *Classical Quarterly*, vol. 43, pp. 168–176.
Grant, J. 1986, 'The Father-Son Relationship and the Ending of Menander's *Samia*', *Phoenix*, vol. 40, n. 2, pp. 172–184.
Greco, J. 2000, *Putting Skeptics in Their Place*, Cambridge: Cambridge University Press.
Greenspan, D. 2008, *The Passion of Infinity: Kierkegaard, Aristotle and the Rebirth of Tragedy*, Berlin: de Gruyter.
Greimas, A.J. and Courtés, J. 1989, 'The Cognitive Dimension of Narrative Discourse', *New Literary History*, vol. 20, n. 3, pp. 563–579.
Griffith, M. (ed.) 1999, *Sophocles: Antigone*, Cambridge: Cambridge University Press.
Griffiths, P. 1997, *What Emotions Really Are*, Chicago: Chicago University Press.
Grimaldi, W.M.A. 1980(a), *Aristotle, Rhetoric I: A Commentary*, New York: Fordham University Press.
——— 1980(b), '*Semeion, Tekmerion, Eikos* in Aristotle's *Rhetoric*', *American Journal of Philology*, vol. 101, n. 4, pp. 383–389.
——— 1988, *Aristotle, Rhetoric II: A Commentary*, New York: Fordham University Press.
Groningen, van B.A. 1930, 'ΧΑΡΑΚΤΗΡΕΣ', *Mnemosyne*, vol. 58, pp. 45–53.
——— 1961, 'The Delineation of Character in Menander's *Dyscolos*', *Recherches de Papyrologie*, vol. 1, n. 1, pp. 95–112.
Groton, A.H. 1987, 'Anger in Menander's *Samia*', *American Journal of Philology*, vol. 108, pp. 437–443.
Guthrie, W.K.C. 1971, *The Sophists*, Cambridge: Cambridge University Press.
Gutzwiller, K. 2000, 'The Tragic Mask of Comedy: Metatheatricality in Menander', *Classical Antiquity*, vol. 19, pp. 132–137.
Guzzo, A, 1978, 'Caratterologia e visione della vita in Menandro', *Filosofia*, vol. 29, n. 1, pp. 35–50.
Habermas, J. 1981, *Theorie des Kommunikativen Handelns*, Frankfurt: Sührkamp Verlag.

——— 2001, *On the Pragmatic of Social Interaction*, trans. B. Fultner, Cambridge: Polity.

——— 2006, 'How to Respond to the Ethical Question', in L. Thomassen (ed.), *The Derrida-Habermas Reader*, Edinburgh: Edinburgh University Press, pp. 115–127.

Hall, E. 1995, 'Lawcourt and Dramas', *Bulletin of the Institute of Classical Studies*, vol. 40, pp. 39–58

Halliwell, S. 1986, *Aristotle's Poetics*, London: Duckworth.

——— 1990, 'Traditional Greek Conceptions of Character', in C. Pelling (ed.), *Characterisation and Individuality in Greek Literature*, Oxford: Oxford University Press, pp. 32–59.

——— 1992, 'Pleasure, Understanding and Emotion in Aristotle's *Poetics*', in A.O. Rorty (ed.), *Essays on Aristotle's Poetics*, Princeton, pp. 241–260.

——— 2002, *The Aesthetics of Mimesis: Ancient Texts and Modern Problems*, Princeton: Princeton University Press.

——— 2008, *Greek Laughter*, Cambridge: Cambridge University Press.

Handley, E. (ed.) 1965, *The Dyscolos of Menander*, London: Methuen.

——— 1968, *Menander and Plautus. A Study in Comparison*, London: Levis.

——— 1985, 'Comedy', in P. Easterling and B. Knox (eds.), *Cambridge History of Classical Literature*, vol. 1, Cambridge: Cambridge University Press, pp. 335–425.

Hankinson, R.J. 1990, 'Perception and Evaluation: Aristotle on the Moral Imagination', *Dialogue*, vol. 29, pp. 41–63.

——— 1998, *Cause and Explanation in Ancient Greek Thought*, Oxford: Oxford University Press.

Harding, P. 'Comedy and Rhetoric', in I. Worthington (ed.), *Persuasion: Greek Rhethoric in Action*, London: Routledge, pp. 196–221

Harrison, A.R. 1968, *The Law of Athens*, London: Duckworth.

Harsh, P.W. 1945, ''Αμαρτία again', *Transactions of the American Philological Association*, vol. 76, pp. 47–58.

Henry, M.M. 1985, *Menander's Courtesans and the Greek Comic Tradition*, Frankfurt: Lang.

Hey, O. 1928, 'AMAPTIA: Zur Bedeutungsgeschichte des Wortes', *Philologus*, vol. 83, pp. 1–17; 137–163.

Heylbut, G. (ed.) 1889, *Aspasii in Ethica Nicomachea Quae Supersunt Commentaria*, Commentaria in Aristotelem Graeca, vol. 19.1, Berlin: Reimer.

——— (ed.) 1892, *Eustratii et Michaelis et Anonyma in Ethica Nicomachea Commentaria*, Commentaria in Aristotelem Graeca, vol. 20, Berlin: Reimer.

Hicks, D.R. (ed.) 1907, *Aristotle: De Anima*, trans. with introduction and notes, Cambridge: Cambridge University Press.

Hokenson, J. 2006, *The Idea of Comedy: History, Theory, critique*, Fairleigh Dickinson University Press.

Hubbard, M.E. 1972, '*Poetics*', in D.A. Russell and M. Winterbottom (ed.), *Ancient Literary Criticism: The Principal Texts in New Translations*, Oxford: Clarendon Press, pp. 85–131.

Humphreys, S.C. 1985, 'Social Relations on Stage: Witnesses in Classical Athens', *History and Anthropology*, vol. 1, n. 2, pp. 313–368.

——— 1988, 'The Discourse of Law in Archaic and Classic Greece', *Law and History Review*, vol. 6, n. 2, pp. 465–493.

Hunter, R. 1985, *The New Comedy of Greece and Rome*, Cambridge: Cambridge Univeristy Press.

Hurst, A. 1990, 'Ménandre et la tragédie', in E. Handley and A. Hurst (ed.), *Rélire Ménandre*, Geneva: Droz, pp. 93–122.

Ireland, S. 1981, 'Prologues' Structure and Sentences in Menander', *Hermes*, vol. 109, pp. 178–188.

——— 1983, 'Menander and the Comedy of Disappointment', *Liverpool Classical Monthly*, vol. 8, pp. 45–47.

——— (ed.) 1995, *Menander: The Bad Tempered Man*, trans. with introduction and notes, Warminster: Aris & Philip.

——— (ed.) 2010, *The Shield and Arbitration*, trans. with introduction and notes, Warminster: Aris & Philip.

Irwin, T. 1978, 'First Principles in Aristotle's Ethics', *Midwest Studies in Ancient Philsophy*, vol. 3, pp. 252–272.

——— 1988, *Aristotle's First Principles*, Oxford: Oxford University Press.

——— 1990, 'The Good of Political Activity', in G. Patzig (ed.), *Aristoteles 'Politik'*, Göttingen: Vandenhoeck & Ruprecht, pp. 71–98.

Iversen, P.A. 1998, 'Menander and the Subversion of Tragedy', (Diss. Ohio State University).

——— 2001, 'Coal for Diamonds: Syriscos Character in Menander's *Epitrepontes*', *American Journal of Philology*, vol. 122, pp. 381–404.

Jäkel, S. 1982, 'Euripideische Handlungsstrukturen in der *Samia* des Menander', *Arctos*, vol. 16, pp. 19–31.

——— 1984, 'Die Tüke der Faktizität in der *Epitrepontes* des Menander', *Arctos*, vol. 18, pp. 5–21.

Janko, R. (ed.) 1984, *Aristotle on Comedy: Towards a Reconstruction of Poetics II*, trans. with introduction and notes, Berkeley: University of California Press.

——— 2001, 'Aristotle on Comedy', in Ø. Andersen and J. Haarberg (eds.), *Making Sense of Aristotle. Essays in Poetics*, London: Duckworth, pp. 54–58.

Judson, L. 1991, 'Chance and "always or for the most part" in Aristotle', in L. Judson (ed.), *Aristotle's Physics*, pp. 73–99.

Kahan D.M. and Nussbaum M.C. 1996, 'Two Conceptions of Emotion in Criminal Law', *Colombia Law Review*, vol. 96, pp. 269–374.

Kantizios, I. 2010, ''Old' Pan and 'New' Pan in Menander's Dyskolos', *Classical Journal*, vol. 106, pp. 23–42.

Katsouris, A. 1975, *Tragic Patterns in Menander*, Athens: Hellenic Society for Humanistic Studies.

——— 1976, 'Menander Misleading his Audience', *Liverpool Classical Monthly*, vol. 1, pp. 100–102.

Kayser, J. 1906, *'De veterum arte poetica quaestiones selectae'*, (Diss. Liepzig).

Kennedy, G.A. 2007, *On Rhetoric: A Theory of Civic Discourse*, trans. with introduction and notes, Oxford: Oxford University Press.

Kenny, A.J. 1979, *Aristotle's Theory of Will*, New Haven: Yale University Press.

Kent Sprague, R. (ed.) 1972, *The Older Sophists*, trans. by several hands of *Die Fragmente der Vorsokratiker*, edited by Diels-Kranz, Columbia: University of South Carolina Press.

Keuls, E. 1973, 'The *Samia* of Menander: An Interpretation of its Plot and Theme', *Zeitschrift für Papyrologie und Epigraphik*, vol. 10, pp. 1–20

Knox, B.M.W. 1957, *Oedipus at Thebes*, New Haven: Yale University Press

——— 1964, *Heroic Temper*, Berkeley: University of California Press.

——— 1980, 'Exit Oedipus?', *Greek Roman and Byzantine Studies*, vol. 21, pp. 321–332

——— 2001, 'Euripidean Comedy', in E. Segal (ed.), *Oxford Readings in Menander, Plautus and Terence*, Oxford: Oxford University Press, pp. 3–24.

Kommerell, M. 1940, *Lessing und Aristoteles: Untersuchungen über die Theorie der Tragödie*, Frankfurt: Klostermann.

Konet, R.J. 1976, 'The Role of *Tyche* in Menander's *Aspis*', *Classical Bulletin*, vol. 52, pp. 90–92.

Konstan, D. 1983, 'A Dramatic History of Misanthropes', *Comparative Drama*, vol. 17, pp. 97–123

——— 1995, *Greek Comedy and Ideology*, Oxford: Oxford University Press.

——— 1997, *Friendship in the Classical World*, Cambridge: Cambridge University Press.

——— 2006(a), *Aspasius: On Aristotle's Nicomachean Ethics 1–4, 7–8*, trans. with introduction and notes, Ithaca: Cornell University Press.

——— 2006(b), *The Emotions of the Ancient Greeks*, Toronto: University of Toronto Press.

——— 2013, 'Menander's slaves: the banality of violence' in B. Akrigg and R. Tordoff (ed.), *Slaves and Slavery in Ancient Greek Comic Drama*. Cambridge; New York: Cambridge University Press, pp. 144–158.

Körte, A. 1929, 'ΧΑΡΑΚΤΗΡ', *Hermes*, vol. 64, pp. 68–86.

——— (ed.) 1938, *Menandri quae supersunt*, 2 vols., Leipzig: Teubner.

Kovacs, D. 1989, 'Euripides, *Electra* 518–544. Further Doubts about Genuineness', *Bulletin of the Institute of Classical Studies*, vol. 36, pp. 67–78.

Laird, A. (ed.) 2006, *Ancient Literary Criticism*, Oxford: Oxford University Press.

Lamagna, P. (ed.) 1994, *La fanciulla tosata di Menandro*, Naples: D'Auria.

Lape, S. 2004, *Reproducing Athens: Menander's Comedy, Democratic Culture, and the Hellenistic City*, Princeton: Princeton University Press.

——— 2010, 'Gender in Menander's Comedy', in A.K. Petrides and S. Papaioannou (eds.), *New Perspectives on Postclassical Comedy*, Newcastle: Cambridge Scholars, pp. 51–78.

Lauriola, R. 2007, 'Wisdom and Foolishness: a Further Point in the Interpretation of Sophocles' *Antigone*', *Hermes*, vol. 135, n. 4, pp. 389–405.

Lawrence, S.E. 1978, 'Dramatic Epistemology in the *Trachiniae*', *Phoenix*, vol. 32, pp. 288–304.

Lear, J. 1988, *Aristotle. The Desire to Understand*, Cambridge, Mass: Cambridge University Press, 1988.

Lefèvre, E. 2001(a), *Die Unfähigkeit, sich zu erkennen: Sophokles' Tragödien*, Leiden: Brill.

——— 2001(b), 'Menander, *Dis exapaton* 6–113 und Plautus, *Bacchides* 500–561', in L. Benz (ed.), *ScriptOralia Romana: die römische Literatur zwischen Mündlichkeit und Schriftlichkeit*, Tübingen: Narr, pp. 141–167

Lennox, J.G. 1984, 'Aristotle on Chance', *Archiv für Geschichte der Philosophie*, vol. 66, pp. 52–60.

Lesky, A. 1961, *Göttliche und Menschliche Motivation im homerischen Epos*, Heidelberg: Winter.

——— 2001, 'Divine and Human Causation in Homeric Epic', in D. Cairns (ed.), *Oxford Readings in Homer's Iliad*, Oxford: Oxford University Press, pp. 170–202.

Lever, K. 1956, *The Art of Greek Comedy*, London: Methuen

Liddell, H.G., Scott, R. and Jones H.S. (eds.) 1996, *Greek-English Lexicon* (first edition 1843), Oxford: Clarendon Press.

Lloyd, M. 1986, 'Divine and Human Action in Euripides' *Ion*', *Antike und Abendland*, vol. 32, pp. 33–45.

Lloyd-Jones, H. 1961, 'Some Alleged Interpolations in Aeschylus' *Choephori* and Euripides' *Electra*', *Classical Quarterly*, vol. 11, n. 2, pp. 171–184.

——— 1971, *The Justice of Zeus*, Berkeley: University of California Press.

Longo, O. 2006, '*Oedipus mathematicus*: la matematica di Edipo', *Dioniso*, vol. 5, pp. 24–35.

Lyons, J. 1963, *Structural Semantics*, Oxford: Cambridge University Press.

MacCary, W.T. 1970, 'Menander's Characters: Their Names, Roles and Masks', *Transactions of the American Philological Association*, vol. 101, pp. 277–290.

MacDowell, D. 1982, 'Love versus the Law: an Essay on Menander's Aspis', *Greece and Rome*, vol. 29, pp. 42–52.

——— 1995, *Aristophanes and Athens*, Oxford: Oxford University Press.

MacIntyre, A. 1981, *After Virtue: A Study in Moral Theory*, London: Duckworth.

Macua Martinez, E. 2008, *Técnicas de Caracterización en Menandro*, Vitoria: Universidad del Pais Vasco.

Mansion, S. 1984, "'Plus connu en soi', 'Plus connu pour nous': une distinction épistémologique importante chez Aristote" in J. Follon and S. Mansion (eds.), *Études aristotéliciennes: Recueil d'articles*, Louvain-la-Neuve: Éditions de l'Institute Superieure de Philosophie, pp. 213–222.

Markus, J. 2009, 'Der sophokleische Eros und sein Dialog mit Euripides', in E. Düsing and H.D. Klein (eds.), *Geist, Eros und Agape: Untersuchungen zu Liebesdarstellungen in Philosophie, Religion und Kunst*. Würzburg: Königshausen und Neumann, pp. 63–96.

Martina, A. 1979, 'Note Giuridiche sul *Discolo* di Menandro', *Atti dell'Accademia delle Scienze di Torino*, vol. 113, pp. 33–55.

Mastromarco, G. 1985, "L'inizio della Perikeiromene, un problema di restauro scenico" in G. Mastromarco e P. Totano (eds.), *Sileno XI: Studi in onore di Adelmo Barigazzi*, vol. 2, pp. 33–40.

Mercken, P.F. (ed.) 1973, *The Greek Commentaries on the Nicomachean Ethics of Aristotle in the Latin translation of Robert Grosseteste, Bishop of Lincoln (1253)*, Leiden: Brill.

Meyer, S. 1994, 'Self-movement and External Causation' in M.L. Gill and J.G. Lennox. (eds.), *Self-Motion from Aristotle to Newton*, Princeton: Princeton University Press, pp. 65–80.

Mignucci, M. 1975, *L'Argomentazione dimostrativa di Aristotele*, Padua: Antenore.

Miller, F.D. 1984, 'Aristotle on Practical Knowledge and Moral Weakness', in R. Porecco (ed.), *The Georgetown Symposium on Ethics*, Lanham: University Press of America, 131–144.

Miles, S. 2014, 'Staging and Constructing the Divine in Menander', in A. Sommerstein (ed.), *Menander in Contexts*, New York: Routledge, pp. 75–89.

Millett, P. 1991, *Landing and Borrowing*, Cambridge: Cambridge University Press.

Mingay, J.M. and Walzer, R.R. (eds.) 1991, *Aristotelis Ethica Eudemia*, Oxford: Oxford University Press.

Montmarquet, J. 1986, 'Epistemic Virtue', *Mind*, vol. 96, pp. 482–497.

Moravcsik, J.M.E. 1974, 'Aristotle on Adequate Explanations', *Synthèse*, vol. 14, pp. 622–638.

Moser, P.K. and Vander Nat, A. 2003, *Human Knowledge: Classical and Contemporary Approaches*, Oxford: Oxford University Press.

Mossman, J.M. 2001, 'Women's Speech in Greek tragedy: the Case of Electra and Clytemnestra in Euripides' *Electra*', *Classical Quarterly*, vol. 51, n. 2, pp. 374–384.

Müller, C.W. 2000, 'Elektras Erkenntnisproblem: zu Eur. *El.* 503 ff.', *Rheinisches Museum*, vol. 143 n. 3–4, pp. 251–255.

Munteanu, D. 2002, 'Types of *Anagnorisis*: Aristotle and Menander. A Self-Defining Comedy', *Wiener Studien*, vol. 115, pp. 111–126.

——— 2011(a) 'Comic Emotions: Shamelessness and Envy (Shadenfreude); Moderate

Emotions', in D. Munteanu (ed.), *Emotion, Genre and Gender in Classical Antiquity*, London: Bloomsbury, pp. 89–112.

——— 2011(b), *Tragic Pathos: Pity and Fear in Greek Philosophy and Tragedy*, Cambridge: Cambridge University Press.

Nervegna, S. 2013, *Menander in Antiquity. The Contexts of Reception*, Cambridge: Cambridge Univeristy Press.

Nesselrath, H. 1990, *Die attische mittlere Komödie: ihre Stellung in der antiken Literaturkritik und Literaturgeschichte*, Berlin: Walter de Gruyter.

Nightingale, A.W. 2004, *Spectacles of Truth in Classical Greek Philosophy*, Cambridge: Cambridge University Press.

Noël, M.P. 1998, '*Kairos*, Sophistique et Mises en Forme du *Logos* chez Gorgias', *Revue de Philologie, de Littérature et d'Histoire Ancienne*, vol. 72, n. 2, pp. 233–245.

Nussbaum, M.C. (ed.) 1978, *Aristotle's De Motu Animalium*, trans. with introduction and notes, Princeton: Princeton University Press.

——— 1982, 'Saving Aristotle's Appearances', in M. Schofield and M.C. Nussbaum (eds.), *Language and Logos: Studies in Ancient Greek Philosophy presented to G.E.L. Owen*, Cambridge: Cambridge University Press, pp. 267–293.

——— 1986(a), 'The Discernment of Perception: An Aristotelian Conception of Public and Private Rationality', J.J. Cleary and W. Wians (eds.), *Proceedings of the Boston Area Colloquium in Ancient Philosophy*, Boston: University Press of America, pp. 151–201.

——— 1986(b), *The Fragility of Goodness: Luck and Ethics in Greek Tragedy and Philosophy*, Cambridge: Cambridge University Press.

——— 1990, *Love's Knowledge*, Oxford: Oxford University Press.

——— 1994, *The Therapy of Desire: Theory and Practice in Hellenistic Ethics*, Princeton: Princeton University Press.

——— 2001, *Upheavals of Thought: the Intelligence of Emotions*, Cambridge: Cambridge University Press.

Omitowoju, R. 2002, *Rape and the Politics of Consent in Classical Athens*, Cambridge: Cambridge Univeristy Press.

——— 2010, 'Performing Traditions: Relations and Relationships in Menander and Tragedy', in A.K. Petrides and S. Papaioannou (eds.), *New Perspectives on Postclassical Comedy*, Newcastle: Cambridge Scholars, pp. 125–145.

Onions, C.T. (ed.) 1983, *The Shorter Oxford English Dictionary*, Oxford: Oxford University press.

Orsi, R. 2007, *El Saber del Error: Filosofía y Tragedia en Sófocles*, Madrid: Plaza y Valdés.

Pack, R.A. 1937, 'A Passage in Alexander of Aphrodisias Relating to the Theory of Tragedy', *American Journal of Philology*, vol. 58, pp. 418–436.

——— 1939, 'Fate, Chance, and Tragic Error', *American Journal of Philology*, vol. 60, pp. 350–356.

Paduano, G. (ed.) 1980, *Menandro: Commedie*, trans. with introduction and notes, Milan: Mondadori.

——— 2008, 'Plauto traduttore', in P. Arduini et al. (eds.), *Studi offerti ad Alessandro Perutelli*, Rome: Aracne, vol. 2, pp. 301–310.

Paoli, V.L. 1961, 'Note giuridiche sul Δύσκολος di Menandro', *Museum Helveticum*, vol. 18, pp. 53–62.

Papachrysostomou, A. 2008, *Six Comic Poets: A Commentary on Selected Fragments of Middle Comedy*, Tübingen: Gunter Narr Verlag.

Papadimitriopulos, L. 2006, 'On the structure of Sophocles' *Trachiniae*', *Acta Classica*, vol. 49, pp. 183–189.

Patterson, C. 1998, *The Family in Greek History*, Cambridge Mass: Harvard University Press.

Perrin, B. 1909, 'Recognition Scenes in Greek Literature', *American Journal of Philology*, vol. 30, n. 4, pp. 371–404.

Petrides, A.K. 2010, 'New Performance', in A.K. Petrides and S. Papaioannou (eds.), *New Perspectives on Postclassical Comedy*, Newcastle: Cambridge Scholars, pp. 79–124.

——— 2014, *Menander, New Comedy and the Visual*, Cambridge: Cambridge University Press.

Petrides, A.K. and Papaioannou, S. 2010, *New Perspectives on Postclassical Comedy*, Newcastle: Cambridge Scholars.

Pickard-Cambridge, A.W. 1968, *The Dramatic Festivals of Athens*, Oxford: Clarendon Press.

Pitcher, S.M. 1945, 'Aristotle's Good and Just Heroes', *Philological Quarterly*, vol. 24, pp. 1–11, 190–191.

Pompella, G. 1996 (ed.), *Lexicon Menandreo*, Hildesheim: Olms-Weidmann.

Post, L.A. 1931, 'The "Vis" of Menander', *Transactions of the American Philological Association*, vol. 62, pp. 203–234.

——— 1938, 'Aristotle and Menander', *Transactions of the American Philological Association*, vol. 69, pp. 1–42.

——— 1960, 'Virtue Promoted in Menander's *Dyscolos*', *Transactions of the American Philological Association*, vol. 91, pp. 152–161.

——— 1964, 'Menander and the *Helen* of Euripides', *Harvard Studies in Classical Philology*, vol. 68, pp. 99–118.

Porter, J.R. 1997, 'Adultery by the Book: Lysias 1 (*On the Murder of Eratosthenes*) and Comic Diegesis', *Classical Views*, vol. 40, pp. 421–453.

Preaux, C. 1957, 'Menandre et la societé Athenienne', *Chronique d'Egypte*, vol. 32, pp. 84–100.

Prescott, H.V. 1918, 'The Antecedents of Hellenistic Comedy', *Classical Philology*, vol. 13, pp. 113–137.

Price, A.W. 1989, *Love and Friendship in Plato and Aristotle*, Oxford: Oxford University Press.

——— 2008, 'Particularism and Pleasure', in M.N. Lance, M. Potrĉ and V. Strahovnik (eds.), *Challenging Moral Particularism*, New York: Routledge, pp. 192–208.

——— 2009, *Contextuality in Practical Reason*, Oxford: Oxford University Press.

Price, H.H. 1952, 'Image Thinking', *Proceedings of The Aristotelian Society*, vol. 52, pp. 136–166.

Pritchard, D. 2005, *Epistemic Luck*, Oxford: Oxford University Press.

Pütz, B. 2007, *The Symposium and Kosmos in Aristophanes*, Oxford: Oxbow.

Questa, C. 1970, 'Alcune strutture sceniche di Plauto e Menandro', in O. Reverdin (ed.), *Ménander. Sept exposés suivis de discussions*, Vandœuvres-Geneva: Fondation Hardt, pp. 181–228.

Quijada, M. 2002, 'La Escena de Reconocimiento en la *Electra* de Eurípides: una Muestra del Desarrollo Intertextual de la Tragedia', *Quaderni Urbinati di Cultura Classica*, vol. 71, pp. 101–109.

Raeburn, D. 2000, 'The Significance of Stage Properties in Euripides' *Electra*', *Greece & Rome*, vol. 47, n. 2 pp. 149–168.

Ramage, E. 1966, 'City and Country in Menander's Dyscolos', *Philologus*, vol. 110, pp. 194–211.

Reden, von S. 1998, 'The Commodification of Symbols', in C. Gill, N. Postlethwaite, R. Seaford, (eds.), *Reciprocity in Ancient Greece*, Oxford: Oxford University Press, pp. 256–278.

Reeve, C.D.C. (ed.) 1988, *Aristotle: Politics*, trans. with introduction and notes, Indianapolis: Hackett.

Reinhardt, K. 2003, 'The Intellectual Crisis in Euripides', in J. Mossman (ed.), *Euripides*, Oxford: Oxford University Press, pp. 16–46.

Richardson, N.J. 1984, 'Recognition Scenes in the *Odyssey* and Ancient Literary Criticism', *Papers of the Latin Liverpool Seminar*, vol. 4, pp. 219–235.

Rorty, A.O. (ed.) 1980 *Essays on Aristotle's Ethics*, Princeton: Princeton University Press.

——— (ed.) 1992, *Essays on Aristotle's Poetics*, Princeton: Princeton University Press.

——— 1994, 'The Psychology of Aristotle's *Rhetoric*', in J.J. Cleary (ed.), *Boston Area Colloquium in Ancient Philosophy*, Boston: University Press of America, pp. 39–79.

Rosen, R.M. 1988, *Old Comedy and the Iambographic Tradition*, Atlanta, Georgia: Scholars Press.

Rosivach, V.J. 1998, *When a Joung Men Falls in Love: The Sexual Exploitation of Women in New Comedy*, London: Routledge.

Ross, W.D. (ed.) 1924, *Aristotle's Metaphysics*, 2 vols., Oxford: Clarendon Press.

——— (ed.) 1936, *Aristotle: Physics*, Oxford: Clarendon Press.

——— (ed.) 1949, *Aristotle: Prior and Posterior Analytics*, Oxford: Clarendon Press.

Rostagni, A. 1922, 'Aristotele ed aristotelismo nella estetica antica', *Studi Italiani di Filologia classica*, vol. 2, pp. 1–147.

Rowe, C. 1977, *An Introduction to Greek Ethics*, New York: Barnes and Noble.

Russell, D.A. 1981, *Criticism in Antiquity*, London: Duckworth.

——— 1990, '*Ēthos* in Oratory and Rhetoric', in C. Pelling (ed.), *Characterisation and Individuality in Greek Literature*, Oxford: Oxford University Press, pp. 197–212.

Russell, D.C. 2009, *Practical Intelligence and the Virtues*, Oxford: Oxford Univeristy Press.

Saïd, S. 1978, *La Faute Tragique*, Paris: Maspero.

Sandbach, F.H. 1970, 'Menander's Manipulation of Language for Dramatic Purposes', in O. Reverdin (ed.), *Ménandre. Sept exposés suivis de discussions*, Vandœuvres–Geneva: Fondation Hardt, pp. 113–143.

——— (ed.) 1972, *Menandri: Reliquiae Selectae*, Oxford: Clarendon Press.

——— 1977, *The Comic Theatre of Greece and Rome*, London: Chatto and Windus.

Sander, E. 2014, *Envy and Jealousy in Classical Athens*, Oxford: Oxford University Press, 2014.

Scafuro, A.C. 1997, *The Forensic Stage*, Cambridge: Cambridge University Press.

——— 2003, 'When a Gesture was Misinterpreted: *didonai titthion* in Menander's *Samia*', in G.W. Bakewell and J.P. Sickinger (ed.), *Gestures: Essays in Ancient History, Literature and Philosophy presented to Alan L. Bolgehold*, Oxford: Oxford University Press, pp. 113–135.

Schmitt, A. 1990, *Selbständigkeit und Abhängigkeit menschlichen Handelns bei Homer: hermeneutische Untersuchungen zur Psychologie Homers*, Stuttgart: Steiner.

Schofield, M. 1979, 'Aristotle on the Imagination', in J. Barnes, M. Schofield and R. Sorabji (eds.), *Articles on Aristotle. Psychology and Aesthetics*, vol. IV, London: St. Martin Press, pp. 103–132.

Seaford, R. 1994, *Reciprocity and Ritual: Homer and Tragedy in the Developing City-State*, Oxford: Oxford University Press.

——— 2003, 'Tragic Tyranny', in K.A. Morgan (ed.), *Popular Tyranny*, Austin: University of Texas Press, pp. 95–115.

——— 2004, *Money and the Early Greek Mind*, Cambridge: Cambridge University Press.

Segal, C. 1981, *Tragedy and Civilization. An Interpretation of Sophocles*, Cambridge, Mass.: Harvard University Press.

——— 2001, *Oedipus Tyrannus: Tragic Heroism and the Limits of Knowledge*, Oxford: Oxford University Press.

Segal, E. (ed.) 2001(a), *Oxford Readings in Menander, Plautus and Terence*, Oxford: Oxford University Press.

——— 2001(b), *The Death of Comedy*, Cambridge, Mass.: Harvard University Press.

Shaw, B. 2007, *Euripides: Hippolytus*, trans. B. Shaw with introduction by P. Easterling, Cambridge: Cambridge University Press.

Sherman, N. 1989, *The Fabric of Character*, Oxford: Oxford University Press.

——— 1992, '*Hamartia* and Virtue', in A.O. Rorty (ed.), *Essays on Aristotle's Poetics*, Princeton: Princeton University Press, pp. 177–196.

——— 1993, 'The Role of Emotions in Aristotelian Virtue', in J.J. Cleary and W. Wians (eds.), *Boston Area Colloquium in Ancient Philosophy*, Boston: University Press of America, pp. 1–33.

——— 1997, *Making a Necessity of Virtue*, Cambridge: Cambridge University Press.

Sherman, N. and White, H. 2003, 'Intellectual Virtue: Emotions, Luck, and the Ancients', in M. DePaul and L. Zagzebski (eds.), *Intellectual Virtue: Perspectives from Ethics and Epistemology*, Oxford: Clarendon Press, pp. 34–54.

Sidwell, K. 2009, *Aristophanes the Democrat*, Cambridge: Cambridge University Press.

——— 2014, 'Fourth-Century Comedy before Menander', in M. Revermann (ed.), *The Cambridge Companion to Greek Comedy*, pp. 60–78.

Silk, M.S. 1988, 'The Autonomy of Comedy', *Comparative Criticism*, vol. 10, pp. 3–37.

——— 1990, 'The People of Aristophanes', in C. Pelling (ed.), *Characterisation and Individuality in Greek Literature*, Oxford, pp. 150–173.

——— (ed.) 1996, *Tragedy and the Tragic: Greek Theatre and Beyond*, Oxford: Oxford University Press.

——— 2000, *Aristophanes and the Definition of Comedy*, Oxford: Oxford University Press.

Solmsen, F. 1982, 'Electra and Orestes: Three Recognitions in Greek Tragedy', in F. Solmsen (ed.), *Kleine Schriften*, Hildesheim: G. Olms, vol. 3, pp. 32–63.

Solomon, R. 1984, *The Passions: The Myth and Nature of Human Emotions*, New York: Doubleday.

Sommerstein, A. 1983, *Aristophanes: Wasps*, Warmister: Aris & Philip.

——— (ed.) 1993, *Tragedy, Comedy and the Polis: Papers from the Greek Drama Conference, Nottingham, 19–20 July 1990*, Bari: Levante Editori.

——— (ed.) 2014, *Menander in Contexts*, New York: Routledge.

Sorabji, R. 1973, 'Aristotle on the Role of Intellectual Virtue', *Proceeding of the Aristotelian Society*, vol. 74, pp. 107–129.

——— 1980, *Necessity, Cause and Blame: Perspectives on Aristotle's Theory*, Ithaca: Cornell University Press.

——— 1992, 'Intentionality and Psychological Process: Aristotle's Theory of Sense-perception', in M.C. Nussbaum and A.O. Rorty (eds.), *Essays in Aristotle's De Anima*, Princeton: Princeton University Press, pp. 195–225.

——— 1993, *Animal Minds and Human Morals: The Origin of the Western Debate*, London: Duckworth.

Sosa, E. 1980, 'The Raft and The Pyramid: Coherence versus Foundations in the Theory of Knowledge', *Midwest Studies in Philosophy*, vol. 5, pp. 3–25.

Stafford, E.J. 2002, *Worshipping Virtues: Personification and the Divine in Ancient Greece*, London: Duckworth.

Stafford, E.J. and Herrin J. (eds.) 2005, *Personification in the Greek world: from Antiquity to Byzantium*, Aldershot: Ashgate.

Stanford Encyclopedia of Philosophy, http://plato.stanford.edu.

Starr, C. 1986, *Individual and Community*, Oxford: Oxford University Press.

Ste Croix, de G.E.M. 1972, *The Origins of the Peloponnesian War*, London: Duckworth.

——— 1992, 'Aristotle on History and Poetry', in A.O. Rorty (ed.), *Essays on Aristotle's Poetics*, Princeton: Princeton University Press, pp. 23–32.

Steinmetz, P. 1960, 'Menander und Theophrast. Folgerungen aus dem *Dyskolos*', *Rheinisches Museum*, vol. 103, pp. 185–191.

Stinton, T.C.W. 1975, '*Hamartia* in Aristotle and Greek Tragedy', *Classical Quarterly*, vol. 25, pp. 221–254.

Stockert, W. 1997, 'Metatheatralisches in Menanders *Epitrepontes*', *Wiener Studien*, vol. 110, pp. 5–18.

Stuart, D.C. 1918, 'The Function and the Dramatic Value of the Recognition Scene in Greek Tragedy', *The American Journal of Philology*, vol. 39, n. 3, pp. 268–290.

Susemihl, F. 1884, *Eudemi Rhodii Ethica*, Leipzig: Teubner.

Süss, W. 1910, *Ethos: Studien sur älteren griechischen Rhetorik*, Liepzig: Teubner.

Taplin, O. 1978, *Greek Tragedy in Action*, London: Routledge.

Taylor, C.C.W. 1990, 'Aristotele's Epistemology', in S. Everson (ed.), *Companions to Ancient Thought: Epistemology*, Cambridge: Cambridge University Press, pp. 117–142.

Tierney, M. 1935, 'Aristotle and Menander', *Proceedings of the Royal Irish Academy*, vol. 43, pp. 241–254.

Todd, S.C. 2007, *A Commentary on Lysias, Speeches 1–11*, Oxford: Oxford University Press.

Traill, A. 2008, *Women and the Comic Plot in Menander*, Cambridge: Cambridge University Press.

Treu, M. 1969, 'Humane Handlungsmotive in der *Samia* Menanders', *Rheinisches Museum für Philologie*, vol. 112, pp. 230–254.

Tuominen, M. 2007, *Apprehension and Argument: Ancient Theories of Starting Points for Knowledge*, Dordrecht: Springer.

Untersteiner, M. 1949, *I Sofisti*, Torino: Einaudi.

Usher, S. 1965, 'Individual Characterisation in Lysias', *Eranos*, vol. 63, pp. 99–119.

Vernant, J.P. 1981, 'Intimations of the Will in Greek Tragedy', in J.P. Vernant and P. Vidal-Naquet, *Myth and Tragedy in Ancient Greece*, trans. J. Loyd, Brighton: Harvester Press, pp. 49–84.

Vogt-Spira, G. 1992, *Dramaturgie des Zufalls: Tyche und Handeln in der Komödie Menanders*, München: Beck.

——— 2001, 'Euripides und Menander', in B. Zimmerman (ed.), *Rezeption des antiken Dramas auf der Bühne und der Literature*, Stuttgard: Metzler, pp. 197–222.
Walsh, M.M. 1999, 'The Role of Universal Knowledge in Aristotelian Moral Virtue', *Ancient Philosophy*, vol. 19, pp. 73–88.
Webb, R. 1997, 'Imagination and the Arousal of Emotions in Greco-Roman Rethoric', in S.M. Braund and C. Gill (eds.), *The Passions in Roman Thought and Literature*, Cambridge: Cambridge University Press, pp. 112–127.
Webster, T.B.L. 1950, *Studies in Menander*, Manchester: Manchester University Press.
——— 1953, *Studies in Later Greek Comedy*, Manchester: Manchester University Press.
——— 1974, *An Introduction to Menander*, Manchester: Manchester University Press.
Wehrli, F. 1936, *Motivstudien zur griechischen Komödie*, Zürich: Max. Niehans.
——— 1970, 'Menander und die Philosophie', in O. Reverdin (ed.) *Ménandre. Sept exposés suivis de discussions*, Vandœuvres–Geneva: Fondation Hardt, pp. 145–155.
Whitman, C. 1951, *Sophocles: A Study of Heroic Humanism*, Cambridge, Mass: Harvard University Press.
——— 1964, *Aristophanes and the Comic Hero*, Cambridge, Mass: Harvard University Press.
Wiggins, D. 1981(a), 'Deliberation and Practical Reason' in A.O. Rorty (ed.), *Essays on Aristotle's Ethics*, Berkeley: University of California Press, pp. 221–240.
——— 1981(b) 'Weakness of will, Commensurability, and the Objects of Deliberation and Desire', in A.O. Rorty (ed.), *Essays on Aristotle's Ethics*, Berkeley: University of California Press, pp. 241–265.
Wilkins, J. 2000, *The Boastful Chef*, Oxford: Oxford University Press.
Williams, B. 1976, 'Moral Luck', *Proceedings of the Aristotelian Society*, vol. 50. pp. 115–135.
——— 1993, *Shame and Necessity*, Berkley: University of California Press.
Williamson, T. 2002, *Knowledge and its Limits*, Oxford: Oxford Univeristy Press.
Winnington-Ingram, R.P. 1969(a), 'Euripides: *Poiêtês sophos*', *Arethusa*, vol. 2, pp. 127–142.
——— 1969(b), 'Tragica', *Bulletin of the Institute of Classical Studies*, vol. 16, pp. 44–54.
——— 1980, *Sophocles. An Interpretation*, Cambridge: Cambridge University Press.
——— 2003, '*Hippolytos*: a Study of Causation', in J. Mossman (ed.), *Oxford Readings in Classical Studies: Euripides*, Oxford: Oxford University Press, pp. 201–217.
Woodruff, P. 1990, 'Plato's Early Theory of Knowledge', in S. Everson (ed.), *Companions to Ancient Thought vol. 1: Epistemology*, Cambridge: Cambridge University Press, pp. 60–84.
Woods, M. 1982, *Aristotle's Eudemian Ethics*, trans. with introduction and notes, Oxford: Clarendon Press.
——— 1986, 'Intuition and Perception in Aristotle's Ethics', *Oxford Studies in Ancient Philosophy*, vol. 4, pp. 145–166.
Worthington, I. (ed.) 1994, *Persuasion: Greek Rhetoric in Action*, London: Routledge.

Wright, M.E. 2005, *Euripides' Escape-Tragedies*, Oxford: Oxford University Press.

Yanal, R.J. 1982, 'Aristotle's Definition of Poetry', *Noûs*, vol. 16, pp. 499–525

Zagagi, N. 1990, 'Divine Interventions and Human Agents in Menander', in E. Handley and A. Hurst (eds.), *Relire Ménandre*, Genève: Droz, 1990, pp. 63–91.

——— 1994, *The Comedy of Menander*, London: Duckworth.

Zagzebski, L. 1996, *Virtues of the Mind*, Cambridge: Cambridge University Press.

Zeitlin, F.I. 1985, 'The Power of Aphrodite: Eros and the Boundaries of the Self in the Hippolytus', in P. Burian (ed.), *Directions in Euripidean Criticism*, Durham, N.C.: Duke University Press, pp. 52–111.

——— 1990, 'Playing the Other', in J.J. Winkler and F.I. Zeitlin (eds.), *Nothing to Do with Dionysus?*, Princeton: Princeton University Press, pp. 63–96.

General Index

This index also includes the names of modern scholars whose works are discussed or particularly relevant to the argument of the book.

Index of Ancient Sources

The ancient sources listed in this index are only those discussed in the text and notes. The index does not include ancient sources quoted without discussion.